Encyclopedia of
Antique Tools
& Machinery

C.H. Wendel

Published by

**krause
publications**

700 E. State Street • Iola, WI 54990-0001
Telephone: 715/445-2214
www.krause.com

Please call or write for our free catalog of publications. Our toll-free number to place an order or obtain a free catalog is 800-258-0929 or please use our regular business telephone, 715-445-2214.

Library of Congress Catalog Number: 2001091079
ISBN: 0-87341-607-4
Printed in the United States of America

Table of Contents

Introduction 4

Introduction

To suppose that this book is an all-inclusive reference would be grossly incorrect! I have spent the past forty years gathering information, literature, and old catalogs of antique tools—amassing a fair-sized collection. Despite this, I have found numerous items that I wish had been included. The problem with research is that one must arbitrarily make a cut-off despite the pain of doing so. Without doing this, the research would remain as research, and the book would never be completed.

Along with including as many categories as possible, there is no doubt that some areas are deficient, mainly due to a lack of images or information. I hope to rectify that problem in future editions of this book. My hope is that through this book, further information, literature, or even old trade catalogs may be obtained to help the cause. As it stands, this book was completed entirely from material in my own collection.

Obtaining current collector values for some items has been relatively easy, and very difficult or impossible for others. To this end, we have made notes of values at numerous antique shops and collector shows, as well as at auctions. At best, these values are always subjective, and are included here only as a general guide. I assume no responsibility for pricing information included in this book; it is given to the best of my ability and is not intended as an absentee appraisal of your property.

Before electric saws became popular, I recall the days of handsaws. On our farm, a new corncrib was built in 1947. All of the boards, planks and sills were cut with handsaws. One of my uncles was a carpenter, and as a youngster, taught me how to file a saw by hand. It was a lesson that is still remembered with fondness.

I also recall that about that time, my father was building some small semi-portable hog houses. In order to do this job he had several different handsaws, one of which he bought for 25¢ at an auction. I still have that saw…it remains as one of the best handsaws I have ever owned. My dad was also quite proud of himself on that building project when he bought a brand new rip saw. He was using 1' x 12' boards for the siding, with wood battens over the joints. At the ends, it was necessary to rip down the boards to fit, and that is when I learned to use a rip saw…I thought I was a real big shot when I could rip an eight-foot board in only a few minutes! A few years later we got our first power saw, and that pretty much ended the career for the rip saw.

Various sections of this book have held a special interest for me. As an erstwhile letterpress printer, I had a special liking for the many composing sticks and other trivia I could find for this book. There was a strong urge to also include old printing presses, but I remained strong and tried to keep the section on printing within bounds. Perhaps by the next edition I will succumb and include more items for this section. As noted above, the same holds true for many sections of this book. We have found many more images that really should have been included in this edition. However, it creates real havoc when going back and adding things after the fact, so again, we resisted the temptation.

It has been a real joy to compile this book. We hope that you, the reader will enjoy it as much as we have. We again urge anyone who can assist us for future editions by the way of literature and catalog information to contact us in care of Krause Publications. Thanks in particular to Brad Hahn, my supervisor at Wendler Engineering & Construction Company. He allowed me to take a leave of absence so that I could finish this book in a timely manner. Also my thanks to many different people at Krause Publications for their help in getting this book completed. And thanks be to God for having given me the talent to put my research into words.

A

Adzes, Picks and Mattocks

By definition, an adze has a curved blade set at a right angle to the handle, differing from the axe, which has the blade parallel to the handle. The adze is a very ancient tool, going back to ancient Egypt. Many different forms have been made, with the principal ones being the carpenter's adze, the ship adze, used mainly in marine construction; the cooper's adze built in various forms and used in barrel making; and the railroad, or track adze, used primarily for railway work.

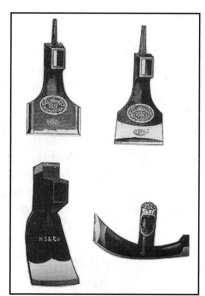

Carpenter's adze shown at top, ship adze left and carpenter's adzes center and railway adzes at right. Among tool collectors, values for these tools run the entire gamut from $10-$15 for a common carpenter's adze up to $150-$200 for a fine example of a ship adze. As with any collectible, condition is a major factor of value. An adze for instance, having an original handle and in good condition will bring a premium, compared to a rusty derelict without a handle.

Augers (Wood Boring)

Literally hundreds of different companies designed and/or built auger bits, many of them for special purposes. In construction, there was a great need for many different-sized holes. Watch for bits in good condition.

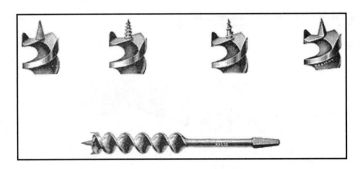

Various auger bit styles are shown at left. While the standard thread was normally supplied, the double thread could be used for wood that was gummy or extremely hard. It is shown to the left of the illustration. A quick boring style could be used for boring end grain, and the double quick thread was used only in softwoods. To the extreme right is the square point; it was used in power boring machines with a forced feed. The standard extension lip style is shown at the illustration bottom.

Axes

As with picks and mattocks, the axe goes back to antiquity. It is not our purpose to illustrate museum pieces, but rather to show various styles of axes that the collector or interested reader is likely to encounter.

Pricing of axes runs the entire gamut from a few dollars to several hundred. For example, a fairly nice double-bit axe might bring $15-$30, while a German-made broad axe of the 1800s might fetch $400-$500 at auction. Examples of well-made axes would include the Plumb, White, Kelly, Miller and numerous others.

Beyond these were axes of sometimes lesser quality, but built to a price, and sold by the thousands. Exceptional examples might include handmade axes, perhaps from a local blacksmith, or from a factory that specialized in the handmade article, regardless of price. Axes with the original handles usually sell for much more than those with a replacement. Also of note, early day woodsmen often preferred to make their own handle, and oftentimes these were fitted to a high-quality axe head.

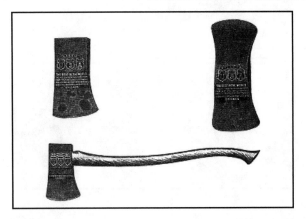

Hibbard, Spencer & Bartlett Company, Chicago, was a huge hardware wholesaler that offered a variety of axes to hardware stores under the USA brand. These were offered in single- and double-bit designs and in the Yankee or the Wisconsin pattern. Shown are two unhandled Hibbard, Spencer and Bartlett axes.

Early hardware catalogs often devoted a full-color page to their line of axes, as shown in the *1914 Hibbard, Spencer & Bartlett* book. Large companies like H.S. & B. oftentimes contracted with a manufacturer to supply an item under its own name. In the case of H.S. & B., the tradename of OVB or Our Very Best was the title ascribed to its line.

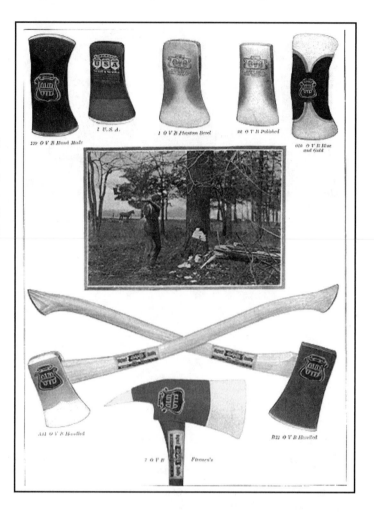

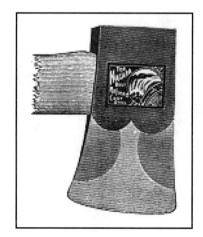

Standard axes usually were fitted with a handle of 32 to 36 inches in length. However, the Boys' Axe was generally fitted with a 26- or 28-inch handle. The head for the latter style usually weighed about 2-1/4 pounds. A standard single-bit axe was usually offered in sizes ranging from 3 all the way up to 5 pounds. Handmade axes often varied somewhat in weight from one to another, sometimes as much as half a pound.

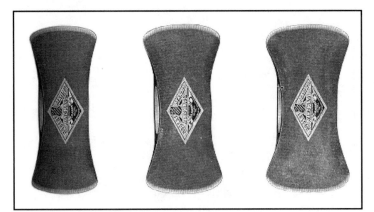

Advertising of the day claimed the double-bit axe from Robert Mann at Mill Hall Pennsylvania, to be the "best double-bit axe in the world." It was made of premium crucible steel and was offered in six sizes, ranging in quarter-pound increments from 3-1/4 to 4-1/2 pounds. High-quality axes such as this one will often auction at $25 and upward, depending on condition. The Mann axes are at left the Young's Pattern, center is the Humbolt Pattern, and at right is the California Reversible.

Broad axes took many forms, depending largely on local custom and personal preferences. One example is the California pattern from Baker & Hamilton of San Francisco. Other patterns might include the Yankee, or New York Pattern, the Canada pattern, or the Pennsylvania pattern. All styles evolved to suit local conditions and requirements. Hunt's style was made by Douglas Axe & Mfg. Co., East Douglas, Massachusetts. White's style was made by L. & I. J. White Company, Buffalo, New York. Axes from the latter firm are particularly sought after, and may bring $250 or more on auction. Those from Douglas are also very desirable, with prices going well over $100 at times. Shown at top is a broad pattern and the two below are ship axes with the Hunt's at left and the White's at right.

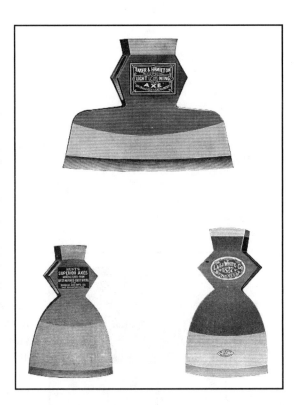

B

Beekeeping

Honeybees have been esteemed from time immemorial. Many different methods were developed to domesticate bees and harvest the honey they produced. For example, in old England the hives were made of braided straw that were formed into a circular hive about 12 inches in diameter and 12 inches high. These hives had a tapered top to shed water.

By the 1860s, the American practice was to build a wooden hive with removable frames. Although these were available from a few manufacturers, many of them were built locally. Their dimensions were about 13 inches wide, 18 inches deep, and about 20 inches high. Eventually, this design was surpassed by the Climax hive, which was in reality a further development of the original American hive design. Ultimately, the beehive evolved into the form which still remains to the present time.

Honey extractors were developed by the 1860s. Virtually all of them used centrifugal force to throw the honey from the combs, whereupon it drained to the bottom of the tank and was drawn off, ready for use. The honey knife was developed especially for use in uncapping the combs. Bee smokers were developed to temporarily stun the bees while working around the hives.

The bee smoker is occasionally found in antique shops, and a nice example will often bring $25-$40. Other beekeeping items are seldom seen in the collectibles market, and no known price guides have been located.

Belting Tools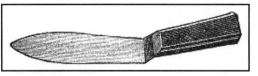

During the 1800s, with the rapid development of industrial tools in the United States, came the need for transmission belting. Rope drives were used to a minor extent, but leather belting was rapidly developed to transmit power in shops and factories. Eventually, canvas belting was available as a cheaper alternative to leather, and finally, rubber belting was developed as a practical answer. With the advent of the V-belt drive in the 1930s, the days of flat-belt drives drew to an end.

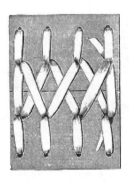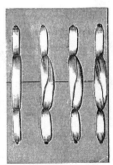

Rawhide or lace leather was used to make the joint, and various styles were made, with the butt joint being shown. Various lacing methods were used, but invariably, the joint was secured with lace leather. With the development of various metallic fasteners the laced joint fell into disuse. A permanent joint was secured with a glued joint. In this style the ends were tapered so that the finished joint was virtually invisible. This was a time-consuming job and required a fair amount of skill.

The belt groover was used on the inside of a laced joint. By grooving the inside of the belt, the laces dropped into the groove and ran smoothly over pulleys without an objectionable noise.

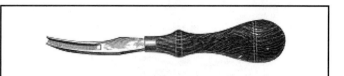

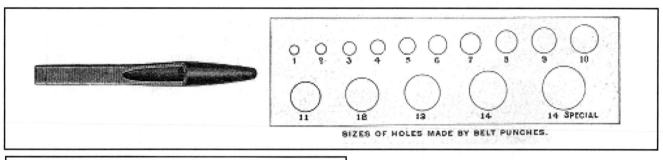

SIZES OF HOLES MADE BY BELT PUNCHES.

Various sizes of belt punches were available. Round punches were the most common, but oval punches were also available. Some were designed to a particular need, and some to the whim of the inventor.

Catalog pages illustrate several styles of belt punches and awls, as well as a combination tool and two styles of belt cutters. Belt studs came into use by the early 1900s, and required some special tools for installation. The combined tool was for that purpose, and the belt cutters shown in this illustration were used to adjust the belting's holes to accept belt studs.

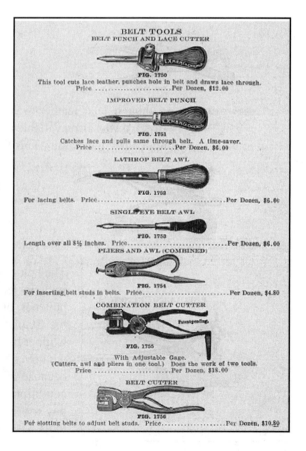

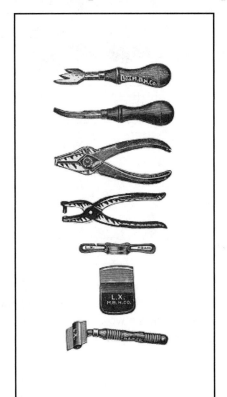

Various other belt tools were required. The belt marker was used for gauging the distance between holes in laced belts, and a belt groover is also shown. A combination belt cutter and plier is shown in this figure, along with a belt punch. The belt slicker was available in several sizes, and as its name implies, was used to smooth out a finished glue joint. Heel shaves were used in making the tapered glue joint. Once it was fitted out, hot glue was applied, the two halves were put in place, and then clamped under heavy pressure. Also shown is a glue scraper for removing old glue from a lapped joint.

Although lace leather was available in bundles of pre-cut strips, it was also available in full sides. It was then cut to size with a belt lace cutter. This little tool is seldom found today.

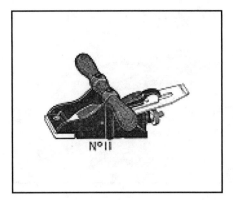

The belt plane was designed specifically for scarfing the ends of a glued lap joint in leather belting. Prices of belting tools vary a great deal. Awls, punches, and similar items usually bring only a few dollars, but items like the Stanley No. 11 plane (in good condition) might bring $75 or more. Clipper belt lacers usually sell from $40 and upwards, sometimes going for well over $100. The Rogers belt punch often sells for $15 or more, perhaps because of its unique design. As with all vintage tools and equipment, its condition is the largest determining factor of the price. Always expect to pay a premium price for tools in pristine condition. By the same token, tools with heavy rust often sell for little more than scrap value.

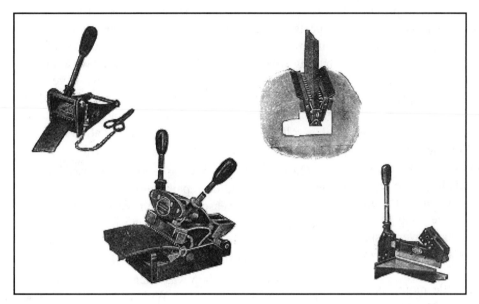

The coming of the Clipper lacer and others of its kind, about 1910, brought an end to laced belts. Within a short time the Clipper and its wire belt hooks dominated the market, although there were a few other manufacturers. Numerous styles were made, and the hooks were (and still are) made in various sizes to accommodate various belt thicknesses. Shown are a few models of the Clipper line.

Also shown is the rather popular Rogers Belt Punch. The semicircular sharpened blade could be extended from the handle as desired so that holes from 1/16 to 3/8 of an inch could be cut in any belt. Also shown in this 1924 illustration at right is a set of hollow punches neatly put up in a circular wooden canister. Revolving punches were suitable for rather light belts, but punches were necessary for the heavier styles.

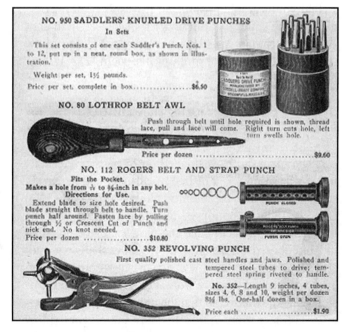

Blacksmithing

The art and practice of blacksmithing goes back to antiquity. For the purposes of this book, we pick up the profession as it stood in the 1800s. In order to provide greater clarity, carriage and wagonmaking tools are under that classification, and farrier (or horseshoeing) tools are also in a separate class. Although this section is fairly extensive, even without farrier's and wagonmaker's tools, it makes no pretense of approaching completeness.

In the days of the American frontier, and during the early settlement of the American West and Midwest, the blacksmith occupied a position of vital importance to a community. Not only was he called upon to repair almost anything that was bent or broken, but many implements of the day were built in the shop of the local blacksmith. Oftentimes, there wasn't even a sign advertising his shop; the ring of his anvil was all the calling card that was needed.

The early blacksmith shop was little more than a simple shed, almost impossible to heat in winter, and virtually unbearable in summer. It wasn't at all uncommon for the smith to work under a shade tree in the hot summer weather. Yet, Henry Wadsworth Longfellow immortalized the blacksmith in his poem, *The Village Blacksmith:*

Under a spreading chestnut-tree
The village smithy stands…

The blacksmith was called on to be the veterinarian, a wagon maker, a farrier, repairman, and in certain seasons was the community plowmaker. With John Deere's 1837 invention of the steel plow, it was the blacksmith who sharpened the plowshares or polished the moldboards. The edge of the plowshare was not sharpened on a stone; it was drawn out with a hammer. This was hard and heavy work, but it also required considerable knowledge so that the plow would work properly. Farmers were quick to sniff out a good plow mechanic, so the good ones got most of the work in the locality. Thankfully, the trip hammer started coming into blacksmith shops in the early 1900s, and it made sharpening of plowshares a much easier task.

Once a plowshare was drawn out or sharpened, it was then necessary to polish it. This was hard work, and was done on an "emery stand." In the early days, felt wheels were charged with emery powder, but eventually improved abrasives were developed and cemented to a buffing wheel. A blacksmith shop would have a number of these wheels on hand. Once the abrasive wore off, a new wheel was put on and work continued. Toward the end of the day, the used wheels were again coated with glue, rolled across a bed of abrasive, and allowed to dry. Then they were ready for use the next day.

Once the spring plowing season had passed, it was time to make and/or repair cultivator shovels. Then came the harvest season and the need to repair sickles, and by then the fall plowing season was at hand. Meanwhile, horseshoeing was a constant job, along with fixing wagons and other machines.

The blacksmith shop was often one of the first customers for a gasoline engine. With an engine, some line-shafting, and a few belts, the shop could be mechanized to a degree. A belt-powered drill press, an emery stand, a trip hammer, and perhaps a few other tools could all be operated from the gasoline engine. All of these innovations often made the blacksmith shop a point of interest and curiosity in a community. However, many blacksmiths zealously guarded their methods, and gadflies or curiosity seekers were not usually welcomed.

One could easily write an entire book about the mystique of the blacksmith and his shop. For this writer, an early memory was watching the sparks fly from the emery stand, and hearing the trip hammer working from a block away. My father was a reasonably good blacksmith, and I learned from him. Three of his uncles were blacksmiths, all of the highest caliber.

Times change and technology changes, too. By the 1950s, the days of the blacksmith were coming to an end. Although there were a great many plowshares to sharpen, the "throwaway" plowshares were coming onto the market, and by the 1960s, minimum tillage farming, or no-till farming was becoming popular. Machines were being built with highly-technical components far beyond the scope of the village blacksmith,

and the number of farms began to decline. Quietly, the blacksmith all but disappeared from the scene. Today, there has been a revival of the art, and a substantial number of shops carry on a profitable business—albeit blended with modern technology.

A few of today's blacksmiths specialize in ornamental ironwork. As in any other vocation, there are those with an inordinate amount of skill. Watching one of these highly-skilled smiths turn out a beautifully formed fire poker or some other object in just a few minutes is quite a sight.

Ordinarily a blacksmith would make his own fire set, but occasionally they were offered for sale. A complete set in reasonable condition will likely fetch $25 or more.

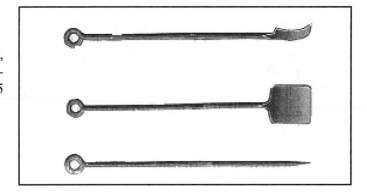

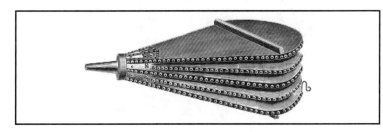

The bellows dates back to antiquity. Early forges used bellows for draft, but most of these were replaced with some type of blower by 1900. Despite this, a few sets of bellows remained in use. Large blacksmith bellows are an uncommon sight, so no market value has been found.

By 1900, a variety of forge blowers had come onto the market. The new forges were almost always equipped with a blower. Some shops had the forge built up of brick, and these blowers were intended for use with forges of this kind, or as a replacement to the bellows. Ordinarily, blowers of this kind sell from $20 and upwards.

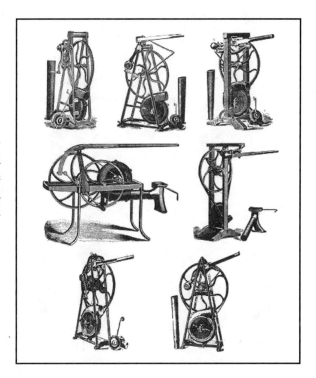

A wide variety of anvil tools was available. Blacksmith's punches were available in square and round patterns, and chisels were made for cutting cold iron, or for hot iron. Center punches and countersinks were also available, along with numerous styles of rock drill sharpening tools. As the name implies, the heading tool was used for forming heads of bolts, pins, and rivets. Most of these tools sell for only a few dollars apiece today.

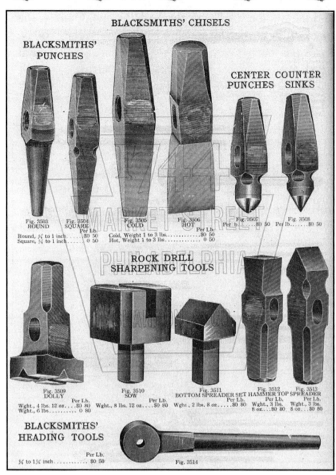

Numerous metal forming tools were available, but in addition, blacksmiths often made their own tools to suit a particular job. This illustration from an early machinery catalog shows some of the many different anvil tools that could be purchased. Current values usually run upward from $5.

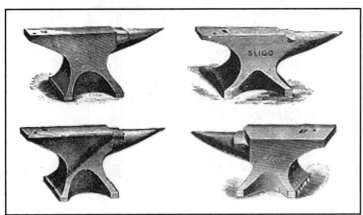

Many different companies manufactured anvils, and each smith had a certain preference. Among the famous makes were the Peter Wright, the Eagle, and the Hay-Budden. Styles varied from the ordinary blacksmiths' anvil to the horseshoers' anvil, to the plowmakers' anvil. The horseshoers' anvil was built with a special nib at the back of the horn that was used for drawing out toe clips on horseshoes. Generally, shop anvils weighed from 125 to 160 pounds. For some years, anvils have been valued at $1 or more per pound, depending on the make and the condition of the face.

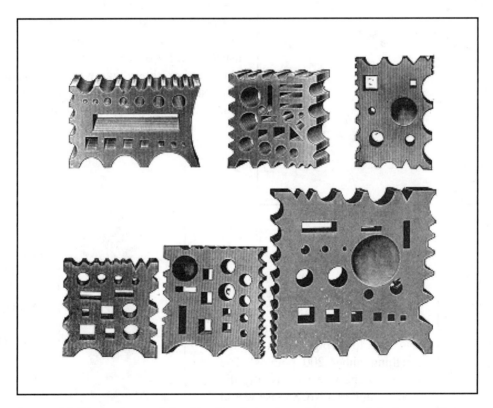

Swage blocks were used for hot forming of steel into special shapes. Various styles were made, usually of cast iron, and weighing anywhere from 100 to 600 pounds. A separate stand was available, but most smiths built their own stand. Swage blocks sell for $100 to $250, depending on size, condition, and style.

Blacksmith mandrels were made in solid and slotted styles, with the size being the diameter of the cone's base. Height varied from 40 to 60 inches, depending on the style and size. Mandrels were sometimes called a "blacksmiths' whistle." The logic was that anyone who had been a blacksmith long enough was also stout enough to pick it up and use it for a whistle. Current values run from $1 a pound and upward, depending on size and condition.

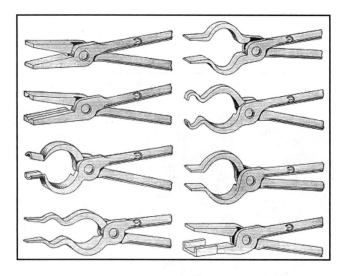

The variety of blacksmith tongs is endless. In addition to the standard styles available from supply houses, most smiths made tongs to suit their needs. Tongs usually sell for only a few dollars each, although very old ones, or those that were handmade sometimes bring substantially more. Imagine the work involved to make a pair of tongs with nothing but iron, a forge, anvil, and simple tools.

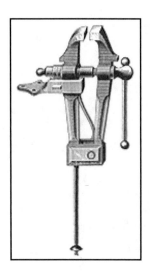

The solid box blacksmith vise is also known as a post vise, a leg vise, or a staple vise. These were made in numerous sizes, ranging from a small model with 3-inch jaws, up to a big 8-inch model, weighing about 200 pounds! The weight of the vise was usually the model number; a No. 85 vise would weigh about 85 pounds. Blacksmith vises usually bring upwards of $50, with the largest sizes being worth substantially more.

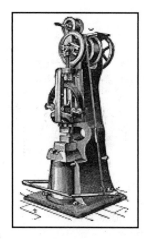

The Scranton hammer was one of many styles available in the late 1890s. It was built by Scranton & Company at New Haven, Connecticut. Presumably it was offered in various sizes.

The advent of the power hammer greatly eased the work of the blacksmith. During the 1890s, various styles of power hammers began to appear. One of the best known was the Little Giant from Mayer Bros. at Mankato, Minnesota. In about 1900, its first power hammers appeared. By 1910, the line was well developed, and ranged in sizes from 25 to 500 pounds. A special design was also available for driving the irons onto neck yokes and single trees.

A number of power hammer manufacturers were located in Iowa. The Grinnell Mfg. Company at Grinnell, Iowa, offered this unit in 1908, and for perhaps a few years surrounding that time. This 1,400-pound unit had the advantage of an adjustable stroke, which could be changed while the machine was running.

An 1887 advertisement for the Bradley Hammer noted that 800 of these machines were already in use. This machine was a helve hammer, and was intended to imitate the hammer blows delivered by the smith himself.

Hawkeye helve hammers first appeared in 1903, and were built up to about 1920. This unit was built by Hawkeye Mfg. Company, Cedar Rapids, Iowa.

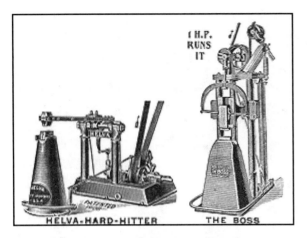

For 1911, Novelty Iron Works at Dubuque, Iowa offered a helve hammer which they christened the Helva-Hard-Hitter. It also offered a power hammer called The Boss.

MacGowan & Finigan Foundry & Machine Company at St. Louis, Missouri offered three sizes of its hammer in 1911. The 30-, 40-, and 80-pound models could be used for everything from light to moderately heavy work.

In the early 1900s, Kerrihard Company at Red Oak, Iowa, offered its power hammer in various sizes. Its design differed somewhat in the operating mechanism, but the frame was essentially the same as that of its contemporaries.

West Tire Setter Company, Rochester, New York, offered its helve hammer for a few years either side of 1910. It could be furnished with welding dies and drawing dies, as desired.

The 1900-1910 period saw countless new innovations in power machinery, and the development of the power hammer reached its height during this time. One example was the helve hammer from Foglesong Machine Company, Dayton, Ohio. The model shown here was introduced in 1908.

In 1916, this unusual helve hammer was advertised. It used a regular blacksmith's anvil, and the helve was fitted with an 8-pound sledge. The mechanism was designed to provide light or heavy blows at the will of the operator.

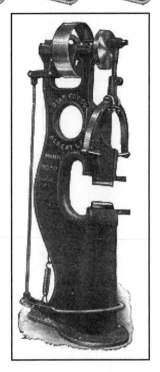

For 1911, the Star power hammer was offered only in a 50-pound size. This model differed slightly from many others because the dies were set at a 45-degree angle to the machine. Shown is a model built by Star Foundry Company at Albert Lea, Minnesota.

The Fairbanks Company with headquarters in New York City, was a major jobbing house for industrial machinery. Its 1908 catalog includes the Fairbanks Power Hammer in various sizes.

Champion Blower & Forge Company at Lancaster, Pennsylvania was a major manufacturer of blacksmith forges, blowers, and related equipment. Its 1913 model of the Champion power hammer was offered in 30- and 65-pound sizes. The unique double treadle design enabled the smith to work the hammer from either side. If the shop was built with two fires, the hammer could be placed between them.

Numerous styles of threading outfits were available to the blacksmith. One was the Champion Thread Cutting Machine of 1913, as shown here. It was a complete outfit, packed in a substantial wooden case. Various other styles are shown under *Screw Plates and Taps*.

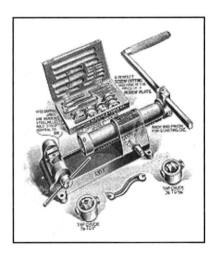

The Edwards shear first appeared in 1893. The No. 5 was capable of cutting a 4 x 1/2-inch bar, and the No. 10 could cut 4 x 3/4-inch soft steel. The shear was a great labor saver for the smith, since it eliminated the need to cut iron over the anvil. It was built by C. D. Edwards at Albert Lea, Minnesota.

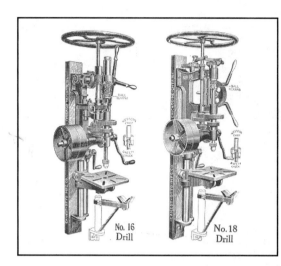

No. 16 Drill   No. 18 Drill

Various kinds of drills were available to the blacksmith already in the 1870s, but many shops did not have a "post drill" until the 1890s, or even later. Most of those available were hand operated, since many small shops did not have a small steam engine for power. With the coming of the gasoline engine, many smiths were able to afford a limited number of power machines. For the early 1900s, this might have included a power drilling machine from Canedy-Otto Mfg. Company, Chicago Heights, Illinois. Depending on the size and style, blacksmiths' post drills often sell in the range of $100 to $300.

Already in the 1880s, the Little Giant Punch & Shear was available to the blacksmith. At the time, most blacksmiths were fortunate to have a hand-operated post drill, so holes were punched through the hot metal over an anvil. A machine that would punch holes was, therefore, quite an addition to the shop. This unit would punch a 3/8-inch hole through 1/2-inch soft iron, and would shear iron up to 1/2-inch thick and 4-inches wide. It was built by Little Giant Punch & Shear Company at Sparta, Illinois.

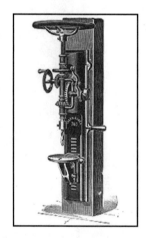

Numerous companies built drill presses. Early on was the post drill. It was designed for mounting to a suitable post in the shop, or perhaps on the wall. Drill presses were self-contained units designed for bench or floor. This 1909 model was built by Wiley & Russell Mfg. Company, Greenfield, Massachusetts. Post drills in good condition now bring $50 and more. Fancy ones might bring $150-$200.

Under the section *Screw Plates and Taps* in this book are illustrated various styles, but for this section, it is to be noted that some of the early advertising depicted, are *Blacksmiths' Tap & Die Sets*. After all, the blacksmith was usually the only one in a community to have such a precision tool. This particular set was offered by Wells Bros. Company, Greenfield, Massachusetts. Vintage tap and die sets, complete and in a well-fitted case often bring $50 to $100.

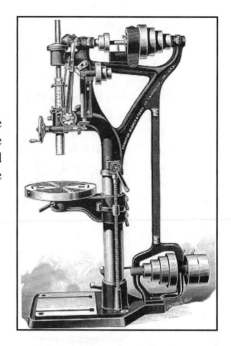

By 1910, the drill press was becoming a common sight in the blacksmith shop. By that time also, various other machine tools were creeping into the blacksmith shop. Proud indeed was the smith who had this Champion drill press, complete with power feed and numerous other features.

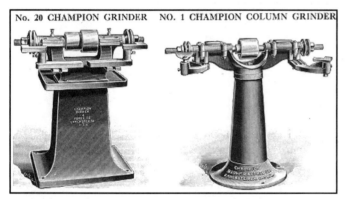

With the coming of steam or gas power to the blacksmith shop came various power equipment. The emery stand was also known as the grinder, and by various other names. Many different companies built them, and some were especially designed for certain jobs such as polishing plow moldboards and plow lays. While many of these have been scrapped, they are occasionally found, and usually sell for $50 to $100, but sometimes for much less.

The forge is nearly as old as civilization itself. For our purposes though, the built-in brick forge of the old blacksmith shop is not illustrated, nor are the hundreds of different styles developed for everything from horseshoes to locomotive parts. Today, the most common forge is the small farmer's style (shown at left), or the small blacksmith forge (shown at right). Those that have been in the weather for many years are often cracked or otherwise spoiled, and are suitable for little else than yard ornaments. However, a small forge in reasonably good condition will usually bring $50, and sometimes much more.

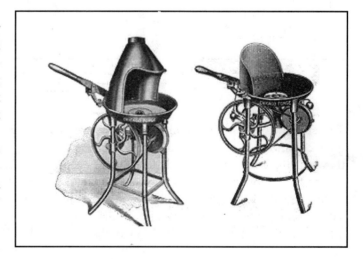

Blacksmith forges generally took on a rectangular form as shown here with this rather common Buffalo forge. Although some blacksmith shops had a built-in brick forge, many others used a forge of this style; it was sometimes called a plow forge. Plow lays were sharpened by heating the edge and drawing it out with a hammer. Plowing was the primary form of soil tillage, so a great many shops survived by sharpening plow lays for area farmers. In good condition, a blacksmith forge might fetch $100-$300.

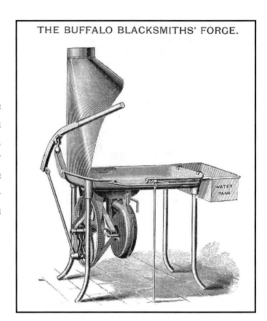

THE BUFFALO BLACKSMITHS' FORGE.

Blowtorches

By the 1920s, blowtorches were available at many hardware stores. Using gasoline fuel, the blowtorch was the first means that was readily available for providing a concentrated heat source. This was invaluable for thawing pipes, heating soldering irons, and many other uses. Shown here is a sampling of the Clayton & Lambert line. An unrestored torch might bring from $5 to $20. Those which have been restored and polished might bring slightly more.

Turner blowtorches were well known and are still quite common. As with the Clayton & Lambert line, they usually bring from $5 to $20. Numerous companies built blowtorches, and some of the unusual makes and models command slightly higher prices. The advent of propane torches and electric heaters effectively limited the market for blowtorches.

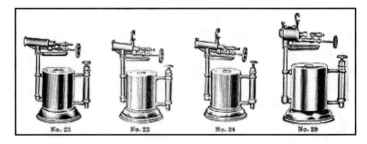

Boiler Tools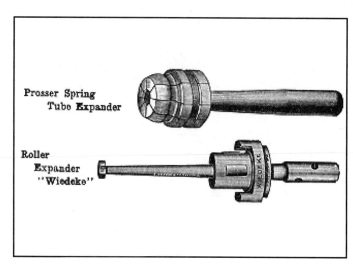

Steam boilers used steel fire tubes, making them much more efficient than a flueless boiler. The tubes were cut to length and then secured with a tube roller. The roller expanded the tube within the flue sheet so that it was water and steam tight. Occasionally a tube would start leaking, and oftentimes a good engineer could "touch up" the offending tube by expanding it slightly with a tube expander. The Prosser spring expander used a number of segments held together by an endless coil spring. It was used primarily when installing new tubes. The Wiedeke roller expander was usually used for repair work, as well as for new tubes. In 1927, a new 2-inch roller was priced at $3.50. Good tube rollers now bring $10 to $20, and are usually grabbed up by those who own vintage steam traction engines.

Prosser Spring Tube Expander

Roller Expander "Wiedeke"

Beading Tool

Boiler Ratchet

In 1935, a new beading tool sold for 76 cents! Once the new boiler tubes were cut and set into place with a tube expander, their slight protrusion from the flue sheet was rounded over with a tube beader or beading tool. This was very important, especially on the fire side of the tubes, otherwise the ends would be burned, ruining the tubes. The boiler ratchet was used for replacing boiler stay bolts. This work was entirely done by hand, and was time consuming as well as laborious. Repairing a steam traction engine out in the countryside, far from any sort of electricity or other power equipment required tools like this one. Ordinarily, the beading tool or the boiler ratchet brings only a few dollars today.

Books

There are old hardware catalogs, tool catalogs, instructional texts illustrating old tools, and many other books that could be included. Old hardware catalogs often bring $200 or more, although those after the 1930s can bring substantially less. Then there are machinist tool catalogs; some of the scarce ones will bring $100 and more, especially when in leather bindings. The cheaply-printed ones of later years often sell for $50 or less.

Many of the early manufacturers of pumps and similar items put up their catalog in a highly decorated, hardback book. Some of these, especially from 1900 and earlier, will bring a handsome figure, often running over $100.

As is commonly said, *caveat emptor*, or "Let the buyer beware." We have seen some reprinted catalogs that were passed off as original, and the reprints have an insignificant value. We have noticed that some of the online auction houses seem to get sky-high prices for some of the old catalogs, but the Latin phrase quoted at the beginning of this paragraph once again applies!

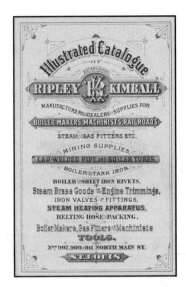

Some of the early tool and hardware catalogs epitomized the Victorian style of book design. This is evident from the title page for the 1882 catalog of Ripley & Kimball of St. Louis, Missouri. This beautiful hardbound book came into the author's possession many years ago for only a few dollars. Today it is probably worth about $200 or a bit more.

Braces and Boring Machines

Many references to these devices illustrate fancy (and ancient) styles ranging from $750 and upwards. As noted in other instances, those interested in pricing these ancient styles should refer to specific price guides, or even consider a professional appraisal. Excellent information is also available on the Internet. For the purposes of this book, we have selected devices dating back to the late 1800s, up to recent times.

The brace (also known as a bitstock) goes back to antiquity. In the 1600s, the brace was improved somewhat, consisting of a wooden frame reinforced with brass plates. The all-metal brace was primarily an American development that originated in the 1860s and gained wide popularity within a few years.

Braces were an essential part of every carpenter's toolbox until recent times. The coming of electric drills, and more recently, the cordless electric drill, have largely replaced the time-honored brace.

Boring machines were used primarily in construction work involving mortise and tenon joints in huge beams. The boring machine permitted easy drilling through the parts for a wooden peg; the latter held the two pieces together.

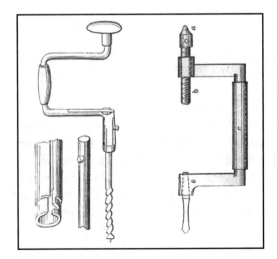

Numerous patents for bit braces and bit stocks were issued after the late 1860s. Most of this activity was in the eastern states. The all-metal bit stock or brace was largely an American invention; Europeans continued with their wooden braces for some years after. Some of the early braces can easily bring $500 or more, but they are seldom found except in a museum or with a dedicated tool collector.

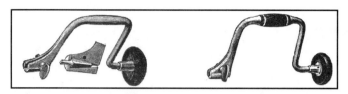

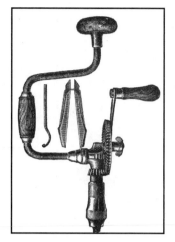

Fray's Plain brace of the early 1900s simply followed the design that had been marketed for a number of years. Apparently, this design followed the work of J. S. Fray at Bridgeport, Connecticut. One of his earliest patents was issued already in 1872. Another design was Fray's Spofford; it apparently was the design of N. Spofford of Haverhill, Massachusetts. The Iron Head Nos. 8-14 are shown above left and the Wood Head Nos. 108-114 are shown above right. The plain all-metal designs sometimes sell for only a few dollars, while the better quality braces with fancy wood handles might bring $40 to $60.

A removable drilling attachment was featured on this ratchet drill brace of 1915. This one had a 10-inch sweep, ball bearings, and used cocobola wood on the head and handle. All the metal parts were nickel plated. In 1915, this brace sold for the tidy sum of $3.

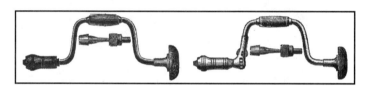

New Haven bit braces were well known, with these two 1915 examples being shown in the plain and ratchet styles. The plain style required room to make the full sweep, while the ratchet could be used in a tight corner. These models featured Lignum Vitae heads and cocobola handles. Depending on condition, these braces can sell anywhere in the $10-$40 range; as with most collectibles, condition is everything!

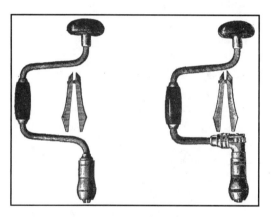

Several companies manufacturing bit braces were centered in Connecticut. In particular, there was considerable activity in the town of Bridgeport. Thus, the Bridgeport braces, shown here in plain and ratchet styles. Like most braces, they were offered in three sizes of 8-, 10-, and 12-inch sweep.

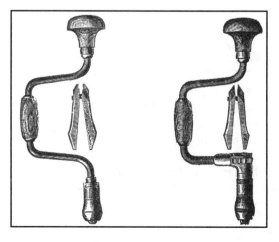

The Farmer's brace was, as its name implies, made expressly for farm use. While it was a very serviceable brace, it lacked the beauty and some of the features found on braces used by professional woodworkers—yet it permitted the farmer to at least drill a hole in a board when necessary. A plain style is shown at left and a ratchet style at right.

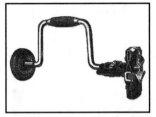

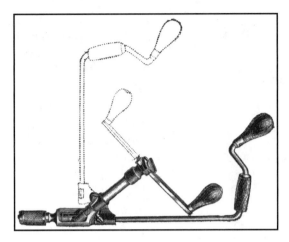

Electricians favored the corner brace because it permitted work in tight corners that would be impossible for the ordinary style. This McClellan's Corner Brace of about 1910 was one such style. Ordinarily, a corner brace in good condition will sell for $20 or more today.

Specialty braces were also available, including Goodell's Hollow Auger and Brace shown above. It was designed especially for cutting tenons, and was adjustable to cut anywhere from 1/4 to 1-1/4 inches in diameter. Specialty braces can often bring $50 or more.

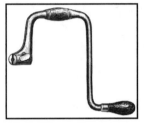

Spofford's Whimble, as shown was designed entirely different than the ordinary bit stock. Also spelled as "Wimble," the term is a throwback to early English times. A whimble in decent shape might bring from $50 to $75 today.

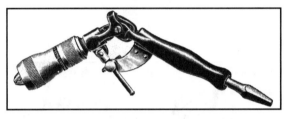

By the early 1900s, all sorts of attachments were available for the brace. Included was this angular borer. It permitted a craftsman to drill holes where an ordinary brace would be impossible to use. Many of these attachments are now quite scarce; no pricing information has been found for any of them.

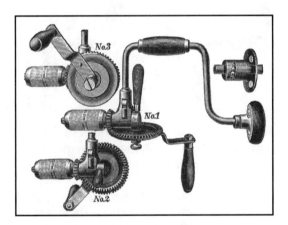

Millers Falls Co. at Millers Falls, Connecticut, offered this combination Brace and Breast Drill as early as 1910, and perhaps even sooner. Known as the M.F. No. 192, it featured the best quality and even permitted the drill attachment to be used in three different positions as shown in the illustration. In 1910, this unit sold for slightly over $4 … a princely sum in those days. Today, examples might bring as much as $100.

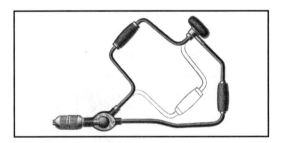

In 1910, this Corner Bit Brace from Millers Falls was priced at nearly $5. Electricians were the biggest users of the corner brace, since they were often required to drill holes at unusual angles and in confined spaces. At the time, many houses were being fitted up for electric lights, so there was a great demand for the corner brace.

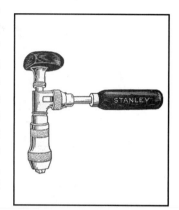

For tight corners, Millers Falls offered its No. 140 Ratchet Corner Brace. This device permitted work in close quarters, and although it was slow, it nevertheless permitted drilling of holes in places that would otherwise be inaccessible.

Among other styles, Stanley offered its No. 984 Ratchet Corner Bit Brace in 1910. This specialty device is seldom seen today, and in fact, we have not seen one in an antique mall for several years. We had no success in determining the market value of this device on today's market. However, we should think that in good condition, it would be of considerable interest to tool collectors.

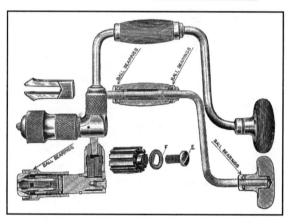

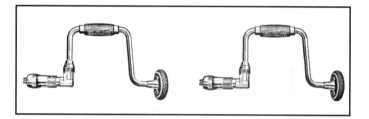

D. Goodell at Millers Falls, Massachusetts, received several patents for bit braces in the 1870s. Early in the twentieth century, Goodell-Pratt offered several styles. To the left of this illustration is the 7008 to 7014 series, all of which were high quality, serviceable braces. To the right are the 6008 to 6014 styles of similar design, except that they were built with a heavier chuck, head, and handle.

The Millers Falls Lion bit brace was a high-quality tool. It offered good centering accuracy using tapered square shank bits, and was even capable of holding a No. 1 Morse taper bit style when necessary. Ball bearings were used throughout, and in fact, this style was intended for the professional carpenter and woodworker. A nice example will usually bring $25 and up.

For those wanting precise, state-of-the-art bit stocks and bits, there were few, if any, equals to the Russell Jennings line. This combination set in a fitted wooden box sold for $15 in 1910. In those days, $15 was quite a sum. Finding a complete set like this in its protective wooden case would be quite unusual today.

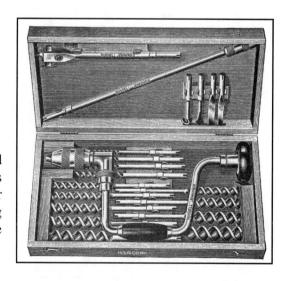

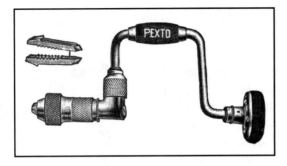

While the name is usually associated with sheet metal equipment, Pexto offered several sizes and styles of braces, at least into the 1920s. The company was officially known as Peck, Stow & Wilcox Co. Occasionally these braces are found with "PS&W" stamped on the sweep.

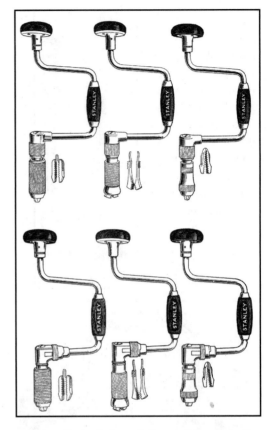

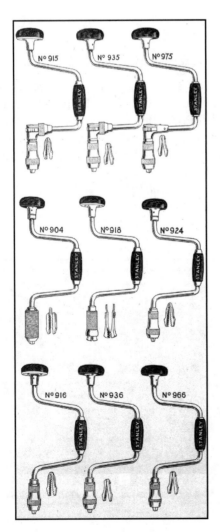

Stanley Rule & Level Co. at New Britain, Connecticut, offered an extensive line of bit braces in its 1911 catalog. Included are those shown here. Within each style were several options, including sweeps ranging from 6 to 14 inches, and various styles of jaws. Something like the No. 921 ratchet brace might bring from $30 to $40. A nice example of these braces still in the original box will bring about $100 or maybe more.

Stanley tools have always been very popular, and in fact, there are many collectors specializing in Stanley tools. Shown here are nine styles of bit braces dating from 1911. The 915, 935, and 975 styles are all ratchet braces, with the remainder being sleeve bit, or plain braces with no ratchet mechanism.

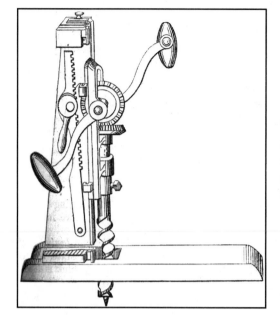

This boring machine of 1871 was an early development for this device. It was used primarily for boring mortise and tenon joints to receive a wooden pin. The latter was driven through the hole to secure the beams together. A boring machine eased the process and ensured that the hole would be precisely square.

By 1900, the boring machine had become very popular with contractors. A contractor in a rural area needed one to build barns and other buildings that used heavy beams. To the left is shown the Millers Falls No. 146 boring machine, and to the right is the No. 6702 from James Swan Company at Seymour, Connecticut. Numerous other companies built boring machines, but by the 1930s construction methods had changed; mortise and tenon construction was being replaced, and the need for boring machines diminished. In 1910, one of these machines sold for $10—but today they often bring ten times that figure.

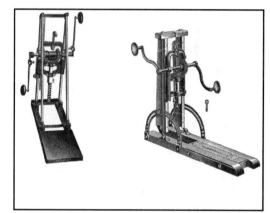

Bricklaying and Masonry Tools and Equipment

This section addresses only those tools used specifically for bricklaying and cement work. For instance, trowels are used for laying brick, with different styles used for concrete work. String lines, levels, and various other devices are also used in carpentry and other building trades. To avoid redundancy, this section has been limited to those items specifically used in bricklaying and concrete work. The list is not at all inclusive; various specialty jobs required special tools, and these have not been included. In addition, there were a great many tools locally crafted.

Numerous styles of trowels have been (and still are) made. The older styles, especially when in good condition are quite collectible. Old tool catalogs illustrate literally dozens of different styles. While some have dropped by the wayside, a considerable number are still made; the craft has not changed dramatically over the years. Some of the collectible trowels are bringing $25 and more, while the common ones sell for only a few dollars.

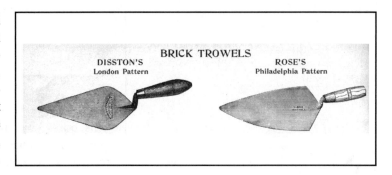

Perhaps it is an exercise in semantics, but what is commonly called concrete work today, has been classified as cement work until recent times. Thus, this 1915 illustration shows a "Cement Workers Trowel." This one was made of aluminum to reduce weight, and is properly called a "float." Older cement trowels in good condition are seldom found.

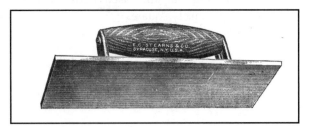

Indentation rollers were used on the green concrete to provide a better grip as might be needed in wet or icy conditions. Only occasionally were they used for a decorative effect. Since this was not a popular tool they are quite scarce today. A good example might bring $25 or more.

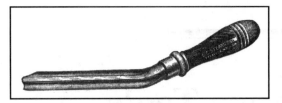

Tuck pointers were another form of trowel; they were usually used to fill in a faulty mortar joint. By holding a trowel carrying a small amount of mortar, the pointer could be used to deftly fill the joint. Pointers or pointing trowels were made in many different styles, and are seldom seen today.

Numerous styles of jointers, groovers, edgers, and corner tools were available. Most were made of cast iron, and a few were made of brass. Some were nickel plated. These tools are found occasionally, but with the coming of concrete saws their need was largely eliminated. Edgers are still used occasionally, but new lightweight steel designs replaced the heavier cast designs of previous years. These tools, when in good condition, often bring $15-$25 or even more.

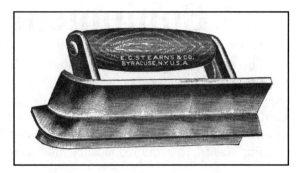

The rotary jointer is rarely found today, even at flea markets and antique malls. Jointing is necessary to provide a place for the concrete to crack as the result of expansion and contraction. Cracking in a straight line along a finished joint is not regarded as being objectionable, but a diagonal crack across the finished work detracts from the job.

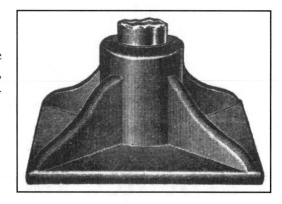

In an effort to compact the poured concrete, hand tampers were available. They were little different than an ordinary dirt tamper, but nevertheless were made especially for concrete work. The coming of concrete vibrators all but ended the need for hand tampers.

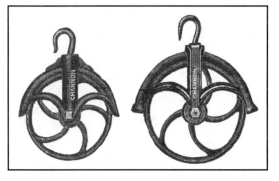

A masonry job of any height at all required scaffolding, and of course, this meant hoisting the brick and mortar up to the level of the workmen. Commonly known as well pulleys, they were on every job so that the laborers could hoist material onto the scaffold. Well pulleys are fairly common, but usually bring $15-$20, and sometimes much more, especially if the pulley is of an ornate design.

Butchering (See Farmstead Tools)

Butter Making (See Dairy Equipment)

C

Calipers (See Machinist Tools)

Carpenter Tools

This section looks at some of the various carpenter tools not already included in other classifications.

For further information on specific tools, the reader is referred to the following sections:

- Augers
- Braces
- Clamps
- Compasses & Dividers
- Draw Knives
- Drills (Hand & Power)
- Hammers
- Hatchets
- Levels
- Mallets
- Marking Gauges
- Planes
- Plumb Bobs
- Routers
- Saws
- Saw Vises
- Screwdrivers
- Squares
- Vises

To include all these categories within the title of Carpenter Tools would have made this section complicated and difficult to read, thus our decision to split many of these groups into separate categories.

As with many sections of this book, we have not attempted to include the wide variety of homemade tools and equipment. For example, my own collection includes various carpenter tools that were obviously made by a talented craftsman. Depending on the tool, its condition, and the skill used in producing it, some of these items are now very pricey among tool collectors. It is nearly impossible to establish a price guide to these items.

Although this section is itself rather small, considerable space has been devoted to specific categories within the realm of carpenter tools and equipment. Also of interest are some of the unique and innovative machines developed especially for various aspects of woodworking.

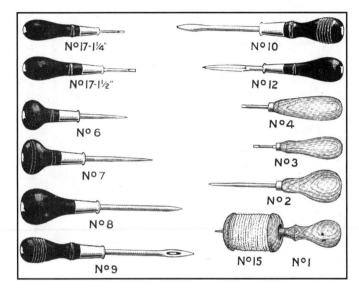

No 17-1¼"
No 17-1½"
No 6
No 7
No 8
No 9
No 10
No 12
No 4
No 3
No 2
No 15   No 1

Only a sampling of awls is shown here, with these being from a 1910 Stanley catalog. There are hundreds of different styles, but all are designed for the same purposes of scribing lines, marking out, and even for punching holes. Of particular interest in this collection is the No. 15 Chalk Line Reel. It could be supplied with or without a No. 1 awl, the latter serving as a convenient handle.

Many different kinds of expansive bits have been designed. All served the same essential purpose of permitting a carpenter to bore a hole of large size. Some expansive bits could be adjusted to as high as 3 inches. Hole saws and similar devices essentially ended the need for expansive bits. Examples shown are Wright's expansive bits.

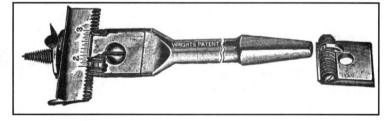

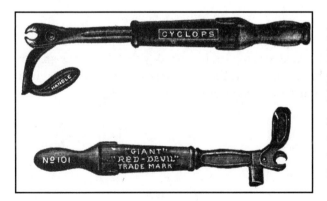

Numerous styles of nail pullers have been offered. The idea was to hammer the jaws into the wood so they could get a grip on the nail head. Then by prying back on the built-in fulcrum the nail could be withdrawn. Professional carpenters held this tool in disdain, using it only when absolutely necessary. The telltale marks of the nail puller indicated to everyone that a mistake had been made. Shown at top is the Cyclops nail puller, at bottom is the No. 101 Giant S&H nail puller.

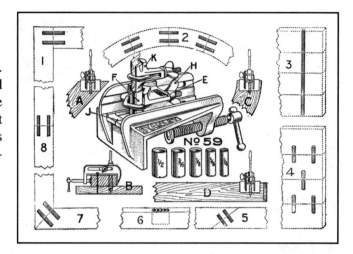

This doweling jig was intended for use with auger bits. By use of this tool, precisely located holes could be bored repetitively, as for instance, when setting the pegs in the edges of table leaves. Doweling jigs are still used, but have been adapted for use with electric power tools. As with many of the tools shown here, prices vary considerably, with none of these tools being terribly expensive.

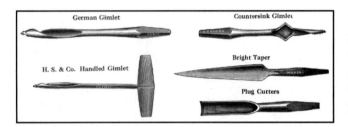

For drilling tiny holes the gimlet bit was often used. Several styles are shown here, including those used as a combination gimlet and countersink. Since they were rather fragile, most of them have now disappeared. Gimlets were sized in 32nds of an inch, usually ranging from Size 2 to Size 7.

For cutting internal and external threads in wood, the iron screw boxes shown here have been used. They are still used today. However, an ancient set of screw boxes is hard to find. We have found no pricing on these tools in the current collectibles market.

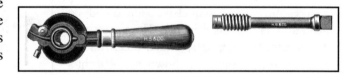

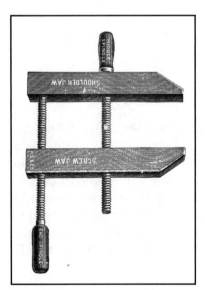

Old handscrews or clamps are found occasionally. Usually they bear the scars of hard use. Many in fact, broke under the strain, so today the older ones are not nearly as common as might be supposed. Carpenters and cabinetmakers might have owned a number of hand screws in different sizes.

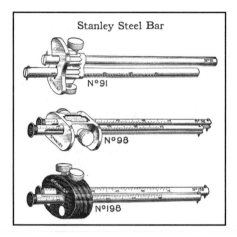

Stanley Steel Bar

N°91
N°98
N°198

Hundreds of different mortise gauges have been offered over the years. Mortise gauges differ from marking gauges. Mortise gauges require two independent marking points, while marking gauges have but a single point. Some are of all-metal construction, and many others are built of wood. Prices vary widely. Ordinary marking gauges are often priced under $20, while some of the fancy ones might bring $80 or more. Occasionally the home-built marking gauge will be found. Some of these will be very ornate, and fully display the maker's skills.

Carpenter's tool chests often bring $200 and upwards, depending on the style, size, and quality of construction. In 1910, this chest, complete with the tools shown, was priced at $90...quite a price for the time. Although factory-built tool chests are found occasionally, a great many were built by the craftsman who was going to use it. Thus, many of them are quite ornate, and very well built.

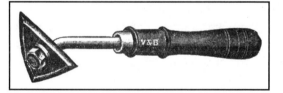

The box scraper was seldom used by the framing carpenter, but found extensive use in furniture and cabinet building. The scraper was an invaluable tool for smoothing wood surfaces. It should be noted that many early carpenters preferred to use a piece of glass as a scraper. It would hold an edge for a long time, and was very sharp.

Lucky indeed was the carpenter of the 1920s who had a combined woodworking machine. This one, from C. H. & E. Mfg. Company at Milwaukee, Wisconsin, was even equipped with the company's own 6-horsepower engine. It could also be furnished with an electric motor drive. This one consisted of a saw, jointer head, and boring attachment, all in one unit. Large construction projects might have one or more of these units. Owing to their weight, most of them were placed into a carpenter shop where they remained throughout their working life.

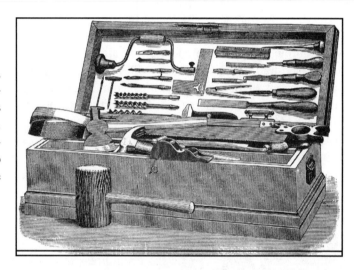

Combination woodworking machines became fairly popular with carpenters of the 1920s. Parks Ball Bearing Machine Co. at Cincinnati, Ohio, built this one, No. 379D. Priced at $165, it included a band saw, table saw, 12-inch jointer, and boring attachment. It could be equipped to run with a gasoline engine, electric motor, or from overhead lineshafting. Very few of these units can be found today.

Wood-turning lathes were another essential tool for the cabinetmaker and related trades. American Saw Mill Machinery Company presented this one about 1910. It could be furnished as a complete unit, or as a kit containing the iron parts and detailed construction drawings. This permitted the buyer to furnish his own timber to construct the legs and the crossbeams. Although these lathes were often seen in old-time shops, very few now remain.

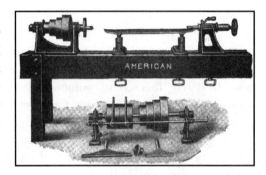

Although intended for larger factories, rather than a local shop, the Drawer Front Press shown here provides an idea of how these designs were fabricated. In use, the clamps were placed over a stack of lumber, placed in the press, and tightly clamped into place. The rod clamps were then tightened down, holding the stack in position. At this point the stack was removed from the press and put into storage until it dried. Meanwhile the press could be readied for yet another batch of drawer fronts.

Cabinetmakers benches are found occasionally. One of these benches in good to excellent condition will usually bring $500 or far more than that in some cases. Usually these benches represented the best of the cabinetmaker's art, especially when built locally by the craftsman who would be using it. For instance, cabinetmaker's benches built locally in Iowa's Amana Colonies, can bring $1,000 or more if in good condition. Some of these were built of local walnut, cherry, oak, and other fine woods.

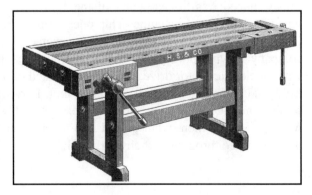

Carriage and Wagon Making

Carriage and wagon making encompassed several different trades. There was the wheelwright who actually crafted the wooden wheels, then set the hubs and tires. There was the blacksmith who crafted the metal parts such as the fifth wheel and the axles. For carriages, a highly-skilled craftsman was needed to fabricate the wooden body. Seats and cushions required a skilled upholsterer.

By the 1880s, most shops needing a replacement hub for instance, would order it from a factory specializing in these goods. Aside from the time element (it might take several weeks to telegraph an order and have it delivered) few shops were equipped to make wheel hubs, nor were the required skills present. On the other hand, a good wagon shop might well have had the equipment to replace broken spokes or felloes. A felloe or felly is one of the segments used to make up the rim of the wagon wheel. These were joined with dowels, and drilled on their inside face to receive the spokes. The steel tire was then shrunk over the outside. Light wheels as used in carriages were often made of bent wood, with two or more of these bent pieces being used to make up the outside of the wheel.

Until about 1900, there were literally hundreds of carriage and wagon manufacturers spread around the United States. Most of their sales were regional in nature, owing to shipping costs. Eventually, a few large firms came to dominate the market, but with the automobile's coming, the carriage trade declined to almost nothing by 1920. Wagons continued through into about 1940, and after World War II, very few wagon builders were left.

Occasionally, it was necessary to reset the tires on a wagon. Usually this was due to shrinkage of the wood. The tire bolts were all removed, and the tire was driven off the wheel. The blacksmith or wheelwright would then measure the inside of the tire, using a "traveler" or a tire wheel. This measurement was recorded and another reading was taken of the wooden wheel's outside. Good judgement then decreed how much the tire had to be shrunk in order to have a good fit. Not enough shrinking, and the tire would be loose again in a matter of weeks. Too much shrinking, and the tire would actually dish the wheels.

A tire shrinker was thus a major tool in every shop. Usually the tire was heated at a certain point, and then moved to the shrinker. Its powerful jaws engaged the tire and compressed the hot metal sufficiently to shrink it, thus decreasing the tire's diameter.

Once the tire was shrunk to its proper size, a circular stack of pine kindling or even corncobs was set up outdoors. The wagon tire was placed in the fire, and when sufficiently hot, it was picked up with tongs, set over the wheel and quickly driven into place. Working quickly, the hot metal was cooled with water to keep it from burning the wood. Any work to replace a spoke for instance, required the metal tire's removal. Today, it is likely that a craftsman will simply cut the tire, shorten it to fit, and then weld the two ends together before refitting it to the wheel.

Also shown in this section are felloe oilers. These were cast-iron troughs which were filled with linseed oil. Corncobs or kindling wood was placed around the troughs to heat the oil. The wheels were then placed in the hot oil and turned every few minutes so that the hot linseed oil would penetrate the wood.

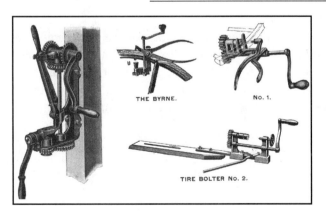

THE BYRNE.   NO. 1.

TIRE BOLTER NO. 2.

As shown with the Byrne tirebolter, this device was used to hold the bolt in place, the nut was started, and by simply cranking a handle, it was tightened quickly and securely. Many of these devices were made, but they are seldom found today.

The cross wrench shown here was used for tightening the nuts on tirebolts. This four-way design handled virtually any size, making it a handy gadget for the wheelwright.

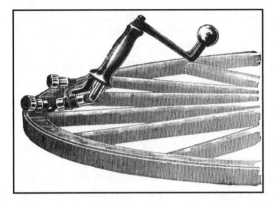

Tirebolters are seldom found today, and when they are, many tool collectors cannot identify their intended use. As noted previously, there are a great many others in addition to the one shown here, Carr Tire Bolter No. 4. Tool collectors specializing in carriage and wagon items would likely pay a premium price for these devices, often $100 or more.

While "tire wheel" is the given name for these devices, they were often known as a "traveler" among blacksmiths and wheelwrights. The traveler was made in many different styles and by many different manufacturers. Some were built with a 21-inch circumference, while many others were made with a 24-inch circumference. Blacksmiths used a

"Green River" Tire Wheel.   "LIGHTNING" TIRE WHEEL.   "LION" TIRE WHEEL.

traveler for many different measuring jobs, but the wheelwright used it to fit the iron tire to the wooden wheel. By careful measuring, the tire could be fitted so that it would fit tightly over the wheel, drawing the entire wheel tightly together for added strength and rigidity. Travelers often bring $50 or more.

When it was necessary to either tighten or remove a tirebolt, the tapered head would often turn in the tire. To obviate this problem, the tire bolt clamp was used to force the bolt's head tightly into the tire, thus permitting the workman to remove the nut. Many different devices were made for this purpose, but few can be found today.

The tire bolt marker was another unique device, and like many others used by the wheelwright, is seldom found today. It was used for locating holes. A pin on the marker's bottom side was placed in an existing hole in the wooden rim. By clamping the device in place, the center punch on top could be driven into the tire, so that a new, matching hole could be drilled. Shown is a Green River tire bolt marker.

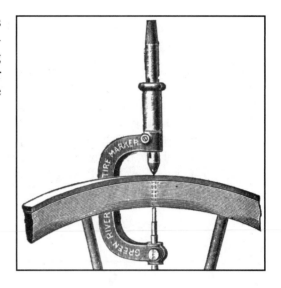

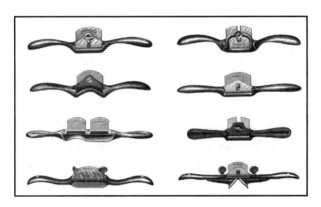

Knight's Mechanical Dictionary of 1871 notes that the name of the spokeshave obviously came from its original use of dressing spokes for wheels. Hundreds of different styles have been made; many of them for a specific purpose. Shown here are a few styles intended primarily for the carriage and wagonmaking trades. Today, wooden spokeshaves (in excellent condition) will bring from $30 to $50 and perhaps more. Metal spokeshaves often sell in the $20-$40 range.

The beading tool was used for beading, reeding or fluting wooden panels. When building a coach body, it was common practice to enhance the appearance by suitable decorative work. Beading tools are found only on an occasional basis.

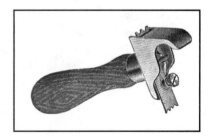

Tenon pointers were, as their name implies, intended to point or taper the tenon of wheel spokes to facilitate driving them into the felloe. Oftentimes they are found for $10 to $20. Shown from left are the Dowell No. 0, No. 1, No. 2, and No. 3.

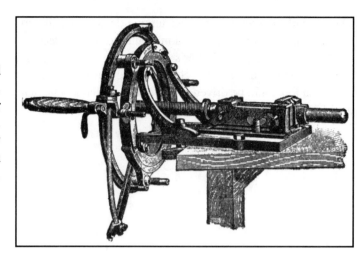

Hub boxing machines were used to bore the hole and could bore the hole straight or tapered as desired. Many of these machines could also cut the shoulder for the box and the rim for the nut, all in one setting. As with many wagon- and carriage-making tools, very few still exist, and usually bring premium prices when found. Shown is the Carr Hub Boxing Machine No. 3.

In 1900, this Carr hand-powered hub boring machine sold for $62.50. Thus, it was seldom seen, except in a wagon shop. Wagon and carriage builders usually were not found in small towns, so today these devices are scarce indeed.

Aside from the hollow augers, there were spoke tenoning machines. These were built specifically to cut the tenon, which was fitted into the felloe. Using this device insured the tenons were cut accurately to provide a better fit into the felloe. In 1900, this device sold for $10.

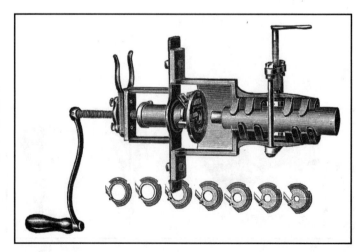

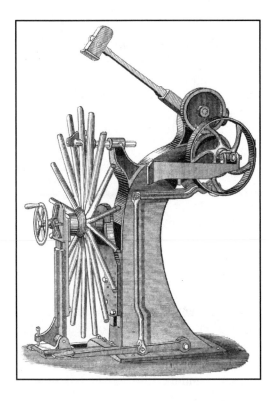

By 1872, there were fifty or more patents on spoke tenoning machines. Prior to the development of this device, tenons were cut by hand or with a hollow auger fitted to a brace. In the machine shown here, the spokes were driven into the finished hub, with the tenons being cut in the next stage. The Carr machine shown here sold for $68 in 1900.

While there are literally many hundreds of different drawing knives, there were designs suited especially to carriage-, coach-, and wagon-making. Today, the metal designs shown here might fetch from $25 to $40. Wooden frame designs might well bring upwards of $40. Shown from left are the Carr Coach Knife and the Carr Carriage Knife.

Dozens of different companies built tire benders. These were used to actually form the iron tire from a piece of flat stock. By moving the adjustable roller noted at the left, the tire size could be precisely regulated. Tire benders are seldom found, and usually bring a premium price because of their scarcity. This one sold for $10 in 1900.

The tire shrinker was simply a device to shrink the tire's inside diameter very slightly. There were hot shrinkers and cold shrinkers, but all had the same purpose. Today, some styles might bring $200 or more. Shown from left are Ideal and Mole's models.

These cast-iron pans were sold singly, but usually used in pairs. In late winter or early spring (before fieldwork), the felloe oilers were nested in some corncobs or kindling to heat the linseed oil. The wagon wheels were then placed into the hot oil so that it could completely penetrate every crevice and pore. Cast felloe oilers will often bring $25 or more.

Various kinds of axle gauges were built. All had the same purpose which was to obtain the correct "set" and "gather" of the wheels for coaches, carriages, and other light vehicles. Even at the turn of the twentieth century, this device sold for $8. Shown is the Wills' No. 470B.

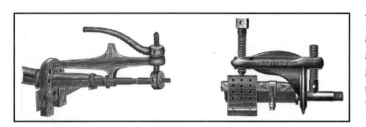

When it was necessary to adjust the set or gather of an axle, several different styles of axle setters were available. All had the same purpose of bending the axle shaft to obtain the proper adjustment. Axle setters are seldom found. Shown left to right are the Universal axle setter and the Little Giant axle setter.

Although the coach, carriage, or wagon shop was equipped with a wide variety of ordinary planes, the T-Plane was adapted particularly to the needs of the carriage maker. T-Planes often bring upwards of $150.

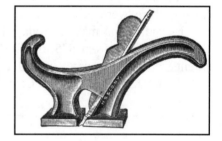

Panel routers were a special tool used primarily by the carriage maker. They could be used for cutting mouldings, or to cut various sizes of grooves, usually for decorative work. These specialized tools seldom sell for less than $50 and those with a wooden frame (rather than metal) often bring upwards of $150.

By 1900, there were numerous companies that specialized in making wheels and wheel components. For instance, a ruined hub could often be replaced by going back to the wagon or coach maker. Otherwise, a company specializing in these parts could usually supply a matching replacement. Although the wagon hub shown here is not a part of our work on carriage and wagon making, a careful look illustrates the tremendous amount of craftsmanship required to make a single wagon hub!

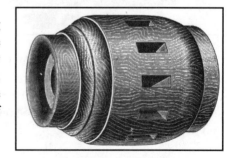

Cement Tools (See Bricklaying & Masonry Tools)

Chisels

The list of chisels is virtually endless. *Knight's American Mechanical Dictionary of 1871* lists 69 distinctively different kinds of chisels. Certainly, there are other styles added since that time. In general terms, however, there are three major classes: chisels for stone, for metal, and for wood. We will concentrate primarily on various kinds of wood chisels.

Until the advent of the milling machine for metal, and the router for wood, chisels have been used for all sorts of jobs. For instance, the ordinary blacksmith shop had no milling machine. If it was necessary to cut a keyway in a shaft, this could be done with a chisel. Old files were often converted to chisels by blacksmiths who knew how to get the desired shape and then temper the steel correctly. I still have some chisels made from old files. They were crafted by some of my ancestors about a century ago.

Wood chisels were often crafted by hand. A skilled artisan would obtain some high-grade steel, or lacking that, he would rework an old file. After shaping the chisel it would be properly tempered, and many times resulted in an excellent chisel, albeit homemade.

Some of the better-known manufacturers include:
Braunsdorf-Mueller Co., Elizabeth, NJ
Buck Bros., Millbury, MA
Buffum Tool Co., Louisiana, MO
Cincinnati Tool Co., Cincinnati, OH (Hargrave)
Greenlee Bros. & Co., Rockford, IL
W. A. Ives Mfg. Co., Wallingford, CT (Mephisto)
Kortick Mfg. Co., San Francisco, CA
Kraeuter & Co., Newark, NJ
Mack & Co., Rochester, NY
Peck, Stow & Wilcox Co., Southington, CT (Pexto)
Smith & Hemenway Co., New York, NY (Red Devil)
Stanley Works, New Britain, CT
James Swan Co., Seymour, CT
Union Hardware Co., Torrington, CT
Vaughan & Bushnell Mfg. Co., Chicago, IL
L. & I. J. White Co., Buffalo, NY
Winchester Repeating Arms Co., New Haven, CT
Winsted Edge Tool Works, Winsted, CT

Firmer chisels are usually thin in proportion to their width. They are shorter than paring chisels and lighter than framing chisels. Usually the handle goes over a tang as shown here, and as compared to the socket chisel. Firmer chisels have generally been made in sizes from 1/16 inch to 1/2 inch by sixteenths. Shown, from left, are the Buck No. 1 plain edge and the No. 2 plain edge.

Firmer chisels are made for hand use, not for use with a hammer, as shown here. In addition to the plain edge style, they are also made in a beveled-edge design. Buck Bros. Chisels, usually bring $10 and up if in good condition. Many other brands will fetch similar or higher prices. Shown, from left, are No. 35 plain edge and No. 36 beveled edge.

Chisels

Paring chisels are used for finishing and fitting. They have the basil on one side, and this is usually 12 degrees for softwoods and 18 degrees for hardwoods. (The basil is the sloping edge of a chisel or plane blade). Good paring chisels often bring $20 and upwards.

Shown here are bent shank paring chisels in plain and beveled edges. Applewood was often used for the handles. Bent paring chisels often bring upwards from $15. Usually they were made in sizes ranging from 1/8- to 3/4-inch in width.

Butt chisels are used primarily for fitting door butts. Since they usually have a blade under 4 inches in length, they are often called pocket chisels. Butt chisels are usually found in widths ranging from 1/8- to 3/4-inch. Prices usually range upwards from $15.

Notching chisels are characterized by a thin, but very stiff, blade. They were usually offered in sizes from 1 to 2 inches. Since they were designed for heavy use, the handle usually was furnished with a leather top to resist hammer impact.

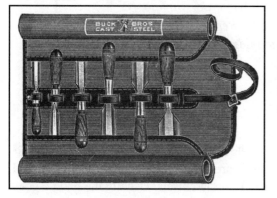

Sets of old chisels in a canvas roll often command a premium price. It is not uncommon for a set of six chisels, as shown here, to sell for $75 or more. Certain makes are more desirable than others, and this also affects the price.

Mortise chisels were made specifically for cutting mortises, as the name implies. They were usually made in sizes from 1/8 to 5/8 inches wide, of socket design, and the better quality chisels were furnished with a leather top on the handle. Mortise chisels are

fairly common and usually sell for $10 to $20 in good condition. Framing chisels are a heavy-duty design, usually offered in sizes from 1/4 to 2 inches in width. Common ones often sell in the $8 to $10 range, although some of the finer designs might bring considerably more. Shown is Bucks Bros. No. 48 left mortise.

A carpenter's slick was used particularly to smooth the edges of mortises and tenons, but it was also used for smoothing and fitting. Usually a slick was available in 3-, 3-1/2-, and sometimes a 4-inch width. A common one might sell for $40, but a nicely built slick might bring $100 or more. Shown is a Witherby No. 45 socket handle.

The Stanley Adjustable Chisel Gauge was also known as a blind nail tool. By attaching a chisel to this tool (with the beveled edge up), a shaving of any thickness could be raised with precision. A nail or other fastener could then be put in place, after which the shaving was glued and pushed back into place. When skillfully done, the joint was virtually invisible. This device is quite rare, and will likely fetch $200 or more.

As the name implies, gouges are used to remove wood in a circular plane rather than the flat aspect offered by a chisel. Gouges are usually found in sizes from 1/4 to 2 inches. Pattern makers often used gouges when developing a new foundry pattern. Prices vary widely for gouges, with the common ones going for about $10.

A complete set of chisels from 1/8 to 2 inches in a fitted wooden case might bring $250 or more if in good condition. As with any of the pricing, a rusty old relic will bring but a fraction of one that has no rust, or only light surface rust. Those that are pitted, even slightly, will bring much less. Chisels that have been badly abused, or with broken or missing handles likewise bring a meager price. Replacement handles also cause the value to suffer.

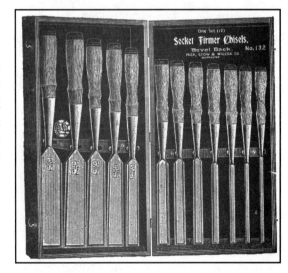

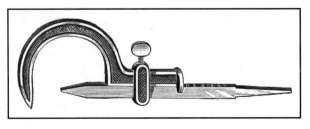

Sizing tools for wood turning are fairly scarce. In good condition and complete with blade, they often bring $50 and more. Most sizing tools would open to 4 inches. This tool permitted accurate repetitive cuts when this was necessary. Shown is a No. 25 sizer. Shown is a No. 25 sizer.

Chisels

Chisel Corner CH 35 Corner chisels were mainly used to square up the corners of a mortise. For instance, in the old days of building barns and other buildings using large beams secured with mortise and tenon joints, a corner chisel was a great help. Corner chisels, while unusual, are not particularly rare. Even so, a nice one might bring $40 or more.

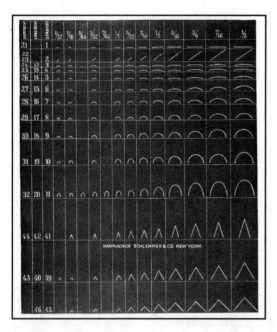

The S. J. Addis wood carving tools made in England are probably the best known, and likely rank among the best in quality as well. Shown here is only a partial listing of the Addis carving tools; they ranged in size from 1/32 to 1 inch. Up to fourteen different styles were available for each width, and within these, most could be purchased with a straight, long bend, or short bend shank. Thus, there were about 250 different styles and widths. Add to this, the choice of three different shanks, and the grand total goes to some 750 distinctly different carving tools! Ordinarily the Addis carving tools sell in the $10 to $20 range. However, a set of, say, ten tools in good condition might bring upward of $200.

Clamps

Literally hundreds, and perhaps thousands of different clamps have been developed for specific purposes. This section limits itself primarily to those styles used in the averages in light industrial work. Many clamps built a century ago are still in use. Thus, their collectible value is quite variable. Ornate or unique clamps might bring $25 or more, but many of the common ones sell for only a few dollars.

Trestle clamps were used primarily in large woodworking and furniture shops. They were seldom found in the small carpenter shop, especially since even the small 4-foot size sold for $7.50 in 1910!

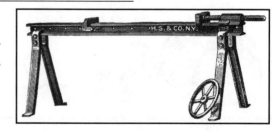

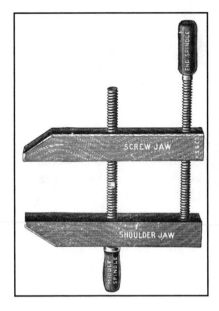

Hand screws were available with wooden screws or with metal screws. The early Jorgensen style with wood screws was fully adjustable, while the metal hand screws were more or less rigid. Large sizes with 18- or 20-inch jaws might sell for upwards of $30, but the smaller sizes are fairly common, and often bring $10-$15 or even less.

Mitre clamps are seldom found. They were intended to hold two pieces perfectly square when closed. Even in 1910 these clamps were priced at $1.75. Numerous styles of mitre clamps were made by different manufacturers.

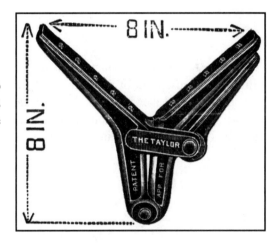

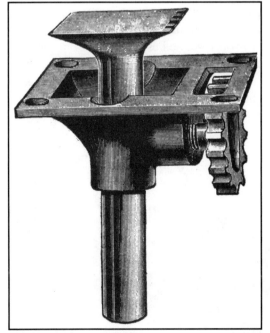

Bench stops were made in a variety of styles. Atum's Bench Stop of 1900 is shown here. Bench stops are not especially rare. Usually they can be bought for a few dollars, with the fancy and unique ones bringing somewhat more.

Of the steel bar clamps, only the older ones are given a substantial collector's value. Steel bar clamps are readily available at many hardware stores. However, a bar like this one (Patented in 1892) might be a desirable collector's item.

Door frame clamps (shown at left) that used a wooden bar have not been made for decades; therefore, they have acquired value as a collectible. Many different styles were made, and were furnished as only the iron parts; the wood beam was furnished by the craftsman. Fine examples might bring $25 or more. The axle bed clamp (shown at right) was used for holding wood axle beds to iron axles. This style is quite scarce.

A machinists' clamp (shown at left) is difficult to find, primarily because most of them were simply worn out and discarded. Likewise, the quick action clamp (shown at right) is now among those curiosities that show up occasionally at an auction or a flea market.

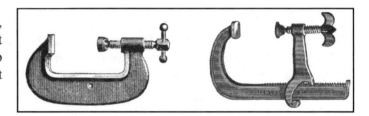

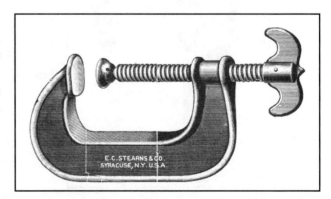

A quilt frame clamp (shown at far left) was (and is) used to clamp the corners of a quilting frame. The Trimmers Clamp (shown second) was intended for carriage trimmers and upholsterers. A Carriage Clamp (shown third) was designed especially for the carriage maker. Snow's Adjustable Clamp (shown at right) had a quick release mechanism on the screw permitting it to be quickly located on the work and then tightened.

Carriagemaker's clamps were a popular style. Although designed for the carriage trade initially, this style came into wide use by woodworkers. It was made in numerous sizes. A fine example might bring $15 to $20, but most of the common ones sell for much less, especially if they are rusty or manifest heavy use and abuse.

Compasses, Dividers, and Calipers

In addition to hundreds of "store-bought" calipers, compasses, and dividers, there are probably thousands more that are "one-of-a-kind" made by an enterprising craftsman for a specific purpose. Granted, some of these are rather crude, but others typify fine craftsmanship. Oftentimes they were made of fine wood reinforced with brass. Instruments like this might well bring $100, and ranging upward to over $300.

Very early manufactured instruments were often made of cast iron. These are now quite scarce, with good examples often bringing in excess of $200. Many others were made of cast steel, but these do not usually command exceptional prices. Others, such as those used in the foundry trades, were often made of brass. These instruments can also fetch considerably more; nice ones might sell in excess of $100. By comparison, later styles with steel legs and a spring back might sell in the $5 to $10 range, especially if rusted or pitted.

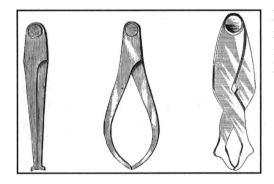

In the 1880s, many calipers were made of cast steel. Shown here are inside, outside, and the "fancy" or "dancing legs" style. Ordinarily the inside and outside styles usually sell for $20 or less, but the dancing legs caliper might fetch anywhere from $40 to well over $100.

Spring calipers were made of fine tempered steel, and usually are found in sizes ranging from 2 to 6 inches. This one from 1890 typifies the selection of the day, with the 6-inch model selling for $1.35. Today this caliper might bring $10-$15.

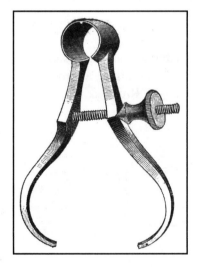

Compasses of this 1880s version were usually made in sizes from 4 to 12 inches. They are not at all scarce, and only the finer examples get across the $15 threshold.

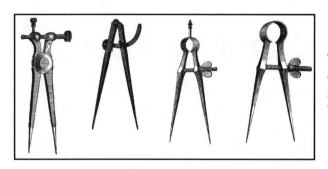

These dividers of the 1880s are commonly found except for the one shown to the left...it was furnished with a thumb screw attachment for fine adjustment. Dividers like this one always bring a premium over the common and ordinary styles.

The inside caliper (shown at left) is a cut above the average with its top screw and fine adjustment. Chances are that it should be in the $10-$20 range. By comparison, the register caliper to the right is rather scarce, with nice ones selling in excess of $50.

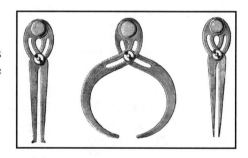

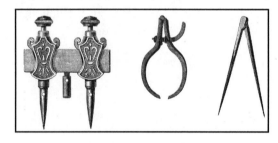

Shown to the left of this illustration are trammel points. These were attached to a steel or wooden beam of the desired length. Fancy ones like this might fetch $20 or more. The small wing caliper at center, and the steel compass at right are both fairly common, selling in the $8 to $20 range.

Unusual caliper designs, as shown here, often bring $20 and sometimes more. These designs are all from the early 1880s, and are, in fact, from the 1882 catalog of Ripley & Kimball at St. Louis, Missouri.

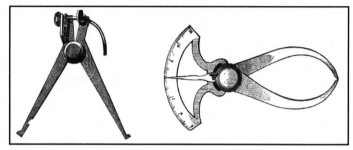

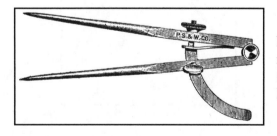

Peck, Stow & Wilcox at Southington, Connecticut offered a wide range of calipers in the early 1900s. The wing dividers shown here are from Pexto, and were made in sizes ranging from 5 to 12 inches. In 1910, the big 12-inch size sold for $1.00.

Various kinds of extension dividers were available. Extension dividers could be furnished with one movable leg, or with both legs movable, as desired. Styles like this Cook's Pattern extension often bring in excess of $20.

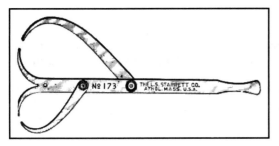

P.S. & W. (Pexto) dividers of this style were available in 4-, 5-, and 6-inch sizes. The 6-inch version retailed for 50 cents in 1910. Often-times, a divider like this one can be purchased for under $10.

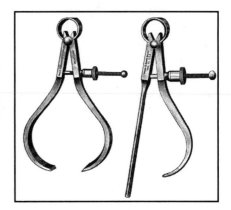

Companies like Brown & Sharpe and Starrett offered various kinds of special calipers for specific needs. Shown here are a thread caliper (at left), with wide sharpened jaws. Also shown (at right) is a keyway caliper. It was used to determine the depth of a keyway on a shaft. These special designs should easily sell in the $15 to $20 range, since they are fairly scarce.

The specialized blacksmith caliper had a long handle to dissipate heat from the hot metal with which it came in contact. Since this design is fairly scarce, the blacksmith caliper often sells in the $50 to $100 range, sometimes higher.

A rather unusual caliper design is the crankshaft style, shown here (No. 80) on the left. Also shown (No. 444) is a "double-jointed" caliper. The intermediate screws permitted adjustment to fit odd shapes or surfaces, but the top pivot was furnished with a fine adjustment screw. These and other unique caliper designs might well bring in the $30 to $50 range. Large sizes and mint specimens always bring higher prices.

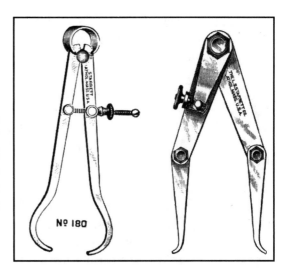

Cooperage

Cooperage is the trade of making wooden barrels and casks. Dry coopering was the making of barrels for flour, grain, sugar, and the like. Wet or tight coopering is for barrels to hold whisky, cider, and similar items. White coopering was for making buckets, tubs, and churns.

The art of coopering goes back to ancient times, and is said to have originated at the foot of the Alps. Like all the early trades, it was learned through a long apprenticeship, and even in the modern age was a trade that had to be learned through experience, rather than from books.

Many of the tools used for coopering were developed over the course of the centuries. By the early 1800s though, the making of barrels had become partially mechanized, and by the end of the nineteenth century, most barrels were made in factories, rather than in a cooper's shop. Only the most common coopering tools are shown here.

Spokeshaves, planes, and other tools used in coopering as well as other trades are not shown here to avoid redundancy.

Various styles of coopers drivers were made. Drivers were used to drive the hoops or bands down tight on the barrel. Like most tools used for cooperage, drivers are fairly scarce, fetching $15-$25. Shown are the Regular Pattern at left, the Nantucket Pattern at center, and the Short and Oval Pattern at right.

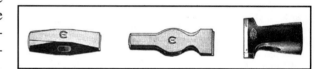

The straight peen hammer shown here was especially for the cooper. It was made in various weights. Although they are not readily available, there seems to be no great demand for them, except perhaps for dedicated tool collectors.

A froe or frow was used to cleave staves from a wood block. Today, froes are fairly scarce, often bringing $75 or more. Also included in the cooper's tool chest were items like the croze, a sun plane, and stave gauges. Perhaps in another edition of this book we will be able to locate additional illustrations of cooper's tools.

The cooper's adze was specially designed for barrel making. Today they are quite scarce, and a good one might bring $100 or more. Sizes from 3 inches and upwards were generally used for tight or wet barrel work. Those with a cutting face of 2-1/2 to 3 inches were usually employed for dry barrels.

Drivers, or hoop drivers, were made in many different styles. In addition to the Nantucket style, shown to the left, there was also the socket style with a leather-topped wooden handle.

D

Dairy Equipment

There was a strong temptation in this section to include items like cream separators, milk pails, and similar items. However, there are titles available dealing specifically with cream separators. Milk pails and numerous other dairy items are often included in other directories. Instead, we concentrated our efforts mainly on home butter making, and a few other items relating to the dairy business.

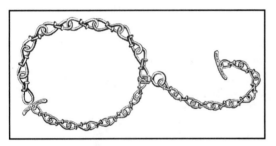

Although once plentiful, cow ties or cow chains are not nearly so common today. While they cannot be classified as being scarce, they nevertheless do not appear very often. Usually they can be acquired with very little outlay. Shown is a Niagara model.

Several pairs of cow hobbles (a.k.a. cow kickers) were once in every barn. Today, they are not nearly so common, most of them having been delegated to the iron pile. Numerous kinds were made, with this one even having a metal tab by which to secure the tail. Anyone who ever milked cows by hand can recall the thrill of being swiped across the face with a dirty tail!

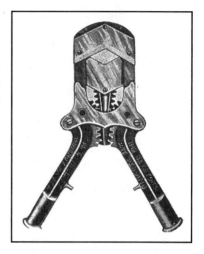

Dehorning cows was a disagreeable task. Sometimes the horns were simply cut off with a saw, but other farmers preferred a dehorning tool as shown here. These are fairly scarce today, and often bring $25 or more…. I recently saw one priced at $65!

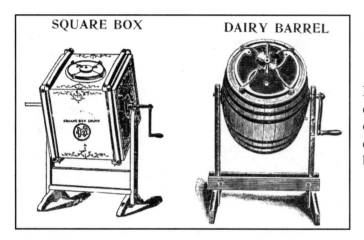

Many different kinds of churns were built. All of the early styles were made of wood. This in itself was okay, but demanded a very thorough cleaning after each use. A nice cylinder or box churn might well bring $300 to $500.

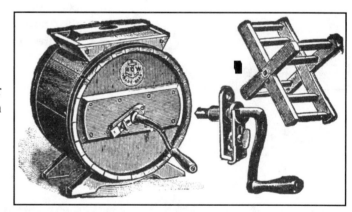

Cylinder churns were yet another variety available for home butter making. In good condition, they often bring upwards from $100.

Hard maple was the preferred wood for many different butter-making tools. Included was this butter packer. It was intended to firm up the butter and eliminate air pockets. Butter tools like this one are not often found, and will likely bring $25 or perhaps much more.

Many different styles and sizes of butter spades were available, with three of the most common being shown here. They are not often found today, and we have not been able to suggest an approximate market value.

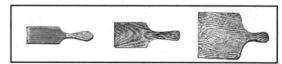

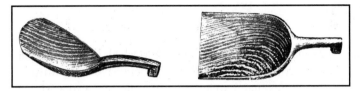

Butter ladles as shown at left and butter scoops as shown at right, were usually made of hard maple. Today they are seldom found, and should probably command an excellent price. However, no pricing information has been located.

A long butter spade (at left) or a curd scoop (at right) would probably be classed among very scarce butter-making items. Likewise, such items as butter molds are often very expensive when made of wood; metal ones have a much lower value. Good wooden butter molds with a nice design will likely bring $200 or more, and a very nice pattern might fetch upwards of $700.

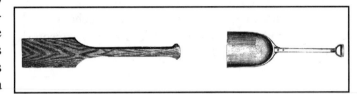

I spent many an hour as a kid cranking a churn just like this one! Sometimes the butter would come up in 15 or 20 minutes and sometimes it would take nearly an hour of steady, slow cranking. Cranking fast did nothing but get the arms tired, and seemed to do nothing towards hastening the butter! Dazey Churn Company was located in St. Louis, Missouri. From there they sold thousands upon thousands of these churns with the glass jar. The latter had the advantage of being easy to clean, compared to the wooden churns of earlier days. A nice Dazey glass churn will likely bring upwards of $100 today.

Dazey Churn Company offered this model with a metal container. After filling, the top and the agitator simply slipped into place. When youngsters (kids or grandkids) were around, it was likely that they would have the pleasure of cranking the churn. Churns like this all-metal design usually bring $100 and more.

Drawknives

Dozens of different drawknife designs can be found. In addition to the many styles, the cheaper ones used a decent grade of steel, but for fine work by professionals, the very finest steels were featured. Prices for drawknives (or drawing knives) vary widely. The ordinary ones (often called a Farmer's Knife) might bring only a few dollars. On the other hand, a nice Wilkinson made of the best cast steel, with folding handles, and no rust or pitting, might bring $75 to $100. Drawknives are fairly common, and this section endeavors to illustrate the various major styles. Chamfer gauges, also as shown in this section, are quite scarce, and a nice pair might easily bring $50. Carpenters drawknives are by far the most common, with the carriage, coach, and wagonmakers knives being far less plentiful.

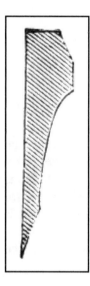

Note this sectional view of the ordinary carpenter's drawknife. It is somewhat different than the coach knife or the carriage knife. From this sectional view, one can get a better idea of what a carpenter knife looks like.

Most carpenter knives had a 1-3/8 to 1-1/2-inches wide blade. The knife on the left used "razor steel" while the Fuchs No. 1 on the right had stubby handles and a 1-1/2-inch blade.

On the left is a Smith Perfect Handle style of 1910; it was made with a solid crucible steel blade. To the right is a Buck Bros. Carpenter knife with a cast steel blade. The latter was made in widths of 4, 5, and 6 inches, while the Smith was made in 8-, 10-, and 12-inch sizes. Narrow knives of six inches or less are rather scarce.

A Witherby No. 165 adjustable handle drawknife is shown on the left. Available in 8- and 10-inch sizes, this attractive drawknife sold for about $1.50 in 1910. On the right is a Wilkinson Folding Handle Drawknife. The folding handles could be opened to various positions while in use; for storage the handles folded in to protect the blade. This one was made in 6- and 8-inch sizes.

The carriage-maker's drawknife is shown on the left. Beside it is a cross-sectional view of the blade...quite heavy and with a rather steep angle. On the right is the coach-maker's drawknife; its cross-sectional view demonstrates a very thin cutting edge, with a heavier back for strength. These styles are quite desirable, since they were often fitted with fancy handles, and usually had excellent care.

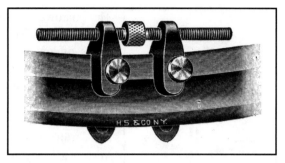

Wagon makers used a drawknife that generally was 10 or 12 inches long, but carried a 1-3/4-inch blade width. To the right is an Adjustable Auto-Body drawknife. Ordinarily this style was furnished with several different cutters. This style is quite scarce, and could be expected to bring a substantial price. However, I have not found one of them, and no pricing has been located.

Chamfer gauges were available for use with a drawknife. They were clamped to the knife, and a screw permitted fine adjustments. They were intended to chamfer the corners of square stock. Chamfer gauges are very scarce, and might bring $50 or more.

Drills (Hand and Power)

This section is mainly concerned with small breast drills, bench drills, and even a few early electric drills. So-called Yankee drills or push drills are included in the *Screwdrivers* section. A few early post drills are included, but the larger drill presses are in the *Machine Tools* category.

Approximate values are shown for many of the items in this section. However, as with any collectible, prices vary widely. For instance, an item that was commonly used in a certain area will likely bring far less in that area because there is an ample supply. On the other hand, an item that was rarely found, say in the Midwest, might bring far more than in the area where it was used.

Personal preferences have a lot to do with values as well. Brand name loyalty is a major factor in determining values. Undoubtedly though, the largest single factor is condition. A breast drill for instance, that might ordinarily bring $25 might easily bring twice that if in mint condition, and will bring even more if still enclosed in its original box or carton.

Auctions are always unpredictable. One auction might have several dealers in a bidding war, while another might have no dealers on hand at all. Frequently, heirs to an estate will "bid in" an item that they want to keep as part of a family heritage. Those who track auction prices might then get a completely erroneous picture as to the ordinary market value of a certain item. As with all buying, the Latin phrase, *caveat emptor,* "Let the buyer beware" always applies.

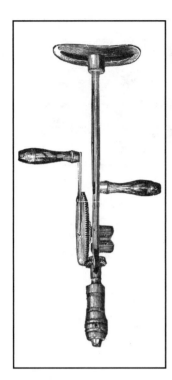

The hardware firm of Ripley & Kimball at St. Louis offered this breast drill in their 1880 catalog. It was of double-geared design, meaning that the spindle could be driven at two different speeds. Very early styles often sell in the $30 to $50 range, especially if they use brass gears or fittings. A breast drill made entirely of brass might easily bring over $100.

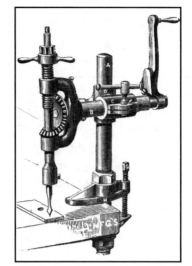

Ancient bench drills like this one from 1880 are scarce, especially if they are still in good usable condition. This model could be easily clamped to any bench, ready for use. Good examples will bring up to $200.

Very early post drills in good condition will often bring over $200, with even the more common ones of the twentieth century bringing $100 or more at times. This simple design was simply mounted to a convenient post within the shop. An automatic power feed attachment permitted the operator to spend his full energy on the crank.

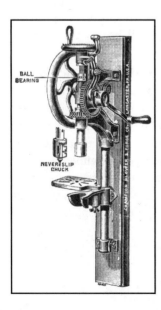

Post drills are fairly common, but still command a decent price. Those in good shape usually bring $75 or more, but a large post drill or one with a fancy feed mechanism might bring $200 or more. This rather ordinary Champion post drill of 1910 sold for $8.50; it weighed 100 pounds!

Bench drills were fairly popular in the 1900-1930 period, but are not very plentiful today. This one from Millers Falls Co. was made in three sizes. The smallest one could drill holes up to 3/8-inch; it weighed 34 pounds and sold for $16 in 1910.

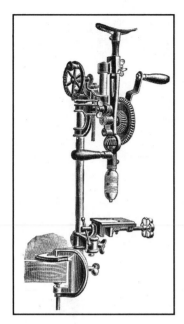

A rather unusual bench drill was this No. 20 Universal model from Millers Falls Company. The bench unit was made especially for the No. 12 and No. 118 breast drills from that company. It was priced without the breast drill at $5 and was packed in a wooden box.

The *1912 Stanley Works* catalog illustrates their Iron Frame Breast Drills in three sizes, and priced at the time from $2.75 to $3.50. Today, good examples will probably fetch $20 or more.

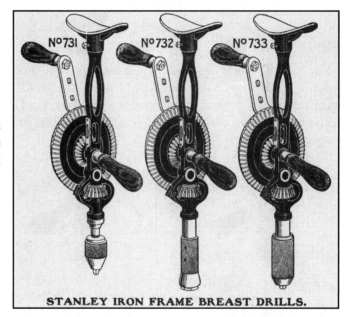

STANLEY IRON FRAME BREAST DRILLS.

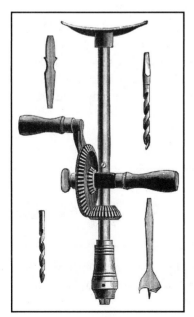

Even in 1890, this small double-geared breast drill sold for $3…a considerable price in those days. The chuck was made to hold ordinary square taper shank bits, but an extra set of jaws was supplied to hold small straight shank bits as well.

Drills

The open frame drills shown here are a typical badge of age…these models are from a 1908 catalog. Drilling holes through steel was a laborious job with a breast drill. Oftentimes it was easier to load the pieces onto a wagon and take them to a local blacksmith shop. The drills shown here were priced at $2 to $4 in 1908.

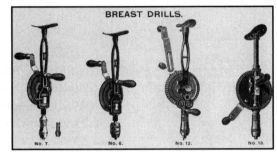

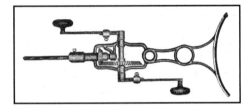

A very unusual breast drill was this double-crank model of 1910. Priced at $5, it featured cranks adjustable to different lengths, a 12-inch breast-plate, and a chuck that would hold drills with 1/2-inch shanks.

In 1910, this Cincinnati 1/4-inch electric drill sold for $45. Weighing 14 pounds, it had a top chuck speed of 900 rpm. Since electrical outlets were not then very popular, it was furnished with a plug that could screw into an ordinary Edison light socket. A working example would be quite a scarcity today.

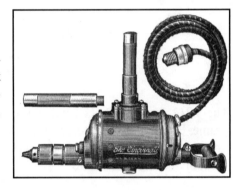

By the late 1920s, the electric drill had come to stay. Black & Decker was a leader in the development of the electric drill. A 1928 catalog shows the 1/4-inch drill, the 1/2-inch drill, a drill stand for the larger size, and a 6-inch bench grinder. This entire package could be purchased for "Only $123." However, the heavy duty 3/16-inch drill shown at the top of this illustration sold at the time for $36, and the B&D electric screwdriver shown here was priced at $48. The development of the electric drill ended the great call for breast drills within a decade. With the development of the battery-powered drill in the past few years, the breast drill is used very little today.

Not to be forgotten is the small hand drill. Developed mainly in the early part of the twentieth century, it had a small capacity, usually 3/16-inch or less. It was a handy device within its capabilities, and was much

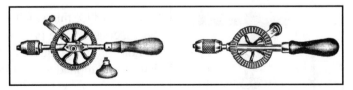

easier to handle than the ordinary breast drill. Bow drills are among the very early styles. They are not shown here, since they are so scarce as to virtually be museum pieces today. Even a mediocre example of a bow drill might fetch $500 or more. Shown left to right are Millers Falls hand drills No. 7 and No. 94.

E

Electrician Tools

Many of the tools used by the electrician will be found under other categories in this book. The tools of the electrician formerly included various items no longer used, such as soldering pots and the like. Also included in this section are pike poles and other equipment formerly used by linemen, but seldom used today.

For handling and raising electrical and telephone poles, linemen resorted to carrying hooks (at center) to move the pole about, pikes (shown at top) to raise the pole into position, and cant hooks (at bottom) to turn the pole into its proper place. Pikes were available in lengths from 10 to 20 feet. The guarded style is shown here, although the plain pike was far more common. Digging the hole was accomplished with a Post Hole Shovel, also called a straight shovel, or a "banjo." It was used to loosen the dirt in the hole, and then lifted out with a spoon. Setting the pole into place called for a heavy wooden tamper…oftentimes these were bound with iron on the sides and bottom to add weight and to protect the wood from rocks and stones.

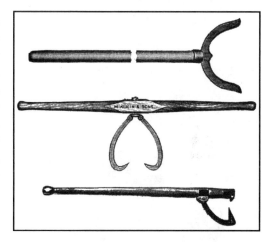

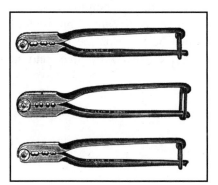

Splicing clamps were used, as the name implies, for splicing wires. Usually they were used for overhead wire on poles. Splicing and sleeve clamps were made in many different styles and sizes. Today they are relatively scarce.

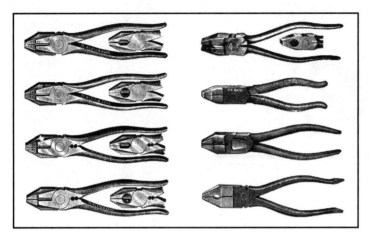

Many different kinds of electricians or lineman pliers have been offered over the past century. Not until the 1880s did the electrician become a part of the building trades. By 1900, however, electricity had come to stay. Lineman pliers usually have no great collectible value, although some early styles are indeed unique, compared to those on today's market.

Seldom found today is a lineman's block, using flat pulleys and a leather strap. They were of a special self-locking design that permitted the lineman to keep taking up slack in the wire without risk of it slipping loose.

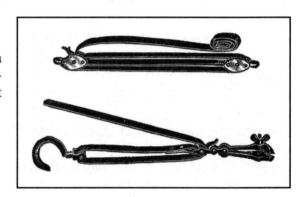

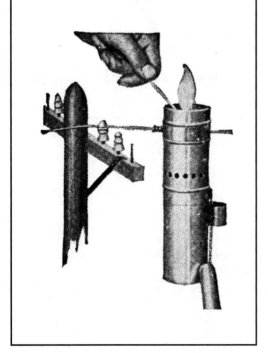

When a field splice was necessary in overhead wires, the completed joint was either assembled with a compression sleeve, or if this was not available, then a soldered joint was used. Weighing only about a pound, the Staysalite Lineman's Torch could be carried on the tool belt. Fueled with alcohol, it could then be hung on the wire, right beneath the splice. In 1930, this torch sold for $10; it is seldom found today.

Engine Room Equipment

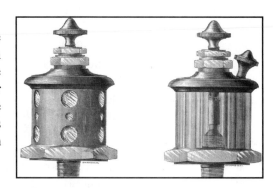

Beginning in the early 1900s, a town or village that had its own electric power plant, or even its own water plant immediately saw this site as a community centerpiece. People for miles around were mesmerized with a big gas or steam engine and all the brass gauges, lubricators, and other fancy things within. This section attempts to illustrate a few such items, since nearly all of them have attained considerable status among collectors.

In the 1870s, crankpin lubricators were often known as Locomotive Rod Cups, and also known simply as *soft oilers*. The latter term meant that oil, rather than grease was used for lubrication. At the time, and for decades after, the comparison was with a *hard oiler* or grease cup. Any lubricator that is complete is sought after by vintage engine collectors, as well as collectors in general. Early examples like these will likely bring $25 to $50. Shown at left is a model with a shield; at right is a model with a valve.

Plain lubricators like this one were found on many steam engines. Initially they were given a highly polished finish, and in today's market a nicely polished lubricator can often bring $100 or perhaps even more.

Glass oil cups of the 1880s and for about four decades following, often were of ornate design, heavily made, and highly polished. A No. 2 size might have a diameter of 2 inches and a height of 1-7/8 inches, for a capacity of 2 ounces. In 1880, a lubricator like this sold for $2.60. Today, a fine example might bring $30 to $50. Note that the early styles did not have a bottom sight glass.

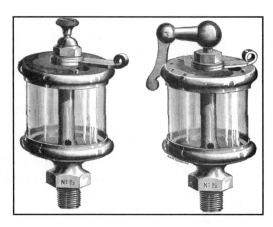

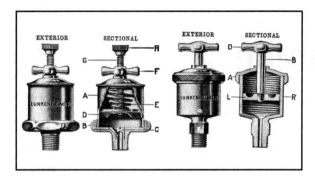

Hard oil, or grease, had largely replaced soft oilers on engines by the 1920s. Lunkenheimer, among others offered numerous kinds of grease cups, including the automatic style shown to the left. On the right are marine grease cups. They used a piston threaded on the outside and engaging threads in the wall of the lubricator. In addition to these styles were the ordinary grease cups, made either of brass or from a steel stamping, suitably machined and threaded. The latter have not acquired any substantial collector value, but brass grease cups today seldom sell for less than $10, and sometimes much more.

By the early 1900s, the glass body oil cup was further refined to include a bottom sight glass. Through it, the engineer could observe the number of drops per minute being delivered to the bearing. Since oil viscosity varies with the temperature, this was an important development, because it permitted the engineer to adjust the flow rate during the operating cycle. Complete glass body oil cups seldom sell for less than $10 today, and a medium-sized one in nice condition might bring $20 to $30, or even more.

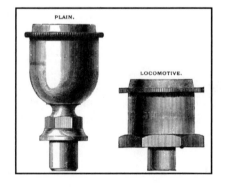

Oil cups were necessary on small or slow speed bearings. They were made in many different sizes. Earlier styles were made of cast brass, but by the 1920s, oil cups could also be secured of stamped brass. The latter have nowhere near the collector value as do the cast brass examples. However, brass oil cups seldom sell for less than $5. Shown at left is a plain model; at right, a locomotive.

Lubricators like the Trident (shown here) were made especially for cylinder lubrication on gas and gasoline engines. To prevent any blow-by from compression feeding backward into the lubricator, it was furnished with a small ball check valve built into its base. Lubricating oil could get past the ball on its way to the cylinder, but if there was any back pressure the ball was forced up onto its seat. Many gas engine lubricators were quite ornate, with even the common ones that are intact and in good condition bringing $20 or more. Those with missing or broken parts bring substantially less. Broken glass also lowers the value considerably. Replacement glass for some styles is virtually impossible to find.

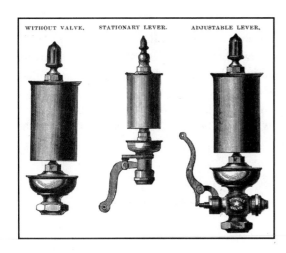

Hundreds of different steam whistle designs have appeared. Every powerhouse, most factories and mills, and every steam traction engine was equipped with one. They were made of brass, but once in awhile a cast-iron whistle is found. Steam whistles in almost any condition usually bring a very high price, while large, ornate styles might bring $300 to $500. Common whistles seldom sell for less than $100.

Finding an Engine Room Combination as shown here is very difficult. I recall seeing one or two over the years, and these were in museums. No effort was spared; the backboard was usually made of walnut, cherry, or some other expensive wood. The gauges were usually furnished with a silver face, and the exterior was usually nickel plated.

Due to the vibration usually present, pendulum clocks were unsuitable in an engine room. In its place an accurate spring-wound clock, highly plated, and built to exacting standards was used. Engine room, or locomotive clocks are indeed difficult to find. While I am certain they would be expensive, I have found no pricing information for them.

For the larger powerhouse, a barometer was part of the standard equipment. If the elevation above sea level was known, the barometer could be shipped with all the adjustments done at the factory. I once acquired an Engine Room Barometer, but they are rarely found today.

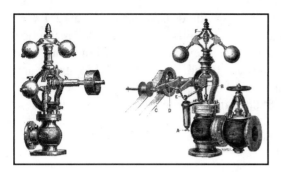

Every steam engine had a governor. For the ordinary slide-valve engine, it appeared as shown here. Complete steam engine governors still have a substantial value. Quite often an engine is found with the governor missing, so steam engine collectors are always on the prowl for a replacement. Thus, any governor that is intact and in good condition will often bring upwards of $100. Shown at left is a Gardner model and at right is a Judson.

An engine room might well have had a set of oilers and tallow pots, complete with an attractive tray. This 1880s set, when furnished with the tray and oilers in a nickel-plate finish, sold for the princely sum of $10.

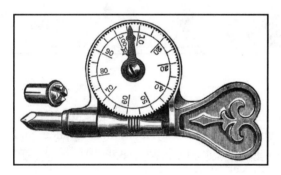

With the powerhouse and its engines came the need to ascertain engine speed, machine speed, or lineshaft speed. Accordingly, a simple tachometer or *revolution counter* was available. Which would record 100 revolutions. The engineer looked at his watch and counted the time it took to make the 100 revolutions. A simple calculation then gave the speed in rpm. In 1880, this instrument sold for $1.50.

By the 1920s, several companies offered tachometers or revolution counters. The Starrett line of the 1920s included several styles. As an extra attachment, the surface speed indicator could be attached to the speed indicator. The wheel was designed to show the lineal travel of a flywheel rim as an example. Shown at top is No. 104, middle No. 106, and at bottom No. 107.

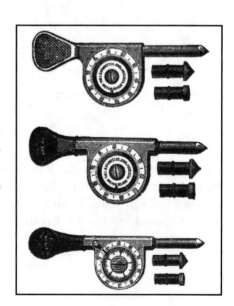

Part of the equipment in an engine room or powerhouse likely included a gauge glasscutter. It was designed to cut gauge glasses to the exact length, needed whenever a replacement was necessary. Gauge glass cutters are relatively scarce today.

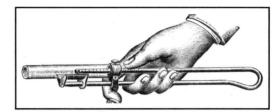

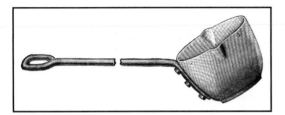

The engine room usually included all the necessary supplies to re-pour a babbitt bearing. If the engine was operating the town's only generator or perhaps the town's water pump, a burned-out bearing brought everything to a standstill. It then became the engineer's work to remove the old bearing, prepare everything, and re-pour it as quickly as possible. If all the supplies were on hand, this might take only a short time. Shown is a Babbitt ladle.

The day-to-day operations in an engine room or in a powerhouse required various kinds of lubricants. These included steam cylinder oil, various kinds of lubricating oils, and of course, hard oil, or grease. The items could be stored in a "Safety Oil Cabinet" to keep dirt and other contaminants away. The cabinet on the right sold for $45 in 1910, while the larger one on the left sold for $110.

F

Farmstead Tools

A great many farmstead tools have now become highly-desirable collectibles. Of course, many tools used on a farm were not unique to it. Many farmers of the early twentieth century for example, were immigrants. In their fatherland, they might have been coopers, or carpenters, or tailors. One of my great-grandparents for instance, was a tailor, one was a gunsmith, and two had been fishermen. Usually, they were able to transfer some of their Old World talents to their new surroundings. As an aside, some of them developed into very successful farmers or tradesmen, while others lived on a meager existence.

Numerous items used on the farm will be found in various other categories of this book. Garden tools, for instance, will be found in that specific section.

For the farmer of 1900, his stock in trade was an assortment of forks, an axe, post maul, felling saw, a sledge, and a variety of wedges for splitting wood. Also included was a hammer, saw, and perhaps a square. Butchering supplies were necessary, and buttermaking was often confined to skimming cream off the milk, allowing it to ripen, and then using a barrel churn. Those without a churn made butter in a stoneware crock, using a homemade dasher to facilitate the conversion.

Of course the usual spade was present, and perhaps a few meager tools to repair the harness. Very few farms of 1900 had running water. There was virtually no electricity, and heating came from endless hours of woodcutting. Farm machinery usually was shipped with the necessary wrenches and even an oil can. Carpentry beyond the simplest repairs was turned over to a professional, as was any metalworking; it meant a trip to the blacksmith. Thus, the farmer of 1900 needed few tools to pursue his agrarian existence. However, with the coming of farm mechanization, all this changed, and by 1930 many farm shops had been set up. By this time, many farmers had learned to repair and maintain their own machinery. The coming of the oxy-acetylene torch to the blacksmith was a great help in repair work, and in the 1940s the electric arc welder was being found in numerous small shops. With these and other machines the days of the proverbial blacksmith shop were numbered.

In apple growing regions, nearly every community had at least one cider press by 1900. In autumn, the press made its way around the neighborhood, or sometimes, neighbors would bring their apples to the press to convert the crop into cider. Some was used fresh, some was allowed to turn to vinegar, and not a little of it was fermented into "hard cider" having up to about 8% alcohol by volume. The cider press shown here sold for $35 in 1890.

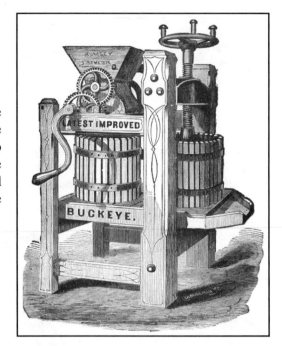

For heating large quantities of water, many farms had a cauldron. Oftentimes it was simply a large cast-iron kettle set in brick. In other instances it took the form shown here with a heavy cast-iron firebox beneath. A 30-gallon cauldron kettle sold for $9 in 1890, but this complete outfit sold for $26 at the time. Today, a cauldron in decent condition might fetch $300 or more.

With the coming of mechanized farm machinery came the need for oil cans, also known as machine oilers. Oil cans have been made in dozens of sizes and styles. Those with a lithographed design always bring more money, especially if from a famous manufacturer such as International Harvester or John Deere. Some of the fancy ones will easily bring from $30 to $50.

A post maul was an essential part of the farmer's tool inventory. Posts were pointed with an axe or hatchet. Usually the fellow with the maul stood in the back of a wagon while an assistant on the ground held the post in place. Cast-iron post mauls were ordinarily made in several sizes ranging from 10 to 20 pounds.

The post-hole auger was an improvement over driving posts into the ground with a maul. Many different sizes and styles have been made. By the 1950s, this job was mechanized with the introduction of posthole augers that either mounted to the front of the tractor, or even better, mounted to the three-point hitch. Posthole augers are still made, but the older styles are found occasionally. Shown left to right are a Fenn's model and an Iwan's Improved.

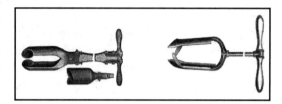

Virtually every farm kept hogs. However, hogs were (and are) prone to root holes in the feedlot, as well as under fences and other places where they weren't supposed to be. Various methods were tried to keep them from rooting, with the macabre hog tamer being one approach. It cut notches out of the rim of the nose, leaving these areas very tender. The hog tamer was said to "positively prevent rooting." Hog tamers are seldom found today. Shown from left are a Hurd's model and a Miller's model.

Hog rings have been used for many decades as a means of preventing rooting by hogs. Many different styles have been used, and hog ringers have been made in many different styles, most of which bring $5 to $10 today, with somewhat more for the unique designs.

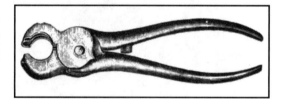

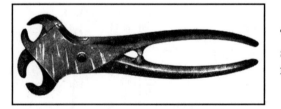

The double-jawed hog ringer shown here was intended to set any size of ring. Pig rings for instance, are somewhat smaller than hog rings; thus two different sizes of ringers were required.

When a farm had considerable timber, livestock could be difficult to locate. Thus, a few were equipped with a bell, making them easier to find. Many different sizes and styles of bells were made. The cowbell on the left was made in several sizes, and many different styles. Sheep bells were somewhat smaller, and the turkey bell shown on the right was usually made of bell metal. Tuned bells were also available. Iron cowbells often bring $30 or more. Sheep bells and turkey bells, especially the high quality ones, frequently bring $25 to $40.

Required equipment for the corn harvest included a husking pin. These were made in many different styles, with only a few of them being shown here. Husking pins and husking hooks were made to ease the job of pulling back the shuck from the ear of corn. Taking a "dirty load" to the crib was not a good idea. Most farmers prided themselves in having removed all the shucks from the corn before it went into the wagon. Today, husking pins with all their leather straps intact bring from $10 to $20. Especially nice examples bring slightly more.

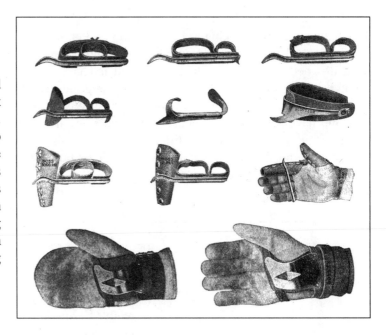

Home butchering required its own set of tools. Many farmers did their own butchering. Generally though, there were a few good butchers in the neighborhood, and one of these fellows came to do the slaughtering, and at least part of the carcass preparation. For hog slaughter it was the usual practice to scald the carcass and then remove the hair. This was done with the hog scraper shown on the left. The block scrapers shown at the center and on the right were used to scrape down and clean the butcher block. Today a nice scraper might bring $25 or more.

The steelyard was a primitive weighing device going back to the Romans. They were still available into the twentieth century, and were made in various forms and capacities. Today a steelyard, complete with the poise can bring upwards from $40.

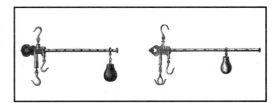

By 1870, there were dozens of patents for wagon jacks, and by the beginning of the twentieth century, there were hundreds! Wagon jacks were among the first lifting devices to be used on the farm, and a great many of them were made in a local blacksmith shop. Most of these never were franchised with patent rights, and it is likely that many others closely followed the design of another. Wagon jacks usually bring $15 to $50.

Butchering and fencemaking were two farm jobs that required a tackle block. These were made in many sizes and styles. Those with all-wood blocks are much harder to find and have a greater value than those of steel or wrought iron. A large farm tackle block would likely be strung with 3/4-inch rope. With six lines it would have a capacity of about 4,000 pounds; each man on the fall line would be able to lift about 900 pounds. Chain hoists, cable hoists, and finally the hydraulic hoist brought the time-honored tackle block to an end.

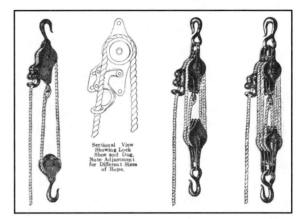

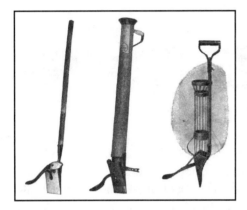

Potatoes were a staple in the farmer's diet. Large quantities were planted each spring and stored in root cellars for use until the next crop was ready. Easing the back-breaking job of planting the seed eyes were numerous sizes and styles of potato planters. Potato planters like those shown here are seldom found today.

Corn planters like those shown here from left to right, a Herschel Rotary and Acme Nos. 306 and 307, were used primarily for planting a small area, a special crop (such as broom corn) or for *plugging*. This practice was continued for many years. It consisted of walking the rows of newly emerging corn, looking for those spots where the seedlings did not emerge. With a planter like this, a farmer (and probably his boys, plus the hired man) would go to the fields and replant any missing hills of corn.

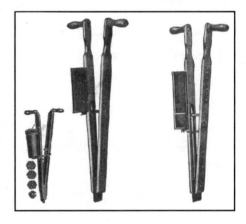

Thousands upon thousands of Cyclone Hand Seeders have been built. They are still available today, although in a modern version. In 1920, this little seeder sold for about $4; an old Cyclone seeder in nice condition might bring $25 or more. Unfortunately, mice had a great affinity for the canvas grain bag, so many of the Cyclone seeders have been patched, sometimes repeatedly.

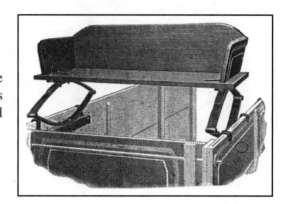

For many farmers having little extra money, a board laid across the wagon box served as the only seat. In 1912, a nice spring seat (as shown) would sell for $10 to $12. Today, a good spring seat will likely sell for well over $100.

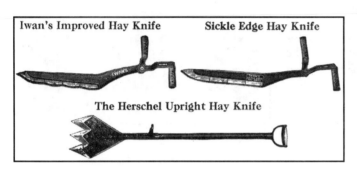

The hay crop was very important, since huge quantities were consumed by the cattle, sheep and horses during the winter months. In addition to the hay loft, there were haystacks for more storage. Long-stemmed grasses made it difficult to load the hay, so the hay knife was offered in various styles. Using it, the farmer could cut through a portion of the stack, making it easier to load the hay onto a waiting wagon. Hay knives are fairly common, but a nice one usually brings $20 to $40.

A grindstone was a virtual necessity for the farm. Not only was it used to sharpen the household cutlery, it was also necessary to sharpen a scythe or a chisel. Grindstones are still fairly common, with a nice example usually bringing $50 or more. Those with a wooden frame are usually rotted away, sometimes so badly there isn't enough left for rebuilding a pattern.

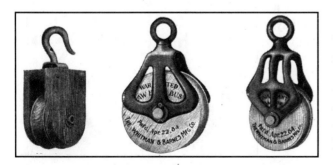

The hay crop was mechanized to a major extent with the introduction of overhead track and hay carriers in the 1870s. By 1900, virtually every new barn was mechanized with this equipment. Among the required components were a multitude of pulleys. Some were equipped with a wooden frame, and the majority used a wooden pulley. Old hay pulleys often bring $20 or more.

In addition to the usual grindstone, there were various kinds of grinding machines for special work. In the center of this illustration is a sickle grinding attachment made especially for mower and reaper sickles. Prior to these machines, the sickle was removed from the machine and sharpened with a hand stone.

The lantern was essential on the farm. They were designed to stay lit, even in strong winds. Although electricity came to many farms in the 1930s, outbuildings had very little light, except perhaps for the barn. About this time, the electric flashlight came onto the scene, but during World War II, it was almost impossible to get replacement batteries. Thus, the lantern experienced a brief revival during the early 1940s.

When farm people ventured out after dark, the only choices for light were a lantern or a pair of driving lamps on the buggy. They were intended to withstand strong winds without the flame being extinguished. They also had a highly-polished reflector to help project the light forward. Driving lamps are rather scarce, usually bringing $75 and upwards.

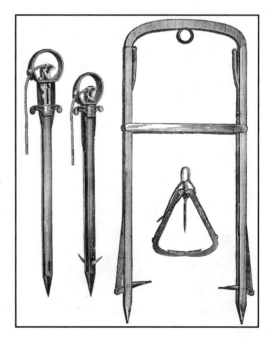

Various kinds of hayforks were available in the 1890s. The Nellis' single harpoon style was among the earliest. A rather scarce style, it often brings $40 to $75. All of these designs were made for loose hay, since the days of a hay baler traveling through the fields wouldn't be widely experienced until after World War II.

By the 1870s, some of the famous agriculturists were advocating the cooking of feed, especially for hogs. It was thought that this provided better feed conversion. Thus, there were numerous companies offering feed cookers. Eventually the practice died out, and today, very few of these devices still remain.

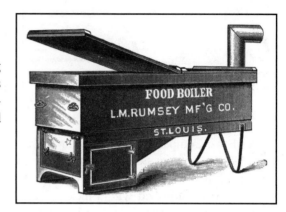

A wheelbarrow was used for almost everything on the farm. It carried feed to the livestock, wood to the stove, and potatoes to the bin. Ordinarily a wheelbarrow (as shown) had a capacity of 4 to 6 cubic feet. However, the sides were removable when necessary. In 1890, this wheelbarrow sold in the $4 to $9 range, depending on the size.

Farrier Tools

The term *farrier* comes from the Latin word *ferrarius* or the word *ferrum*, meaning horseshoe. Until sometime in the nineteenth century, the farrier also was a veterinarian and dispensed drugs for external and internal use on animals, especially horses. The usually descriptive German language termed a farrier as a *Hufschmied* or literally, hoof smith. However, in early times the Germans often referred to the farrier as a *Roßarzt* or veterinary surgeon. Semantics aside, the art of horseshoeing goes back to ancient times, and became quite refined by the Middle Ages.

In our recent history, blacksmithing and horseshoeing were quite often carried out in the same shop. Quite often too, a good blacksmith was not necessarily a good farrier, and vice versa. However, many of the same tools were used by both, and I invite you to look at the *Blacksmithing* section of this book for further information.

A wide variety of farriers' hammers were available. To the left in this illustration is a plain eye style, round pattern hammer; on the right is an adze eye style, also with a round pattern. Both of these styles are Maydole's hammers from the David Maydole Hammer Company at Norwich, New York.

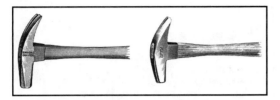

Maydole hammers were forged from solid crucible cast steel. On the left is shown the Boston pattern hammer, and on the right is the whaleback claw, octagon pattern. Farriers' hammers often bring from $10 to $25. Very old hammers or very nice handmade hammers usually bring $25 or more.

Heller Bros. Company at Newark, New Jersey, offered an extensive line of driving hammers and other tools for the farrier. Shown here are two of the Heller styles offered in 1910. A farriers' hammer was almost always furnished with a hickory handle. The styles shown here were made in several sizes, weighing from 10 to 20 ounces.

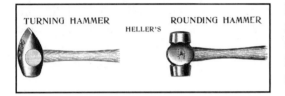

Designed especially for the farrier, the turning and rounding hammers shown here were intended for fitting the shoe. A good farrier took a special effort to see that the shoe was properly fitted to the hoof. These special hammers are seldom found, and usually bring $25 or more when in good condition.

The Scotch pattern driving hammer (shown at top) was yet another style offered in 1910. It was made in sizes from 12 to 18 ounces. Below is shown the Clean Claw Driving Hammer. It was a patented design from Champion Tool Co., Meadville, Pennsylvania.

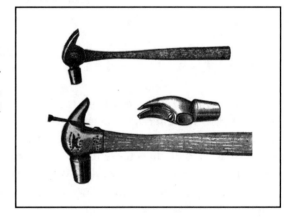

A 1910 catalog illustrates four styles of driving hammers. To the left is the Denver pattern, then the Chicago pattern, followed by the Boston pattern, and on the right is the French pattern. Each was designed for a specific purpose or for personal preference.

In this 1910 illustration, Heller's No. 64 hammer is shown on the left, with Heller's No. 65 hammer next. The Champion No. 13 and No. 14 hammers are also shown. Despite the variety of hammers shown here, there were dozens of other styles, plus many more that were hand forged to a farriers' own liking.

Various kinds of pincers and nippers were needed by the farrier. Shown here are five examples, all made for different purposes. As with driving hammers, each farrier had his own ideas about preference. Of course, it also made a difference whether the subject was a driving horse or a big draft horse.

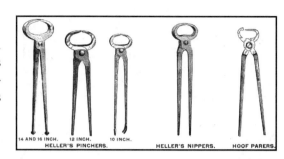

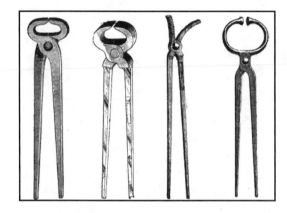

Four different devices are shown here, with two kinds of nippers at the left. Among the scarce items are the clinch tongs, used to clinch the nails after they were driven. A good clinch tong might fetch well over $30. On the right is a hoof tester. It was used to determine whether the hoof was tender in a certain spot, either due to the hoof itself, or due to injury or thrush. (The latter is an inflammatory infection in the frog [of the foot]).

Many different kinds of trimmers and hoof cutters were made. Larson's Pinchers are shown in the two styles on the left. The Gem Hoof Cutter was made for general use, and the Bliss' Hoof Shear on the right was a powerful design when the hoof was very hard. Curiously, many ordinary pincers can be bought for $5 or less, but the hoof cutters, and other specialized instruments often bring $20 or more.

To the left, is shown a nail punch, used by the farrier to punch the nail holes in a new set of shoes. To the right, are two styles of creasers. Prior to punching the nail holes, the creaser was used on the street side of the shoe to create a groove that would recess the nail flush with the shoe, or nearly so. Punches and creasers are fairly scarce.

A pritchel was sometimes used to punch nail holes when making new shoes. More often, the shoe was placed in the forge, heated, and then bent to fit the hoof. Rather than cool the shoe each time, the farrier drove the pritchel into a nail hole. Using the pritchel as a handle, the farrier would then try the shoe to the hoof, as fitting continued. Other tools of the farrier included the toe knife and the buffer. Shown at top left is a pritchel and a toe knife. At right is a buffer.

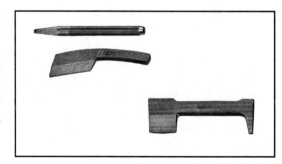

Yet another farrier's tool was the sole knife shown to the left. It was used to trim the sole of the foot, especially since it is imperative that the sole not be lower than the street side of the shoe. The *butteris* shown to the right was a tool used to pare the sole and hoof. The term comes from the French word *boutoir* meaning a tool used by farriers.

Many different hoof knives have been made, all of them to suit a particular need or to satisfy a personal preference. The hoof knife was often used in paring the sole as well as for cleaning the frog area, especially when thrush was present. The farrier would clean the area, pour in some disinfectant, and in a few days (hopefully) all would be well. Hoof knives often bring from $8 to $20.

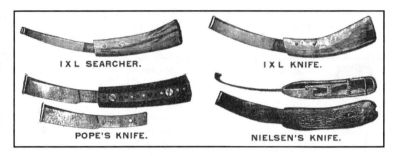

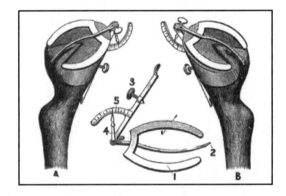

An unusual device was the hoof leveler. With this device the farrier was able to trim the foot to a specified angle. My father was an excellent farrier, and never have I seen or heard of a Hoof Leveler. Even in 1910 this device sold for $3!

A farriers' toolbox is seldom found. When my father sold out his horse equipment in 1971, a shaky old box in only fair condition brought $25. Since that time I have never found another, so any guess of today's value would be pure conjecture.

The butteris was made in numerous forms. Most worked on the idea of pressing the handle against the shoulder to apply the cutting force. At any rate, this instrument is not readily found, and a good example will likely be valued at $25 to $40.

Although the farrier essentially ended his career as a veterinarian by 1850, it still fell his duty to groom and trim the horses in many instances. The roaching shears was one item usually found in his tool kit. It was used to trim the foretop and other areas needing attention. Oftentimes the farrier would also have hand-operated clippers as part of his grooming tool inventory.

Fence Tools

Prior to the mid-1870s, most fencing consisted of boards nailed to posts, or the split rail fence. A couple of barbed wire patents were issued in the late 1860s, but the patent of Joseph Glidden and Joseph Vaughan, DeKalb, Illinois, marked the beginning of barbed wire as a practical fencing material. In 1874, about 5 tons of barbed wire were produced. This climbed to 500 tons the following year, and in 1900, some 200,000 tons of barbed wire were made.

The tools required were quite simple. A spade and posthole digger or an auger, plus a tamper to pack the soil tightly around the post took care of that requirement. The wire was unrolled, tied to the corner post on one end of say, an 80-rod stretch, and a wire stretcher was applied to the other end. When pulled sufficiently tight, the wire was stapled to the wooden posts. Special stretchers were soon developed, as were various kinds of fence pliers. Aside from this, a hammer, and a few ordinary tools completed the tool inventory.

Surprisingly, fence tools usually bring very little in today's collectible market. Fencing pliers seldom bring more than $25, even if unique and unusual.

About 1900 meshed wire appeared, with 50,000 tons being produced that year. By 1907, more than 425,000 tons of mesh wire rolled out of the wire mills. It was variously known as woven wire, Page wire (from the name of a company that made it) or hog wire.

Shortly after woven wire appeared, a few companies developed machines that would weave the fence on-site, traveling across the fencerow and leaving a tightly-woven fence behind. The many strands were carried on rolls of smooth wire which was payed out during the weaving process. This notion never became very popular. Only rarely can one find a fence-weaving machine.

Posthole augers were offered in sizes of 4 to 10 inches, with the larger ones being usually reserved for setting the corner posts. Many different styles were made, and in fact, posthole augers are still available. With posts set a rod apart (16-1/2 feet) that meant drilling about 80 holes in making the way across an 80 rod (1/4 mile) stretch. Shown left to right are a Fenn's model and Iwan's Improved.

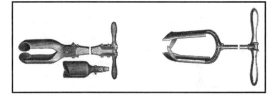

An unusual style of posthole auger was the Vaughan. It literally screwed itself into the ground if the farmer had enough strength. In practice, it was screwed in a short way and then withdrawn with the soil. It was made only in an 8-inch size.

In addition to posthole augers, there were innumerable kinds of posthole diggers. These were used by chopping into the earth, spreading the handles, and withdrawing the loose soil. Shown here are a few examples of 1910. Posthole diggers are still made today.

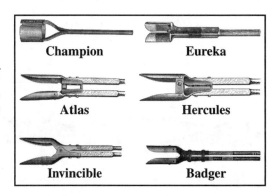

Champion   Eureka
Atlas   Hercules
Invincible   Badger

Fence Tools

The stretcher shown here is set up to stretch woven wire. The 1910 advertising noted that it was a Combination Fence Stretcher, Hoist, Stump Puller, and House Mover. This device is shown in the engraving's center. To the right, it is set up for dressing a steer.

This device used a notched steel bar and a ratchet mechanism for stretching barbed wire. Numerous styles have been made, and fence stretchers of this general pattern are still on the market.

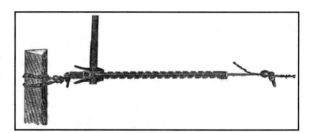

Many styles of tackle blocks were made especially for fence work. The styles shown here were also "useful for butchering hogs, etc." An important part of these devices was a special safety catch that could hold the rope at any point. Tackle blocks like this often bring a few dollars, but are not highly sought after by collectors.

While most fencing pliers have small appeal in the collectibles market, this one might bring $15 to $25 in good condition. Known as Russell's Wire Splicer and Staple Puller, it was a combination tool capable of tightening wire, holding it, cutting it, and served double duty as a staple puller. In 1900, it sold for $1.25.

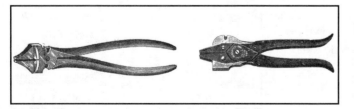

Shown here from left are the Cronk's Fence Plier and the "Elm City" Fence Plier; both are from the early 1900s. Although there are probably hundreds of different styles built over the past century, few bring more than $10 or $15. This is partially because various kinds of fence pliers are still made today.

Forks

Although a great many different styles of forks are still being produced, some of the earlier ones have gained collectible status. It is always surprising to me that forks almost always bring a few dollars at an auction, perhaps because new ones are expensive.

Although nearly thirty different styles are shown here, there are many other varieties that can be found. Nice examples of early forks can sometimes bring $20 or more. Forks with wooden tines, and in good condition, can often bring $50 or more, since they are becoming rather scarce.

Hay forks or pitchforks, were a common item on virtually every farm. Early styles used wooden tines, but the steel tined forks are far more common. Although the three-tine and four-tine styles are shown here, a two-tine fork was sometimes used. The latter is much harder to find than these illustrated styles.

Header forks were used around grain headers of days gone by. Grain headers were used mainly in certain wheat growing regions, and these designs were intended particularly for this need.

Reflecting the needs of Kansas wheat growers, the Kansas Deep Dish Header Fork was a specialized item. Outside of this area, the design shown here would probably be hard to find.

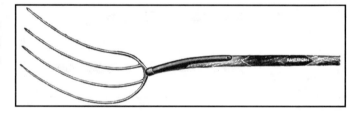

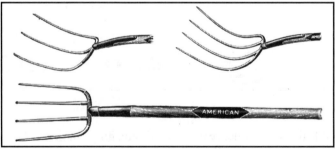

Forks were used to feed early hay presses, and special designs were offered especially for this purpose. Shown here are three-tine and four-tine styles. The Baling Press style could be supplied with a long 4-1/2-foot handle, or with a D-handle as required.

The barley crop required a special fork having a rear bail. One 1910 catalog illustrates both the steel and wood-tine styles offered at the time. Many different styles were made for special crop needs.

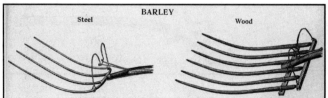

Manure forks were an essential part of the barn tool inventory. Hogs, sheep, cattle and horses were the major part of the average farm, and of course, the chicken house is not to be forgotten. This D-handle style is one of many different varieties offered over the years.

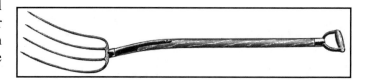

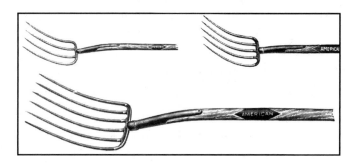

Ordinary manure forks were offered in four-, five-, and six-tine styles. The four-tine was preferable because it weighed less, but at times it was necessary to use a five- or six-tine fork. At farm auctions, a nice manure fork might bring $10-$15.

Spading forks were used mainly for garden work. The average farm of 1900 had virtually nothing that was mechanized, and the home garden would remain unmechanized for another fifty or sixty years. Even then, power rotary tillers only found their way into a relatively small number of gardens.

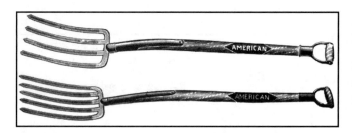

Many different kinds of spading forks have been made. Usually a four-tine style was adapted from the spading fork to produce a potato fork. The latter was intended especially for harvesting potatoes. Most high-quality forks were made in one piece from the best crucible steel.

A specialized design was the Italian Gardening Fork. It was available with a D-handle as shown here, or with a 4-1/2 -foot straight handle. This style was offered by Baker & Hamilton at Los Angeles in 1910.

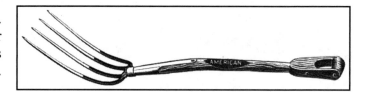

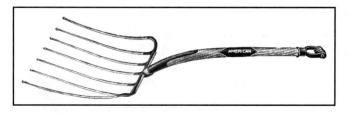

Ball-tipped tines were a distinguishing mark for beet forks, as shown here. Eventually, farm mechanization eliminated the need for many of these specialized designs. Prior to that time, the beet fork was an essential item in handling the crop.

In the 1890s, ensilage became very popular, particularly with Midwestern farmers. Corn or other crops were cut into small pieces and stored in a silo for winter feed. Handling the ensilage required a special kind of fork, and this style was an answer. Ensilage forks are now fairly scarce.

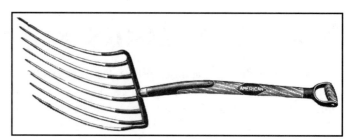

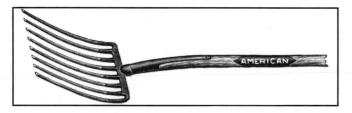

The sluice fork is another design that is now fairly scarce. It was distinguished by having a diamond shape on the front of tines. Like many other designs, this one is now fairly difficult to find.

Coke forks were used mainly in the foundry industry. They were usually made with twelve or fourteen tines and had a total spread of 18 or 20 inches. Coal yards also used these forks to scoop up smaller pieces of coal and coke.

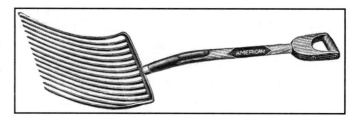

Technically, these two items were classified as Potato Hooks, but sometimes they were called bent forks as well. After digging the potatoes, workers used these hooks to claw through the freshly turned soil, looking for potatoes that were covered by the digger.

On the left is a Hoe Down, also another form of potato hook. On the right is an unusual stone hook. It was made for scratching through the soil and finding rocks which could then be hauled away to a remote area for disposal.

The hop hook shown at the left is a specialized design used by the hop grower and the brewing industry. These are seldom found today. The drag fork on the right had many uses, but in the Midwest it was used mainly for raking ear corn from a crib and into a corn sheller. In the Midwest at least, the corn rake or corn drag is still fairly common.

Foundry Tools

Especially during the last half of the nineteenth century, the foundry arts flourished as never before. During this same period, America saw huge numbers of European immigrants, and many of them helped to propagate the arts of the pattern maker, the molder, and the founder. Pattern making was the heart of things, because he had to accommodate all the various problems that might occur during the remainder of the process. Poor work on the part of the pattern maker would undoubtedly result in a poor casting. The same held true for the molder. A person skilled in this art could provide molds that would faithfully reproduce everything on the pattern.

Shown here are about twenty different tools used by the molder. After ramming the mold into place the pattern was withdrawn. Using various tools, the molder was able to do any necessary touchup work or make any necessary repairs prior to pouring the casting.

Many patterns were very ornate, and to have a mold plugged or otherwise distorting the design works would undoubtedly cause a rejection; this would make the foreman very unhappy. Stove patterns were probably the most ornate of all. It is indeed interesting to look at an ornate casting and then realize the effort involved in its production.

The Victorian era epitomized the arts of pattern making, molding, and founding. Cast iron was cheap and readily available, and even brass was fairly reasonable, and used extensively for small castings. The advent of gas and electric welding processes eventually brought much of the iron casting business to an end, and today, welded sections have largely replaced the large iron castings of a previous time.

The pattern making art is not discussed in this section. Various parts of this book illustrate most of the woodworking tools used by the pattern maker. Likewise, the founders' art required few hand tools and is not discussed in this book to any degree. The primary focus is on the tools used by the molder; the person who set the finished pattern into molding sand, rammed it into place, and withdrew the pattern. At this point, the work was taken over by the founder.

Most of the molding tools shown here are valued at anywhere from $5 to $15 today. While many tools were made of steel or cast iron, some were made of brass, and the latter command a better price. Good molders' bellows will usually bring $100 or more. Even one with dilapidated leather, but still intact will likely bring $75 or more. Molders' bench rammers often bring $40 or more; vintage rammers are now becoming quite scarce, although new ones of a similar pattern are still available.

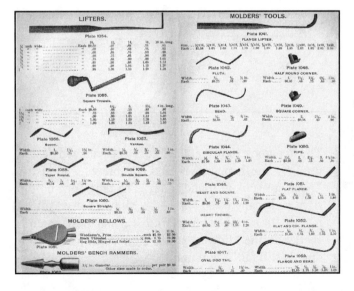

The various molders' tools shown here are from the 1890 catalog of Rumsey & Sikemeier at St. Louis, Missouri. Note that many of the tools shown were offered in various sizes.

G

Garden Tools

Although the required tools for gardening are very basic, a wide variety of different garden tools have been produced over the years. Even taking the simple hoe for instance, one can find dozens of different styles and sizes. Most garden tools do not rank highly among today's collectible items. There seems to be a plentiful supply of many tools, and substantial values only appear for the very unique and unusal ones.

A wheelbarrow was an essential part of garden work. An 1890 catalog illustrates this model with a wooden wheel and removable sides. It was built in three different sizes and priced at $6.60 to $7.50. In good condition, this barrow should bring well over $100 today.

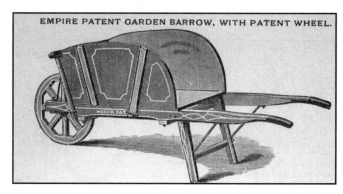

EMPIRE PATENT GARDEN BARROW, WITH PATENT WHEEL.

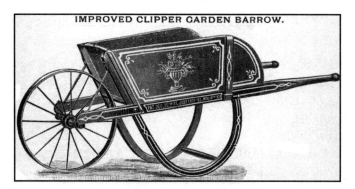

IMPROVED CLIPPER GARDEN BARROW.

This lightweight, unusual design featured jointless bent legs as shown. With a wood wheel it was priced at $5 in 1890; with a steel wheel it was $6. Factory-built wheelbarrows were usually painted, nicely striped, and varnished.

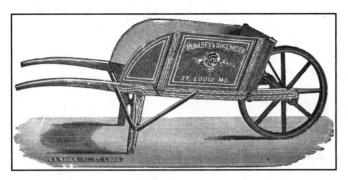

The Eureka "Garden Barrow" shown here was made in four different sizes, and in 1890, the prices ranged from $6 to $10. For all the wheelbarrows that were factory-built, many more were made locally and additional thousands were homemade.

The Lightning Potato Bug Killer was advertised in an 1890 catalog. To the right, is a funnel where Paris Green powder was poured into this bug duster. By working the bellows, the potato plants were covered with this insecticide. Paris Green was a poisonous green powder derived from the salts of copper arsenite and copper acetate. It was used widely at one time to control potato bugs. Lead arsenate was also used widely, either as a spray or as a dust to control various garden bugs. It was a pinkish powder that is no longer used. Numerous kinds of garden dusters were available, some of them being quite unique.

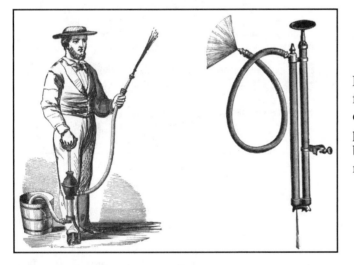

Numerous kinds of garden sprayers were available. In fact, an entire industry sprang up to build power orchard sprayers, ridding the maturing fruit of various pests. The Patent Aquaject shown here was claimed to be capable of "throwing about eight gallons of water a minute." In 1890, this brass and iron pump sold for $6.

Hundreds of different garden cultivators have been built, with the idea making great headway from 1900 onward. This one of 1920 sold for $7.95. It weighed about 25 pounds. Today, garden cultivators usually bring $20 to $40 if the wooden parts are not rotted and if the cultivator is otherwise complete.

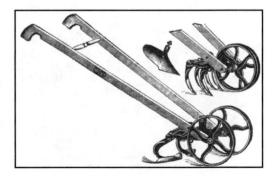

Probably the most popular cultivator was this Hamilton high-wheel style. In 1920, it sold for $5.50. Several different attachments were included, including a moldboard shovel as shown. Today, it is rare that a garden cultivator is found complete with all its original attachments.

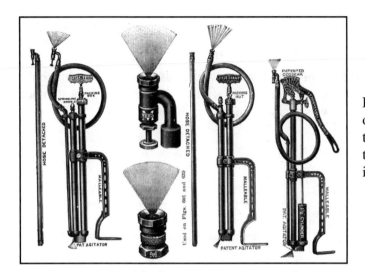

By the 1920s, there were many different companies offering hand spray pumps. Myers for instance, offered these various styles made entirely of brass except for the malleable iron foot stop which secured the sprayer in any convenient bucket.

Garden hoes seldom have a high collector value, except for very old or very unique styles. Ordinary garden hoes are still available, and for every new one sold, there are probably hundreds of others ranging in age up to perhaps a century. A prized possession of mine is a hoe dug from a hedgerow in upstate New York in the 1850s by my great-great-grandfather. It is badly corroded from its years in the soil, and probably goes back to the 1700s. Although it is completely unusable as a hoe, it likely has a substantial collector value because of its age.

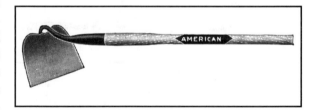

In addition to the ordinary garden hoe, there were many different hoes for specialized purposes. To the left is an onion weeder, found mainly in those areas where onions are grown as a cash crop; on the right is a beet thinning hoe. Again, this style was used primarily in areas where this crop was raised.

For the sugar beet crop, this hoe was designed especially to meet specific needs. With the coming of farm mechanization, the need for hoes and hand work was virtually eliminated.

Certain crops and certain soil types were needed for the scuffle hoe. This was a type of surface cultivator. The hoe passed beneath the top of the soil, lightly cultivating it and cutting off weed shoots beneath the ground.

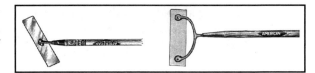

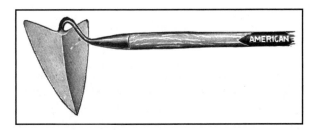

The Warren style hoe was widely used, since its point could work right up to plants without damage. Like most other hoes, it was available in several different sizes.

Various kinds of weeding hoes were available. These were better suited to removing established weeds around the edge of a garden for example. Their design was better suited to chopping and digging than the ordinary hoe.

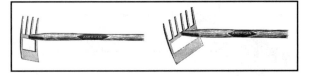

Prong hoes were fairly popular, but are seen only occasionally today. The duplex design permitted hoeing and raking within a single lightweight tool. They are usually found in the four- and six-prong styles shown here.

The familiar garden rake has little collectible value because they are so plentiful and are being made in virtually the same design as this 1910 model. Only the unique and very old designs have acquired a collectible value.

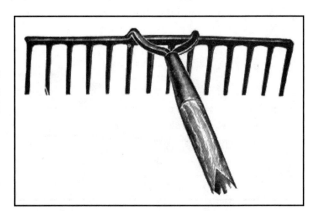

Early garden trowels have a slight collector value, but since this tool is so very plentiful, only the best examples are sold as collectibles. Shown here are various designs of the early 1900s.

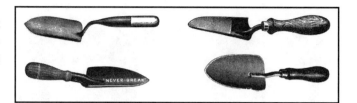

Numerous kinds of weeding hooks and hand forks have been readily available over the past century. Nice hand-forged examples as shown here sell for only a few dollars as collectibles, especially since a great many different styles are still being produced.

Gauges and Meters

The Bourdon pressure gauge was invented in 1845. M. Schinz in Germany got a patent for it that year. To this day, the great majority of pressure gauges follow the basic design. The Bourdon gauge depends on a closed and curved tube that tends to straighten itself when pressure is applied from within.

Only a sampling of meters are shown here, mainly electrical meters. Many of the older styles have now gained a good collector value when still in good condition. Older switchboard meters were often very ornate, and built with a brass case and ring. Quite often a silver face was used. Some of these meters sold for $100 and more in the 1920s. Gauges too, were very expensive in the larger styles. For example, in 1910 a 12-inch pressure gauge with a brass case sold for $80 to $100. Today, a decent one will still bring that much or maybe more.

High quality gauges were an expensive item from their beginning. A 10-inch gauge like this one sold for $80 to $100. When engraved with a company name such as Fairbanks-Morse, the collector value rises appreciably. Today a gauge like this one might bring $100.

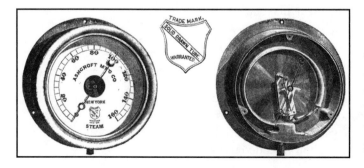

To the right of this engraving is shown the Bourdon tube which is the basis of most gauges. It is a curved tube, closed on one end, and coupled to the meter hand with appropriate linkage. As pressure rises within the tube it tends to straighten, thus providing a reading on the face of the gauge.

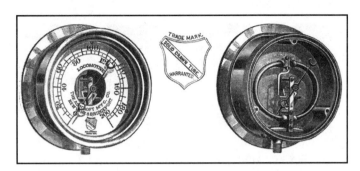

While the single-tube gauge was sufficient in stationary applications, the double Bourdon style was used for locomotives and steam fire engines. These gauges were built so that the entire movement was free from the back of the case in order to minimize vibration. Usually, these gauges were supplied with either an iron case, or one made of brass. The latter is far more valuable in the collectibles market.

Farm traction engines, like the locomotive styles, used a double-tube Bourdon design. These gauges were usually between 4-1/2 and 6 inches in diameter. Usually the engine builders name was engraved on the face. When engraved with J. I. Case, Avery, Rumely, or any of the other traction engine builders, these gauges can become very expensive, sometimes bringing well past $100.

Gauges have been, and still are, built in countless varieties to meet specific needs. This compound gauge could read vacuum or pressure and was widely used on heating systems, condensers, and other apparatus.

Pumping stations and waterworks plants required a special sort of gauge. This one had two scales, one in psi (pounds per square inch) and altitude expressed in feet of water. Altitude gauges, and particularly the combination style are fairly scarce today.

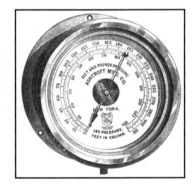

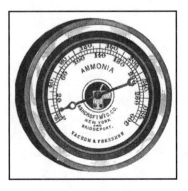

Large refrigerating plants of old used ammonia as the refrigerant, but the chemical makeup of this substance required special materials that would not be destroyed by its presence. Ammonia gauges are now fairly scarce. Oftentimes, a power house or manufacturing plants would have each gauge displaying its use on the engraved face, such as "Condenser vacuum" or "Exhaust pressure." These special use gauges often take on a special value just because of their intended usage.

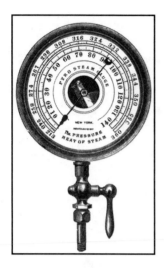

In 1890, Ashcroft Mfg. Company in New York City offered a Pyrometrical Steam Gauge. It was simply a dual gauge that indicated steam pressure, as well as the temperature of the steam at a given pressure. For instance, at 100psi the steam temperature was 338 degrees.

Test gauges were a necessity in the powerhouse and in manufacturing plants. Periodically, gauges would be tested against the master test gauge to verify their accuracy. Test gauges were made to exacting standards and were only used as a reference, never in day-to-day work.

Locomotive and marine duties required a special spring-wound clock that would retain its accuracy despite heat, cold, dust, and vibration. Ashcroft answered this need with various sizes and styles of Locomotive and Marine Clocks. The best of these sold for $125 in 1890.

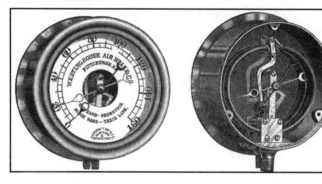

Duplex gauges are seldom found today (except, of course, for new ones made for specialized applications). This one of 1890 was made for Westinghouse Air Brake Co., at Pittsburgh, Pennsylvania. The red hand indicated air pressure in the reservoir, while the black hand gave the pressure of the train line.

Factories, power plants, and waterworks plants were often equipped with a large panel board containing all the necessary gauges to show the activities of various parts of the operation. Usually the gauges were nickel plated, and the board itself was highly ornamented. Panel boards like this one have become virtual museum pieces.

Steam boiler test kits as shown here in a wooden case, are very difficult to find today. A high quality test gauge was part of the unit, along with a nickel-plated test pump and fittings. Already in 1890, this outfit sold for $45.

In order to keep live steam from entering the Bourdon tube and ruining it, a syphon was (and is) used on every steam gauge. Water condensed in the syphon tube, preventing steam from reaching the Bourdon tube. The plain syphon is still in use today, although farm traction engines often had a special bronze syphon that achieved the same purpose.

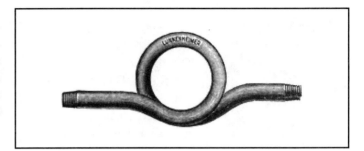

Specialized gauges came into use by the 1870s, including this 1890 model of a hydraulic pressure gauge. This one is set up to read pressure in psi, as well as reading the tons of thrust by an 8-inch hydraulic cylinder. Many different styles of these specialized gauges have been built for specific applications.

With the widespread use of electric power by 1900, there also came a need for instruments to read voltage, amperes, and other electrical functions. Portable instruments were a requirement too, and most of these were enclosed in a cherry or walnut case. Today these instruments are rather scarce, especially if all their accessory parts are still intact. Examples have recently brought well over $100. Shown left to right, a voltmeter and an ammeter.

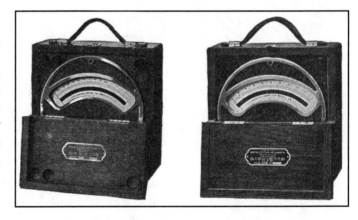

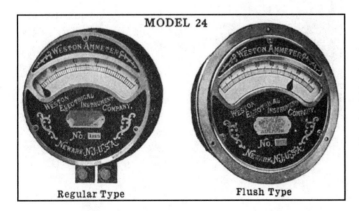

MODEL 24

Regular Type   Flush Type

With the coming of electrical power stations came a wide variety of instruments. Originally the instruments were mounted through heavy slate panel boards, with the electrical connections being on the backside. Although fairly plentiful, most instruments in reasonably good or restorable condition now bring $25 and more.

Switchboard instruments were always of the highest quality, and designed for 24-hour use, years on end. A voltmeter of interest, though, is one that reads 2300 volts at full scale, or an ammeter that reads 500 amperes at full scale. Neither the full voltage was applied to the meter, nor is the amperage. A voltmeter would have a 120-volt movement, and would be connected to the line with a potential transformer. The meter scale would coincide with the voltage of the line being read. Ammeters use a 5-amp movement coupled with a current transformer. The ratio of the current transformer might be 100:5, meaning that 100 amps on the line would give 5 amps or full scale reading on a 100-ampere meter face. The c.t. ratio is almost always inscribed on the face of the meter.

MODELS 151 AND 156

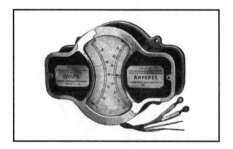

Duplex gauges were often used in direct-current work, especially for home lighting plants and similar applications. This was a simple and attractive design, but these meters are now fairly scarce.

Numerous companies built switchboard instruments, and at least into the 1920s, many of them were quite ornate. Unfortunately, the fancy ones are becoming scarce, while the modern styles introduced in the 1920s are fairly plentiful. The latter were much more economical to build, and were better-suited to mass production techniques than the heavy-cast case models.

Pocket meters are always an attractive collectible and always seem to be highly desired. They were mainly used for testing dry cells as used on telephones, gas engine ignition, and the like. These meters, especially if carrying the name of an engine manufacturer such as Fairbanks Morse, New Holland, or any of countless others, bring phenomenally high prices on occasion, with a recent one selling for well over $200 on an Internet auction.

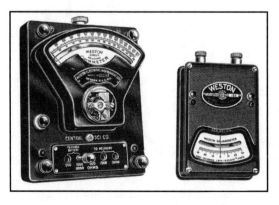

Besides the numerous switchboard and portable instruments used over the years are the many specialized instruments used in certain industries. Telephone and telegraph companies for instance, had wide recourse to the ohm meter for measuring electrical resistance. Oftentimes these meters were built into a fancy wooden case. They are now very hard to find, and probably would bring premium prices.

Grindstones and Grinders

Grindstones have been used for centuries. Initially the type of sandstone used depended largely on what could be found in each area. In England for instance, several different varieties were found that were highly esteemed. In North America, excellent sandstone was found in Nova Scotia and in the area around Berea, Ohio.

Emery, an impure form of corundum, has also been used as an abrasive for centuries. It appears that by the 1850s (and the advent of power tools), that emery was combined with shellac, sodium silicate, India rubber, and perhaps other combinations to form a grinding wheel. Emery polishing wheels consisted of a thick buff, covered with glue, then rolled in emery powder and left to dry. Blacksmiths used these "buffers" for polishing plow moldboards and other parts into the 1950s.

Carborundum is now the primary material used in grinding wheels. It was first developed in the 1890s, virtually by accident. An experiment with an electric furnace that would hopefully lead to artificially produced diamonds yielded the first carborundum. Since that time, it has been the primary material used in grinding wheels.

In the 1920s, numerous companies offered grindstones to their customers. Many of them took the form shown here, with a lightweight tubular steel frame and a pair of foot treadles to turn the stone. A funnel-shaped holder above the stone permitted a constant flow of water to aid in cutting and to keep the stone from plugging.

Although heavier than the tubular steel model, the wood-frame grindstone was also very popular. Most grindstones originated in the area around Berea, Ohio. Today, a grindstone and frame, both in reasonably good condition will bring from $25 to $50.

A hardware catalog of the 1870s illustrates a pair of grindstone frames as might have been used in a blacksmith shop or a factory. Both use a huge cast iron trough needed to keep the stone wet, with the upper one in this engraving having ornate cast-iron feet. Large stones are seldom seen today.

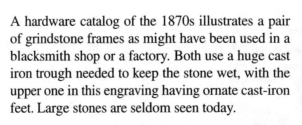

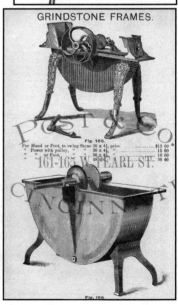

96

An 1890 catalog illustrates several grinders available at the time. Many of the larger blacksmith shops had installed a steam engine to power some of their equipment by this time, and fortunate indeed it was for a smith to have a power grinder. However, carborundum wasn't yet on the market, so the best that could be found was an emery wheel or a sewn buff which was covered with glue and then rolled through emery. After suitable drying, it was ready for use. A smith might use several of these every day, so a number of them were always drying.

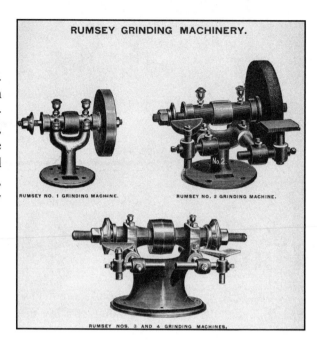

RUMSEY GRINDING MACHINERY.

RUMSEY NO. 1 GRINDING MACHINE.

RUMSEY NO. 2 GRINDING MACHINE.

RUMSEY NOS. 3 AND 4 GRINDING MACHINES.

EMERY GRINDERS.
Fig. 415.

From the 1870s comes this illustration of an Emery Grinder, also called an emery stand. At some point in time, it appears that the speed of overhead lineshafting in shops was established at about 270 to 300 rpm. Given the speed at which the driven machine was to run, it was fairly easy to clamp a pulley of the correct size onto the lineshaft.

International Harvester Company, among others, built a special knife grinder to sharpen sickles. It could be clamped right onto a drive wheel, making it fairly easy to tackle this job. Today these grinders are fairly scarce, and a nice one carrying the name of a famous harvester company in the castings might fetch $100 or more.

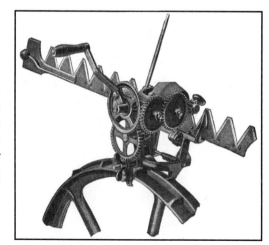

H

Hammers

Most early hammers do not bring more than $10 to $20, and quite often they can be bought for less than $5. Certain brand names always seem to bring a premium price, and exceptionally unusual ones do likewise.

This section illustrates a wide variety of hammers, and beyond these there are many more styles that have yet to be included. High quality hammers were forged from solid steel, with the cheaper ones being made of cast iron. Those with original handles are always worth more than those with a missing one. As with any other collectible, we reiterate once again, *caveat emptor*, Let the Buyer Beware.

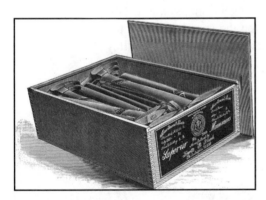

High-quality hammers were shipped to a dealer in a wooden case. Today, the case is probably more valuable as a collectible than the hammers it contained. Most of them were broken up for kindling or used for other things and eventually succumbed to the heating stove.

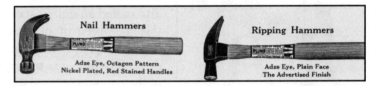

Fayette R. Plumb at Philadelphia was a well-known manufacturer of hammers and related items. A 1920s catalog illustrates its nail hammers with the curved claws and the ripping hammers with straight claws. Many of the Plumb claw hammers were furnished with a nickel-plated finish.

Ripping hammers, as well as claw hammers, were made in several different face styles, as shown here. To the left is a ripping hammer with the ordinary bell face, as is usually found today. To the right is the plain face which is no longer made; or if so, in very small quantities.

In the 1920s, the Plumb Triple-Claw hammer appeared. Advertised as "Two Hammers in One," it was intended to pull nails that could not be reached by any other hammer. It was intended to pull finishing nails, as well as common nails. These hammers are quite scarce, and often bring $50 or more. A few makers made a hammer with two separate sets of claws, and these can bring as much as $200.

F.R. Plumb Company at Philadelphia had its beginning with Jonathan Yerkes in 1856. By 1869, the company was known as Yerkes & Plumb, and by the early 1890s, was bought out by Plumb. One of the best-known Plumb hammers was the "Artisan's Choice," shown here. It was made in various styles and weights.

Plumb and numerous other companies offered a brad hammer as part of their line. Usually these were of four-ounce weight, but were made in various sizes and styles.

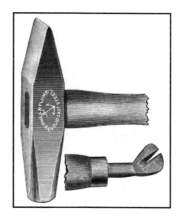

Carpet hammers are fairly scarce today. This style appeared by 1890 and it is not likely that they were especially popular except within the carpet and upholstery trades.

Many different styles of riveting hammers have been made, with many of them being used by the tinsmith. Additional styles are shown in the *Tinsmithing* section of this book.

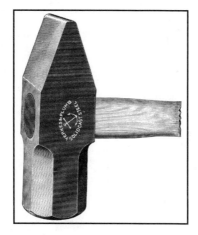

Every farm had a plow, and every plow needed a blacksmith to sharpen the lays. Over the years, hammers were developed especially for plow work, but with the coming of the power hammer, the work was much easier than before.

The double-face, or engineer's hammer, is still made and usually a nice one will sell in the range of $10 to $25. Virtually all of the older ones were forged of solid steel or made of cast steel.

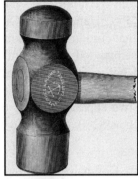

An 1892 Plumb catalog illustrates its Carriage Ironers' Hammer. It was designed especially for those whose job it was to attach the various iron parts to the carriage body. This style is seldom found today.

The cooper or barrel maker needed a specialized hammer, as shown here. Today, these are fairly scarce, but still can be found occasionally for $20 or less. At the other end of the spectrum, a nice cooper's hammer might bring $50 or more.

Bricklayers' hammers have a somewhat different appearance today, compared to this 1892 model from F. R. Plumb. It was made in four different sizes, from 1 pound up to 2-1/2 pounds.

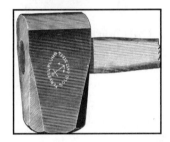

Prospectors used an entirely different hammer in their search for precious metals. Despite their unique design they can often be purchased for $15 to $30.

In the days of brick streets, there were artisans who specialized in this work. Their work called for a special hammer, and Plumb offered its Belgium Pavers' Hammer in its regular style, or the Boston Pattern Hammer shown here. Pavers' hammers are quite scarce and can fetch anywhere from $25 and upward.

The Plumb Bill Posters' hammer of 1892 was fitted with an apple-wood handle and the head was made of tool steel, with a nickel-plated finish. This style is seldom found today.

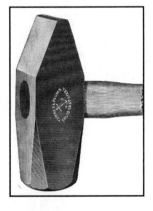

The ordinary blacksmith hammer was, by comparison, somewhat different than a plow hammer. It is likely, though, that they were used interchangeably in some shops. These hammers were made in various styles, and several different sizes.

Prospecting picks were frequently made in 1- or 1-1/2-pound sizes. Despite the mystique associated with prospecting, these tools seldom manifest a high value today.

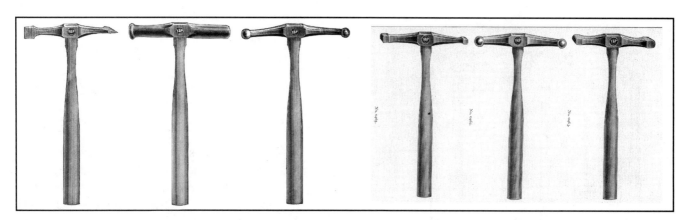

Cornice hammers were especially designed for the metal cornices so popular in the 1890s. In addition to this work, the sheet metal trades of that time built ornate coves and other embellishments on buildings…much of this work was done in copper. Cornice hammers are quite scarce today. Finding a complete set would likely be very difficult.

For those still building cobblestone streets in the 1890s, Plumb offered its Cobble Pavers' Hammer. This unusual design is likely very difficult to find today.

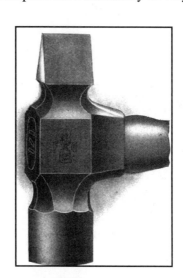

Straight-peen hammers, as shown here, or the cross-peen hammer have not acquired any great collector value, except, of course, for the unique and unusual designs. Like the ball-peen style, they typically have been made in sizes ranging from 4 ounces up to 3 pounds.

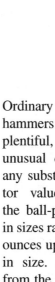

Ordinary ball-peen hammers are quite plentiful, so only the unusual designs have any substantial collector value. Typically, the ball-peen is made in sizes ranging from 4 ounces up to 3 pounds in size. Styles range from the octagon head to a smooth head.

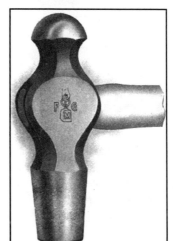

An unusual hammer today is the Boiler Makers' Riveting Hammer. Made in sizes ranging from 1-1/2 to 3 pounds, this style was adapted especially to the needs of the boilermaker.

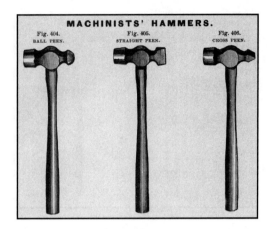

Ripley & Kimball, hardware merchants at St. Louis, offered these three styles of machinists' hammers in its 1877 catalog. Shown here are ball-peen, straight-peen, and cross-peen styles.

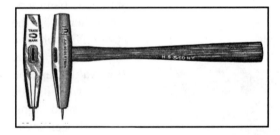

Robertson tack hammers gained a wide reputation in the early 1900s. Its hammers featured a polished head, and the better ones were nickel plated.

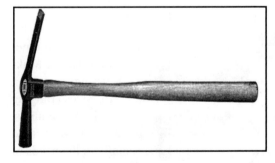

Patternmakers often had this special hammer in their shop, and today it is rarely found. This one was made by Maydole and had a 6-1/2-inch head.

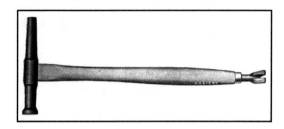

Various kinds of magnetic tack hammers have been made, including the Stanley No. 3 shown here. Numerous tool collectors specialize in the Stanley line, so usually this one would bring a premium over a lesser-known style.

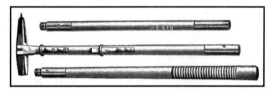

Probably the most expensive hammer for a collector to acquire today would be the Robertson Bill Posters' Hammer, shown here. Depending on the style, the handles could be extended to as much as 45 inches. This enabled a bill poster to reach perhaps 10 feet up on a telephone pole to attach his message. A complete outfit, as shown, would likely fetch $200-$250.

Upholsterers had need of specialized hammers. To the left is the Jahne Pattern hammer, with a Robertson Horseshoe Magnet style to the right. Both are fairly scarce today.

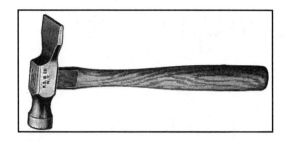

It is likely that the Veneer Hammer, shown here, is quite rare today. It was used in the attaching of veneer to a base wood. This one had an 11-ounce head. In 1910, it could be purchased for only fifty cents.

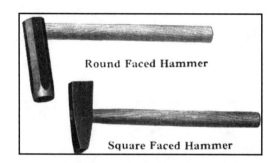

With the widespread use of circular saw-mills, there was also a need for saw mechanics. This trade used many ordinary tools, but also some unique hammers as they did their work. Saw hammers, as shown here, can often bring $100 or more, since they are extremely scarce.

Many different kinds of crating hammers have been made. Oftentimes, they are indeed unique. Thus, it is not uncommon for a nice one with an unusual design to bring $25 or more. Shown left to right are a box opener and a crate opener.

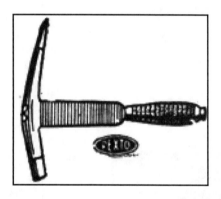

Working in slate, for example, as a roofing material, required special tools, including a Slaters' Hammer. Today these tools are very scarce.

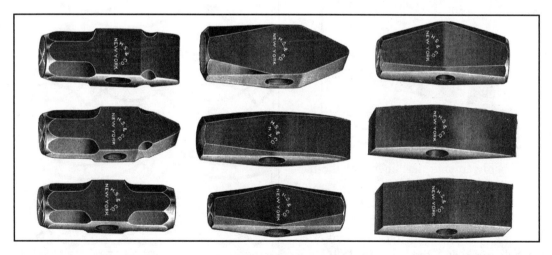

Heavy hammers often bring $15-$35, depending on their intended use. The top four items in this engraving were all used by the blacksmith. The remainder were all intended for various aspects of the stone trade and used for breaking, drilling, and stonecutting.

Harness Making and Leather

An advertisement in an 1884 issue of *National Harness Review* illustrates a harness-maker busy at his craft. He is stitching one of a pair of traces or "tugs" for a harness. The stitching horse was an essential tool to securely hold the work. Today, a stitching horse is not often seen, and can easily bring $100 for a mediocre one, or more than $300 for a fine example.

The above cut represents our Double Rope Wave Crease, ½ inch and 1 inch. The ½ inch can be used as ⅝ inch, by making straight crease on edge of strap, and the 1 inch can be used as 1⅛ in the same way. Price of each, $2.00.

The above cuts represent our Double Rope Wave Crease, ¾ and 1¼ inches. The ¾ can be used as ⅞ by making straight crease on edges of strap, and the 1¼ can be used as 1½ in the same way. Price of each, $2.00.

The above cuts represent our Diamond Wave Crease, ¾ inch and 1¼ inch. The ¾ inch can be used as ⅞ inch, by making a straight crease on the edges of strap, and the 1¼ can be used as 1½ inch in the same way. Price of each, $2.00.

No history concerning C. J. Cooper & Co. has been found, but in 1884, this Chicago firm was offering a wide variety of hardware and machinery for the harness trade. Included was Cooper's Improved Creasing Machine. As shown here, it could be equipped with numerous kinds of rollers to create a rope crease, diamond wave crease, or any of numerous different ornamentations for harness and saddlery. In 1884, this machine sold for $15. Finding an intact Cooper Creasing Machine would be very unusual.

J. O'Flaherty at Montreal, Quebec, advertised this "Newly Improved Lock Stitch, Wax Thread Harness Sewing Machine" in 1884. At the time, only factories or custom shops had a mechanical sewing or stitching machine. Any work done in a local harness shop was usually done by hand. Eventually this would change and virtually every harness shop had its own sewing machine. A harness stitching machine such as this was much heavier than the usual treadle machines made for shoe repair.

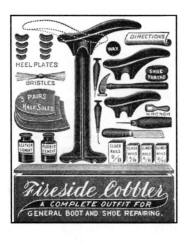

By 1900, and perhaps earlier, major hardware companies offered shoe-repair outfits. Generally, the tools included two or three sizes of shoe lasts and a mounting stand. Also included was a hammer, an assortment of nails, an awl, and some thread, with beeswax for lubricant. It is rather difficult to find one of these outfits complete and in its original wooden box. Many different companies offered a boxed kit of harness and/or shoe-repair tools.

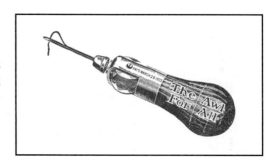

Numerous companies offered sewing awls like the Myers shown here. They are found occasionally, and a nice one still in its original case might bring from $10 to $25.

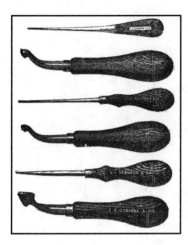

Daily harness and saddlery work required a wide variety of awls, creasers, and ticklers. Today, these tools have become quite scarce, but they still do not generally bring high prices at auction. Harness making and saddlery are trades outside the understanding of the average collector, since they were very specialized.

Collar awls and various kinds of dividers were also part and parcel of the harness-makers tool box. These tools were designed especially for use with leather and were not well suited to other duties.

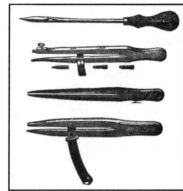

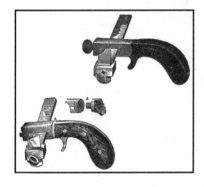

Draw gauges were an important tool for the harness-maker. With it, a piece of leather could be suitably narrowed when necessary. Draw gauges in good shape often bring $25 to $50.

The head knife was one of the most important tools for the harness and saddle-maker. Sometimes this was called a saddler's knife, but technically speaking, the latter was a straight knife having either a square or a rounded end. High quality head knives were made of the finest steel, and today a nice one often brings $25 or more.

A cast-steel shoe hammer from Plumb or some of the other famous hammer makers usually will bring $10 to $25, or even more for an exceptional one. This basic tool is fairly common, although many were made of cast iron or other inferior materials. Many more show the scars of misuse and have little collectible value.

Hatchets

Axe Pattern Collins	Hunters Pattern American A. & T. Co. Ridge Brand Red Enamel Finish	Sportsmans Pattern Plumb

Many different kinds of hunters' and sportsmans' hatchets have been made. Shown here are three different styles. In 1915, there were nearly 50 different companies making hatchets. Included were the common names such as Plumb and Underhill. On the obscure side were small companies like What Cheer Tool Company at What Cheer, Iowa. Certain brand names such as Keen Kutter often bring a premium price, but ordinary hatchets, as shown here, often sell in the $8 to $20 range.

Boy Scout hatchets often sell in the $15 to $30 range, especially if in good condtion and with a decent leather sheath. Pocket hatchets with a built-in blade guard are fairly scarce today. Shown is a model by H.S. & Co.

H. D. Smith & Company at Plantsville, Connecticut, offered this Perfect Handle Shingling Hatchet in 1910, and probably for several years surrounding that time. It was a one-piece forging with wooden sides riveted to the handle.

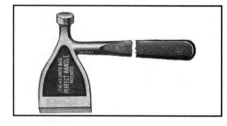

Shown here are two broad hatchets. They were used mainly for smoothing timbers during building construction. To the left is Hunt's design made by Douglas Axe Mfg. Company, East Douglas, Massachusetts. On the right is an Underhill made by Underhill Edge Tool Company at Nashua, New Hampshire. Broad hatchets are beveled only on one side. Oftentimes they can be secured for less than $20.

Claw hatchets were used mainly in warehouses and stores for opening wooden crates and similar work. Shown from left to right are three different examples: a Hunt's, an Underhill, and a Defiance model.

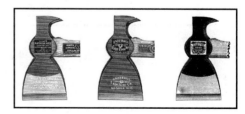

Many different kinds of shingling hatchets have been made, with the Defiance full-bell design shown here on the left. The Clark's half-bell design somewhat resembles the box hatchet shown on the right. While some shingling hatchets might bring more, the majority sell in the $8 to $20 range

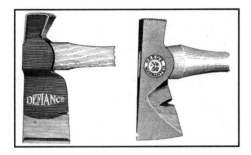

Many different kinds of box hatchets have been produced. Shown here, from left, are the Defiance and Reed's patterns.

In days gone by, a lath and plaster job in a house, for instance, meant wooden lath nailed to the studs with a small gap between each one to key the plaster. Many different styles of lathing hatchets were produced. The hatchets shown here, from left, are a Regular Pattern, Chicago Pattern, and St. Louis Pattern.

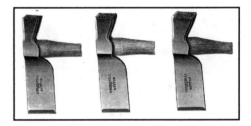

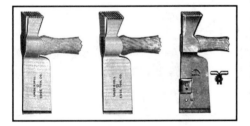

Lathing hatchets from Underhill included the Regular and the Chicago Pattern. Underhill was located at Boston, Massachusetts. Sayre's Chicago Pattern with Positive Gauge, shown on the right, was made by L. A. Sayre Company, Newark, New Jersey.

Other styles of interest include the Haine's Pattern on the left, and Hunt's Pattern on the right. As building methods changed, the wooden lath disappeared in favor of other materials. Today, the lathing hatchet is simply a curiosity that might also find use for totally unrelated purposes. Lathing hatchets seldom bring more than $20, except for those in mint condition, hand forged, or with other unique features.

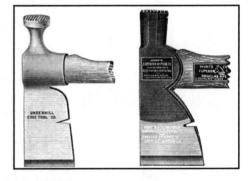

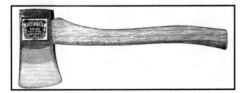

The sportsman's hatchet was usually made with a 1- to 1-3/4-pound head, and usually had a handle of 14 to 18 inches. Some were made of cast steel, and others were forged from the best crucible steel.

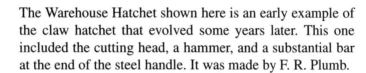

An unusual shingling hatchet is this bell-pattern style made of a solid steel casting. This one was made by F. R. Plumb in the 1890s.

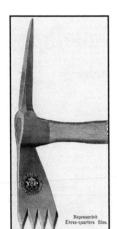

F. R. Plumb Company offered this Ice Hatchet in its 1892 catalog. This style is quite unusual, and probably is rather scarce...I have never seen one aside from this catalog illustration.

The Warehouse Hatchet shown here is an early example of the claw hatchet that evolved some years later. This one included the cutting head, a hammer, and a substantial bar at the end of the steel handle. It was made by F. R. Plumb.

Hay Tools

Various hay tools are shown in the *Farmstead Tools* section of this book. Others are shown on page 202ff of my book, *Encyclopedia of American Farm Implements*, published by Krause Publications in 1997.

Hay tools in general have not acquired a significant collector value, except perhaps for unusual hay forks or wooden hay pulleys.

The Nellis single-harpoon hay fork was one of the earliest designs. It was well suited to the long-stemmed timothy and other grasses commonly used for hay in those days.

Besides the Nellis, there was the Cribbs harpoon fork shown here, along with a few other lesser-known makes. Single-harpoon forks in reasonably good condition often sell above $25.

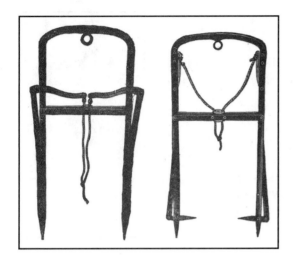

The double-harpoon fork made its appearance in the 1890s, and perhaps earlier. This design was better suited to short-stemmed hay crops, where the single harpoon was a failure. It was very popular, and double harpoons are still fairly plentiful.

For short-stemmed forage crops such as clover, the grapple fork was a much better answer than the harpoon. Not to be forgotten is the hay sling. In practice, two or three slings were required for each load. The first was laid out on the wagon, and when loaded sufficiently, a second one was placed on top. Loading then continued, and a third sling was placed. At the barn, one sling after another was lifted into the barn. When tripped, the basket formed by the sling opened and workers in the barn leveled the hay as the barn was filled.

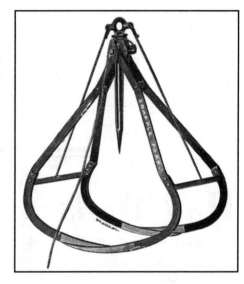

Shows Carrier at Work in Barn where Hay is Taken in from the End.

Artists always had a way of showing menial tasks in an idyllic setting, as typified here. Taken from a catalog of the 1890s, this scene illustrates a double harpoon fork set and headed into the barn. A lively driving horse is pulling in the load, but in fact, it was usually an old horse, or perhaps an old team, led by a youngster pressed into duty by his parents. The fellows in the hay mow were unfortunate victims of heat, dust, and a fair variety of bugs as they did their work. Yet, these tasks were accepted as part of a day's work on the farm. Most of these people also were aware of the much worse alternative…that of having to unload the wagon by hand, as was done in previous times.

I

Ice Making

Prior to the days of refrigeration, the ice harvest was an important part of winter. Once a pond, lake, or river froze sufficiently, the ice harvest began. The area to be cut and harvested was marked, either with a marking plow or by hand. In the right-hand illustration a snow ice plane is shown. It was used to level ice made from snow and watered to make solid blocks.

Various kinds of ice saws were used, and by the 1920s, some thoughtful soul developed a circular saw, usually powered by an old car engine, and mounted on sled runners. Many styles of ice tongs were used to bring the cut blocks to shore for loading on wagons or sleds. Also illustrated here are many different tools unique to the ice harvest. Aside from ice tongs, many of these tools are virtually impossible to find today.

Once the ice was loaded, it was taken to an ice house. This was a building unto itself, and the blocks were often laid on sawdust, with much more of this material being used around the sides, between the layers and over the top of the harvested ice. Carefully done, there was a supply of ice well into the following summer. I recall some of my ancestors talking about the ice house that was on the family farm in the 1870s and that continued in use until the early 1900s, when it was abandoned. There was also a sawmill on the farm at the time, so there was certainly an ample supply of sawdust.

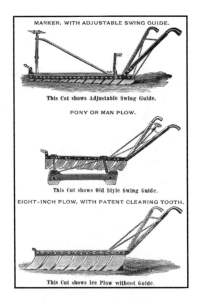

MARKER, WITH ADJUSTABLE SWING GUIDE.

This Cut shows Adjustable Swing Guide.

PONY OR MAN PLOW.

This Cut shows Old Style Swing Guide.

EIGHT-INCH PLOW, WITH PATENT CLEARING TOOTH.

This Cut shows Ice Plow without Guide.

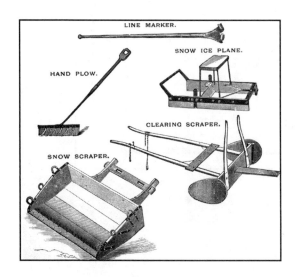

LINE MARKER.

SNOW ICE PLANE.

HAND PLOW.

CLEARING SCRAPER.

SNOW SCRAPER.

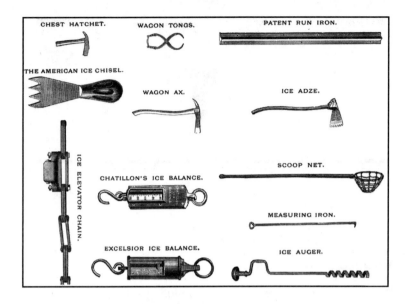

CHEST HATCHET. WAGON TONGS. PATENT RUN IRON.

THE AMERICAN ICE CHISEL. WAGON AX. ICE ADZE.

ICE ELEVATOR CHAIN. CHATILLON'S ICE BALANCE. SCOOP NET.

MEASURING IRON.

EXCELSIOR ICE BALANCE. ICE AUGER.

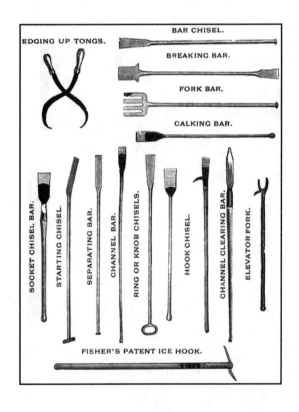

EDGING UP TONGS. BAR CHISEL.

BREAKING BAR.

FORK BAR.

CALKING BAR.

SOCKET CHISEL BAR. STARTING CHISEL. SEPARATING BAR. CHANNEL BAR. RING OR KNOB CHISELS. HOOK CHISEL. CHANNEL CLEARING BAR. ELEVATOR FORK.

FISHER'S PATENT ICE HOOK.

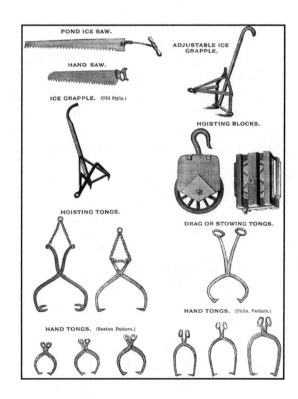

POND ICE SAW. ADJUSTABLE ICE GRAPPLE.

HAND SAW.

ICE GRAPPLE. (Old Style.)

HOISTING BLOCKS.

HOISTING TONGS. DRAG OR STOWING TONGS.

HAND TONGS. (Phila. Pattern.)

HAND TONGS. (Boston Pattern.)

J

Jacks

Regardless of how many different jacks we would illustrate in this section, there would be many more that are not listed. While Barth, Peerless and several large concerns did the majority of jack manufacturing, there were countless small, local companies that made wagon jacks, screw jacks, or automobile jacks.

Prices for old jacks vary considerably. Many of the old automobile jacks will bring $10 to $20, and some-what more if the company trade name is cast into the base, such as Ford or Chevrolet. Screw jacks, especially the large ones, can bring $40 or more, not as a collectible, but as a working tool. This, despite the fact that many of them have reached the century mark and are still quite useable.

Wagon jacks, in particular, have taken on many forms. Unless a wagon was loaded, or very heavy, a jack was not used to grease the wheels. A nut was removed on one side, and the wheel was maneuvered outward nearly halfway, leaving ample room for greasing. The nut on the other side was then removed and the wagon was pushed back into the other hub, the first nut was replaced, the second hub was greased and the second wheel was slid back into place.

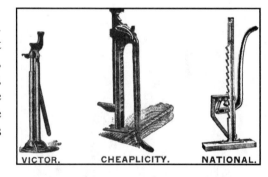

VICTOR.   CHEAPLICITY.   NATIONAL.

Oliver's Wagon Jack was made in various sizes and styles. A noticeable feature was the projecting lug on the lifting pole of the jack. This eliminated the need for wood blocking under the jack and kept everything easy and simple. The smallest Oliver jack weighed about 7 pounds, with the largest one weighing 18 pounds.

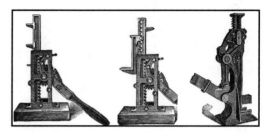

By the 1890s, the steam traction engine was becoming popular. With this and other heavy equipment, bigger and better lifting jacks were needed. Shown here are the Samson No. 1 and No. 2 styles (left), along with the Samson Drop Hook jack (center). The No. 1 could lift 2 tons, but the other models were capable of 5 tons. The Traction Engine Jack (right) could lift 6 tons.

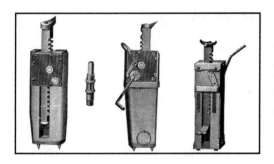

Logging jacks were a necessity, especially in the vast logging country of the western states. Among the better known varieties were the Duncan, the Dawson, and the Garcia, which are shown, from left. Most of these weighed from 40 to 60 pounds. Prices in 1910 ranged from $30 to $40.

Developed especially for the railroads, the Track Jack was soon found in many different industries. The Verona Jack shown here from 1910 was capable of 15 tons. It weighed 90 pounds and sold for $25.

Jack screws in various sizes and styles are an ancient tool going back for centuries. This 1910 offering ran from a small 9-pound style with a 1-1/4-inch screw, up to a heavy 72-pound size with a 3-inch screw. The small one could lift 10 tons, but the huge 3-inch screw was capable of 36 tons. Although seldom used today, jack screws still have considerable sales appeal.

Yet another style of wagon jack was Lane's wrought-steel model. It was made in four sizes to raise from 500 to 4000 pounds. The smallest one cost a dollar in 1910, and the largest one was barely $4.

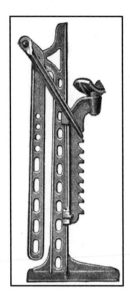

The Reliable Tire Saver Jack was fitted with a yoke that went on the outside of the wheel hub on early automobiles. Manufacturers recommended these lifting jacks to take the weight off the tires when not using the car. In the winter months, many cars were not used at all, so they remained aloft until warm weather.

The Hartford Auto-Jack of 1910 sold for $6.50 and could lift 7 inches. Given the high clearance of early automobiles, it was just a matter of sliding the jack under the axle. Some of these interesting old automobile jacks now bring $10 to $20.

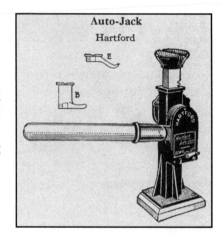

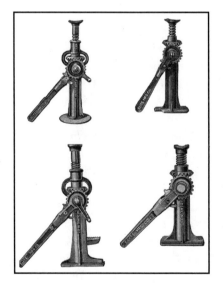

A surprising number of early automobile jacks still exist. Most of them were built very heavy, and remained long after the car had disappeared. Some of these jacks are near the century mark and still used occasionally. Others are polished up as collectibles. The four styles shown here carried a 1910 price ranging from $2 to $10.

L

Levels

The ancient Romans used the *libra aquaria* as a level. This was essentially nothing more than a water level, used to this day. A water level is simply a piece of hose filled with water. When held at a reference point at one end, the other end is moved until the water is still. At that point, the far end is exactly level with the reference point.

The first spirit level to be patented in the United States was under No. 28104, issued to William T. Nicholson in 1860. This patent was used by Stanley Rule & Level Company. Two more patents were issued in 1865 and three in 1867. During the latter year, Leonard L. Davis received the first of several patents for levels built by the L. L. Davis Company at Springfield, Massachusetts. This firm later took the name of Davis Level & Tool Company.

Spirit levels took their name from having alcohol (spirits) within the curved tube. The tangent of the tube is the straight edge of the instrument. In the days of spirit-level development, the bent tube was considered unreliable, but good enough for common work. For work requiring great exactness, the inside of the tube was ground to a specific radius. A curvature of 150-feet radius was considered to be fine for ordinary work, but for the greatest accuracy, the tube was ground to a radius ranging from 700 to 1,200-feet radius.

Although levels have been widely used over the years, the laser levels of recent years have replaced them to a major degree, especially in large building projects.

The *Hardware Buyers Directory* for 1922 lists the following companies as manufacturing levels:

Acme Level & Mfg. Co., Archbold, Ohio
Athol Machine Co., Athold, Massachusetts
Bedortha Bros., Windsor, Connecticut
Bostrom-Brady Mfg. Co., Atlanta, Georgia
Central Hardware Co., Philadelphia, Pennsylvania
Chapin-Stevens Co., Pine Meadow, Connecticut
Henry Disston & Sons, Philadelphia, Pennsylvania
Empire Level Mfg. Co., Milwaukee, Wisconsin
Goodell-Pratt Co., Greenfield, Massachusetts
* (formerly Stratton Bros. Level Co.)*
Millers Falls Co., Millers Falls, Massachusetts
Peerless Level & Tool Co., Sterling, Illinois
Putnam Machine Co., Fitchburg, Massachusetts
Reading Saddle & Mfg. Co., Reading, Pennsylvania
M. W. Robinson Co., New York, New York (Davis)
J. Sand & Sons, Detroit, Michigan
Sawyer Tool Mfg. Co., Ashburnham, Massachusetts
Southington Hardware Co., Southington, Connecticut
Stanley Rule & Level Co., New Britain, Connecticut
L. S. Starrett Co., Athol, Massachusetts
E. A. Stevens, Newton, Iowa
Union Level & Mfg. Co., Chicago, Illinois
Williamsburg Mfg. Co., Williamsburg, Massachusetts

A builder's level of the 1870s took on this form. It was called Sibley's level, and was considered to be a cheap form of better instruments which were then available. Once the level was set, it was then possible to look through the sights to get a reading. Wire crosshairs were placed in the front sight.

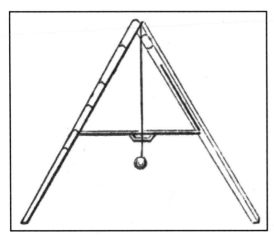

This instrument was sometimes called Brown's level, and was still used to some extent in the 1870s. It is illustrated in *Knight's American Mechanical Dictionary,* published in 1875. This design was used in various forms for centuries.

The 1882 catalog of Ripley & Kimball at St. Louis illustrates its machinists' levels. Included were three styles of cast-iron levels in sizes from 6 to 24 inches. Also available were two kinds of bench levels; the latter were reserved for precision work and kept in storage whenever not in actual use.

Levels

Davis levels are quite scarce and highly collectible. Nice ones seem to be in the range of $75 for an ordinary one, and past $200 for one in fine condition. The Inclinometer styles are very desirable, and usually fetch an above-average price.

Numerous kinds of levels were available by 1900, and at a very reasonable price. The Machinists' Level to the left of this illustration sold for 50 cents in 1910, and the little pocket level, at center, was priced at less than 25 cents at that time. Pocket levels can often bring $20 to $40.

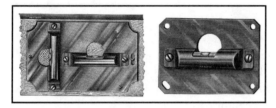

Plumbs and levels for straight edges were available from various companies; this one is from Roe. It could be mounted to a board or a straight edge for use in calibrating long distances. This style is quite scarce today.

The Ridgely No. 2 device could be clamped to any straight edge and could read plumb, level, and also be set to any desired angle. Made of highly polished brass, this instrument is quite scarce today.

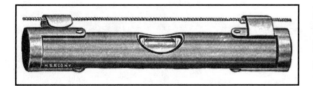

Line levels were in the tool box of many carpenters. Although their accuracy depended largely on the tightness of the string line, they were nevertheless accurate enough for rough grades and other common work. Shown is a Steven's model.

L. S. Starrett Company offered these precision levels in its 1938 catalog. They were made in sizes from 6 to 18 inches long. Being very accurate, they were (and are) widely used in erecting machinery, checking lineshafting and similar duties. Today, much of this work is done by precision laser instruments.

Starrett Iron Bench Levels are quickly picked up by machinists, as well as tool collectors. Their attractive design probably is a factor in their popularity. Since they are fairly plentiful, their value runs anywhere from $10 to $50.

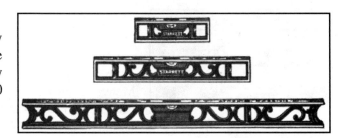

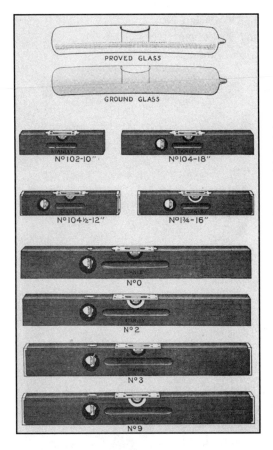

From a 1911 catalog, comes this parade of Stanley levels of the time. The various styles shown here were made in hardwood, mahogany, and rosewood, with the latter being about three times more expensive than the ordinary hardwood design. Some were plain, some had brass tips, some had brass lips, and others were entirely brass bound.

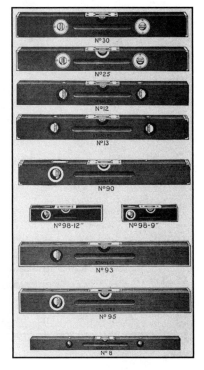

The Stanley level line of 1911 included numerous styles with adjustable plumbs and levels. This was a great advantage when it was necessary to maintain a certain grade or fall in construction work. The No. 8, No. 80, No. 35, and No. 45-1/2 levels were designed primarily for brick and stone work. These Masons levels were available in sizes from 36 to 48 inches.

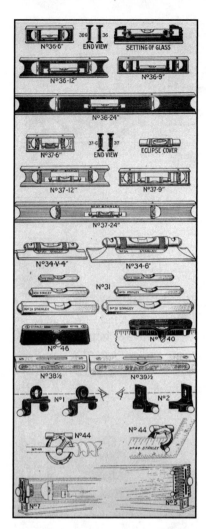

Many specialty levels were available in the 1911 Stanley catalog. Included was the No. 34 Eclipse precision level, the No. 40 and No. 46 pocket levels, and the No. 38-1/2 and No. 39-1/2 machinist levels. The No. 1 and No. 2 level sights are rather scarce today, as is the No. 44 Bit and Square Level. Stanley Pitch Adjusters, No. 5 and No. 7, were designed to clamp to almost any level, and were especially useful when laying pipe or tile to grade.

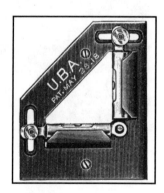

The U.B.A. adjustable level and plumb of the 1920s is an unusual instrument, probably designed to the needs of plumbers and pipelayers. Either the plumb or the level could be adjusted to a specific grade. This device was made by Union Level & Mfg. Co., in Chicago.

Peerless Level & Tool Co. at Sterling, Illinois offered a wide variety of levels in the 1920s. Their previous history has not been ascertained. Shown here are the Masons' Level, the Peerless Carpenter's Level, and the Peerless Plasterer's Level. The latter style would likely be hard to find today.

A single hole corn sheller took many cranks to get the job done.

This collection of tools contains an antique brass blowtorch at right. Also shown are a crowbar, brace, chisel, and two gouges.

Having a bag holder was a great way to make a job go a little quicker. The more free hands a farmer had the better, because they never stayed free for long.

With so much equipment coming into play, a farmer could never have too many wrenches around to make repairs. The above collection includes a variety of open-end wrenches and two pipe wrenches.

The above collection includes a drawknife and a wood auger. Also notice the hog scraper on top of the milk pail at far left.

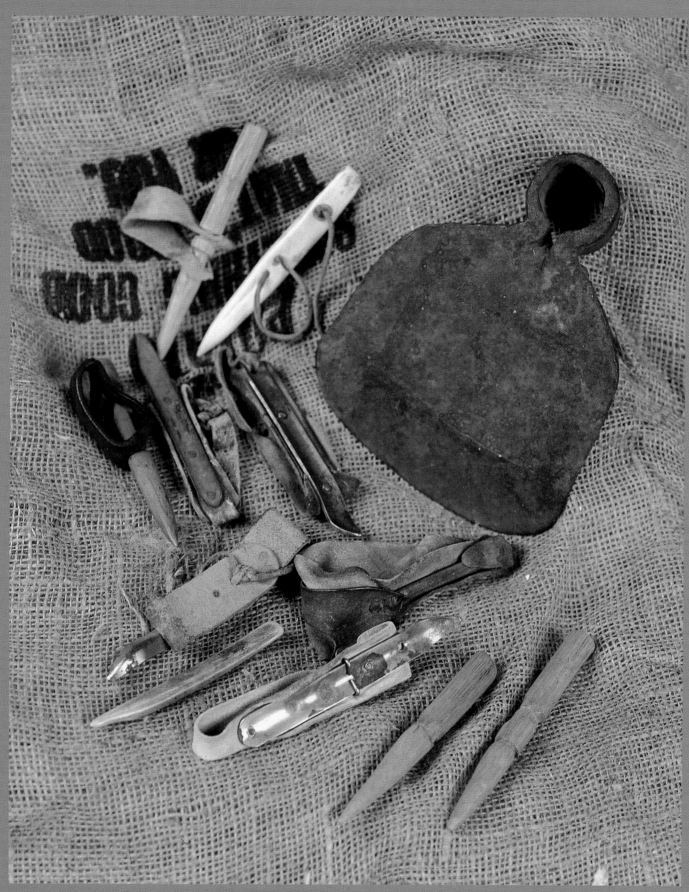

Corn huskers came in many forms, wood, bone, and metal. They were strapped onto the hand with laces and used to pick corn. Also shown is a handle-less hoe.

Antique icebox with tongs. Children in a household were frequently responsible for emptying the drip tray in the bottom. When purchasing an antique icebox, check the condition of this bottom area for rot.

Shown at bottom are a stone chisel and center punch, which were used for heavier jobs. When people had to be handy and fix their own equipment, no tool was unimportant. Here are a pair of pliers, hammer, and screwdriver.

M

Machine Tools

This section includes a variety of machinist's tools as well as machine tools, such as lathes and milling machines. Surprisingly, we have found that there are a great many lathes in use yet today that came out of the factory door a century ago, or even more. The same holds true for many other machine tools. Machinist's hand tools have often been handed down from one generation to another. Although many of the hand tools have been largely replaced with electronic instruments, a great many are still in use.

Books have been written about the development of machine tools, and in fact, the book, *American Machinist's Tools: An Illustrated Directory of Patents* provides a much greater insight into machinist tool developments. This book, by Kenneth L. Pope, was published by Astragal Press at Mendham, New Jersey in 1993. My extensive holdings of *American Machinist* and *Machinery* magazines have also been very helpful. The largest problem was in holding the material within reasonable bounds within this particular book!

Various items in the machinist's tool chest were also used in other trades, and are described in other sections of this book. Also, the average machine shop of 1900 was also a blacksmith shop, or perhaps a carriage business was carried on in another area of the shop. Sometimes a foundry was included.

Machine tool development was spurred forward by the development of the steam locomotive. As they became larger and more sophisticated, so did the need for machines that could make the necessary parts. Setting up a locomotive frame for instance, required precision instruments. This need, and others, prompted the development of precise bench levels such as the one shown here from the 1880s.

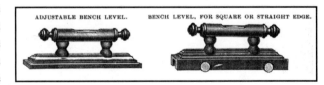

ADJUSTABLE BENCH LEVEL.　　BENCH LEVEL, FOR SQUARE OR STRAIGHT EDGE.

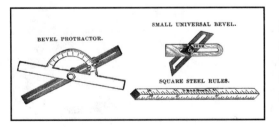

BEVEL PROTRACTOR.　SMALL UNIVERSAL BEVEL.　SQUARE STEEL RULES.

Early machinists were, by necessity, forced to be proficient with mathematics, as well as being able to operate the machines under their care. Bevels, protractors, and other measuring devices were needed to perform each task. Small tools like these always have a market, whether it be with a collector or a home-shop machinist.

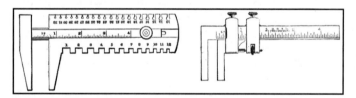

Various kinds of rules were available to the machinist of the 1880s, but nothing as refined as those we use today. Much of the work was done simply by reading a caliper or a rule, and with experience, many machinists were able to do so with amazing accuracy. Shown left to right are a steel-caliper rule and a key-seat rule.

This vernier caliper of the 1880s was graduated to include inches and sixty-fourths of an inch. Close fitting was often done with a gauge. For instance, a very early engine might have had a nominal bore of 4 inches. In reality, this might have been 3.980 or 4.123 inches. However, it made little difference, since all engines of that group were made using the same gauge, and the piston was fitted accordingly. In general though, 4 inches meant 4.000 inches by the early 1900s.

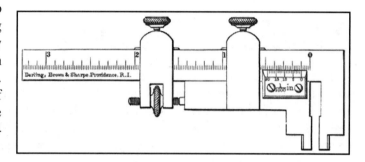

Various kinds of gauges were available by the 1880s. Included was the wire gauge shown to the left. It could size various gauges of wire, as well as determine the diameter of shafting and other articles. A unique combination square and caliper is shown to the right.

The micrometer had its beginnings in the 1870s. Brown & Sharpe Mfg. Co. at Providence, Rhode Island, was an early entrant into this field. In the 1880s, the small micrometer caliper shown here was in vogue. It had a capacity of one inch.

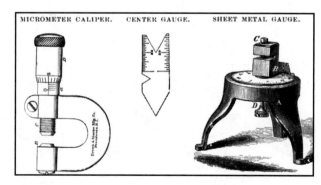

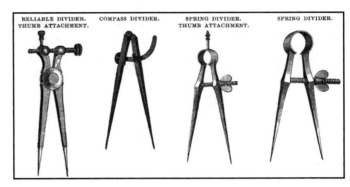

RELIABLE DIVIDER. THUMB ATTACHMENT. COMPASS DIVIDER. SPRING DIVIDER. THUMB ATTACHMENT. SPRING DIVIDER.

Dividers were widely used by early machinists. With some skill and a good basis in mathematics, a machinist could do much of a layout with dividers. They have been made in innumerable sizes and styles, and always have a market with either collectors or active machinists.

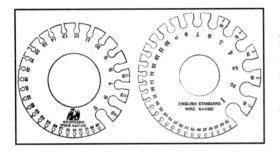

Numerous gauges were available to the machinist of the late 1800s. An accurate gauge made it easy to determine the thickness of materials or to gauge wire sizes. Two major styles were used...the American or "New" Standard Wire Gauge (left), and the English Standard Wire Gauge (right).

Many different kinds of calipers have been made, all with the same purpose of measuring the inside (left) or the outside (center) of an object. Usually these devices find a ready market, especially the Fancy or Dancing Legs style shown to the right. The latter style often sells at $50 or more today.

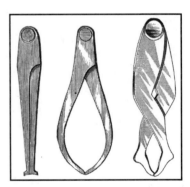

Numerous tool companies appeared in the 1890s, especially on the eastern coast of the United States. Standard Tool Company at Athol, Massachusetts, offered their No. 545 Knife Edge Straight-Edge in 1898. It had a stiffened back and was ground to a beveled edge. Tools like this, still in good condition, have now acquired collectible status, but are rarely found.

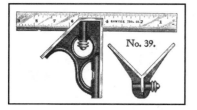

Companies like Sawyer Tool Company at Athol, Massachusetts, offered an extensive tool line. In 1898 they offered their No. 39 Combination Square for machinists. At the time their 12-inch style, complete with the centering head, sold for $2.50.

J. Stevens Arms & Tool Company of Chicopee Falls, Massachusetts had been in the tool business for some years prior to this 1898 advertisement. In this instance they were offering their No. 125 Stevens Universal Bevel. It sold for $1.50 in the 2-inch size.

J. Wyke & Company of East Boston, Massachusetts illustrated their Patent Universal Screw-Cutting and Twist Drill Gauge in the May 1898 issue of *Machinery*. As with many other industries, once the developments started in the 1870s, inventive minds came up with new and creative methods.

Poured babbitt bearings were commonly used until the 1930s. Most machinists were adept at pouring bearings, as well as fitting them after the metal cooled. Careful fitting required the use of bearing scrapers as shown here. This set, in a wooden box, sold for $3.30 in 1910. A set of scrapers in a similar wooden box can sell for $150 today.

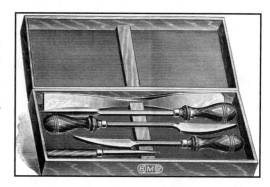

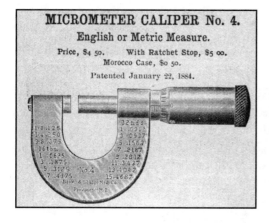

Brown & Sharpe was a major player in the development of the micrometer caliper. Their 1900 catalog illustrates many different styles, with the No. 4 shown here being a typical style. This one would measure up to one-half inch, and sold for $5.

L. S. Starrett Company at Athol, Massachusetts was built on the designs of Laroy S. Starrett. The Starrett line developed into an extensive offering of machinist tools for both the ordinary job work, as well as specialized applications. Their Universal Bevel Protractor No. 360 was a very useful tool, and in 1938 this instrument with a 12-inch blade and in a fitted case, sold for $17.75.

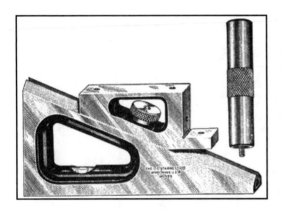

The No. 599 Planer & Shaper Gauge in a fitted case sold for $9.50 in 1938. Considering the times, this was an expensive tool. It has many uses in addition to setting planer or shaper tools, but is not at all common today.

Envied indeed was the machinist of the early 1900s who owned this fine Machinsts' Set No. 21 from J. T. Slocomb Company of Providence, Rhode Island. It comprised 1, 2, and 3-inch micrometers in a fitted case bound in morocco leather.

Star foot-powered lathes were advertised into the early 1900s. They were built by Seneca Falls Mfg. Company at Seneca Falls, New York. These lathes were built in 9-inch and 11-inch sizes. For light work, they could be operated with one foot, but for heavier work, both feet could be used. Several other companies made these machines at the time, including W. F. & John Barnes Company.

Many different companies were building lathes by the late 1890s, including the W. C. Young Mfg. Company of Worcester, Massachusetts. Lathes of this period were furnished with the overhead countershaft. It carried the top cone pulley, and the two clutch pulleys needed to drive the lathe. These pulleys ran from the line shaft; one pulley ran with a straight belt and one with a crossed belt, so that the machine could be run forward or reverse at will. Hardware was included for the shifter, and the wooden shifter bar was made to suit the installation. Also included was a stack of change gears for thread cutting.

This 14-inch lathe from 1900 typifies a common size of the time. Weighing 1,400 pounds, it used a separate feed rod for the carriage. The lead screw was reserved only for threading. Cone pulleys on the extreme left operated the feed rod, and provided a variable feed as required. This machine was sold by E. A. Kinsey Company of Cincinnati, Ohio.

Typical of a 30-inch lathe from 1900 is this model from E. A. Kinsey Company. Weighing 8,500 pounds, it could be furnished with a cross feed graduated either in thousandths, or in sixty-fourths of an inch, as desired. It could cut from 1 to 12 threads per inch.

Not until about 1900 did the quick change gear box gain any real popularity. This eliminated the cluster of gears, or loose gears ordinarily furnished with a lathe. It also raised the price considerably. This machine could cut threads having a pitch of 1 to 48 threads per inch. Also shown here is the overhead countershaft with its cone pulley and clutch pulleys. A face plate and a dog plate came as regular equipment. Three-jaw and four-jaw chucks were extras, as were the tool holders. Tooling for a lathe often cost nearly as much as the machine itself.

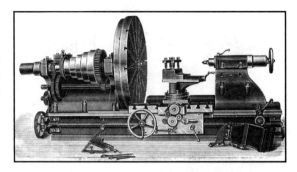

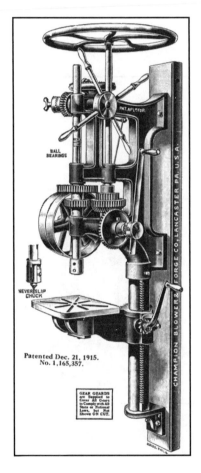

This huge 60-inch lathe weighed over 11-1/2 tons. It could swing 60 inches over the bed and 45 inches over the carriage. The spindle was 8 inches in diameter. Only the largest shops had a machine of this size. Besides the speed changes available with the five-step cone pulley, there were two different gearing changes that made a total of 15 different spindle speeds.

Occasionally a machine shop would have a large post drill, but ordinarily the machine shop preferred a drill press. Usually the post drill could use only those bits with 1/2 inch shanks. Most large drill presses used the Morse taper shank in various sizes. This post drill was made by Champion Blower & Forge Company of Lancaster, Pennsylvania.

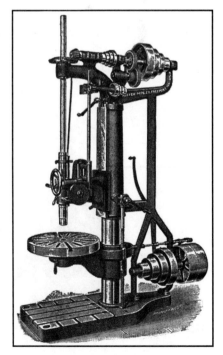

Dozens of different companies were offering drill presses by the early 1900s, and a surprising number of these machines are still in use. Fighting for a share of the market, each company pointed out specific advantages their machine had over all the others. The Hoefer, shown here, touted the accuracy of the column as being paramount to a good design. This machine was made by Hoefer Mfg. Company at Freeport, Illinois.

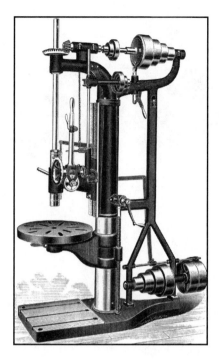

By the 1900s, many drill presses took on the same general appearance shown here. The design of the top end gave them the nickname of camel-back drills and sometimes even hump-back drills. Weighing almost 1,400 pounds, this 26-inch drill press was only fitted with a No. 3 Morse taper. By the 1920s, designers were not so conservative, and would likely have built the spindle with a larger No. 4 taper. Note the tight and loose pulleys on the bottom countershaft. A shifter lever is partially visible, whereby the operator could start and stop the machine at will.

Numerous companies, including Brown & Sharpe, built surface grinders. These machines marked a new epoch in machine tools since they permitted finishes that were never before attainable. This one is from 1900, and I still use one that is virtually identical, even though it is probably past the century mark.

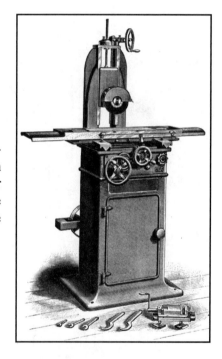

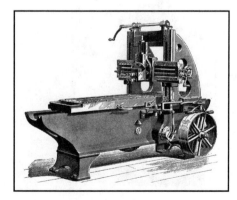

Most machine shops had a planer. These machines are no longer used as they were in the early 1900s. A planer was the machine of choice, to smooth an engine base, or to perform numerous other duties. Occasionally they would be equipped with grinding heads or milling heads for certain kinds of work. The 24-inch model shown here weighed about three tons.

The shaper was found in virtually every machine shop. Work was suitably secured and the shaper ram worked back and forth until the job was done. The shaper had an advantage (recognized by early machinists) that when the bit dulled they had but to sharpen it. By comparison, when using a milling cutter and it got dull, they usually had to send it out to a firm that was equipped with regrinding equipment—thus, the advantage of a single-point tool over a milling cutter.

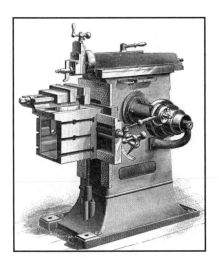

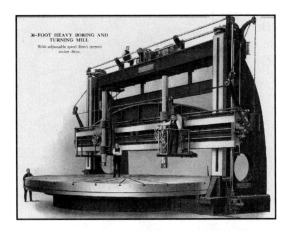

In 1920, Niles-Bement-Pond Company had its offices in New York City. The Niles Tool Works was located at Hamilton, Ohio, and Bement Works at Philadelphia. Pond Works was at Plainfield, New Jersey, with Ridgway Works and Crane Works both being in Pennsylvania. Pratt & Whitney Works was at Hartford, Connecticut. The company built an extensive line of machine tools from small to large, even gigantic sizes. Their 1920 catalog consists of over 600 pages of machine tools. Included is this 36-foot boring and turning mill equipped with adjustable speed direct-current motor drive. Note that the operator worked from a cage mounted on the carriage.

In about 1980, I bought a Gould & Eberhardt shaper, slightly older than the machine shown here from a 1903 advertisement. It had been used in the same shop on a regular basis for all its life, and remains today virtually as good as it was when new. Of course, this resulted in part from good care, but it is also a tribute to the early American machine tool builders. Although my machine sees only occasional use, it is always a pleasure to operate. Originally this machine, like all others in the shop where it served much of its life, ran from lineshafting. The hush of the belts, the clicking of the belt hooks on their pulleys, and the slight rush of air from the pulleys, is an experience that can never be adequately described to those who missed out on those glorious times.

Many different companies built shapers in the early 1900s. Included was this interesting design from George D. Walcott & Son of Jackson, Michigan. This 1903 design was unique in that it used an elliptical gear crank. This design permitted a rapid return on the ram and a slow feed on the cutting stroke.

Hendey Machine Company at Torrington, Connecticut, had become a well-known machine builder by the early 1900s. Part of their line included this unique design. Hendey claimed their machine was "radically different from other shapers." In its general appearance at least, it certainly displays some differences.

NEW SEVEN INCH
CRANK SHAPER

In addition to the usual heavy shapers found in machine shops, there were small machines designed to do light jobs that were too cumbersome for the ordinary shaper. From a 1904 advertisement comes this seven-inch crank shaper. It was built by L. E. Rhodes, Hartford, Connecticut.

Ingersoll Milling Machine Company of Rockford, Illinois began business in 1887. By 1909, they had developed this huge machine with a 10-foot capacity, four separate heads, and complete electric motor drive. The company's first milling machine of 1887 is on the table of this giant.

Kempsmith Mfg. Company of Milwaukee, Wisconsin was well established by the time this 1904 advertisement came out. Shown here is their No. 5 Universal Mill. It offered full power feeds. A universal mill has the capability of turning the table out of a right angle axis to the spindle. This, plus the use of a dividing head geared to the machine permitted the machine to cut spirals and other difficult jobs.

KEMPSMITH MILLING MACHINES

are relatively, size for size, the biggest, heaviest, most powerful, and have greatest productive capacity.

The entire operative mechanism is simple and concentrated.

One gear box provides *all* changes, any one obtainable while machine is *operating under cut. One* trip lever controls *all* feeds. *One* bolt effectually clamps the swivel table.

Altogether the machine is *reliable* and *safe* in severe milling.

The plain milling machine has a table running at a right angle to the cutter, compared to the universal which can be moved to a desired position away from the exact 90 degrees. One such mill was the No. 4 from Burke Machinery Co., Cleveland, Ohio. Small mills like this one were ideal for cutting keyways and many other jobs.

A 1900 catalog from Brown & Sharpe Company illustrates many different models of milling machines. Included was this No. 2 Plain Milling Machine; it weighed 3,800 pounds. Brown & Sharpe developed a tapered arbor somewhat different than the Morse taper. It is called the B&S taper, and in the case of this mill, the spindle was fitted for No. 11 B & S arbors. No. 10 and No. 11 were the most popular sizes, but this arbor has been replaced with other designs.

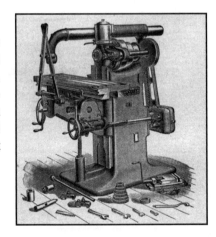

The No. 4 Brown & Sharpe Universal Mill shown here was illustrated in the company's 1900 catalog. It carried numerous patents, the earliest of them being 1893. It is shown here with the necessary change gears for use with the dividing head (index centers), along with required tools and accessories. Arbors, collets, and other tools were all at extra cost.

Universal Index Centers are usually called dividing heads today. Most dividing heads come with three different plates having different numbers of holes. By properly using the tables with a given head, indexing almost any number of spaces is possible. Gears and splines could be cut, along with many other jobs.

Not to be forgotten in the early machine shop was the assortment of wood pulleys on hand. It is curious that lineshafting usually ran in sixteenths of an inch. A main shaft in a machine shop might be 2-3/16 inches, but for most shops 1-7/16 inch shafting was the common size. Split pulleys as shown here could be attached anywhere along the shaft. There were no keyways, the pulley was simply clamped fast to the shaft with bolts. We have been unable to find any history on this development, but it is a certainty that the combination of leather belts on wooden pulleys could transmit power more efficiently than anything else of the time. Today, the few wooden pulleys that have not been turned to kindling are often falling apart from age and humidity. Occasionally, they retain some value as a collectible.

Mallets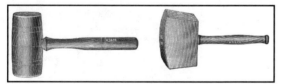

Round and square mallets were quite commonly used in the early 1900s. Common mallets were usually made of second-growth hickory, but the better grade was made of lignum vitæ. This wood from the West Indies is fairly soft and easily worked when green, but when dry becomes very hard. These mallets often sell in the $12 to $30 range.

Carpenter's mallets were typically of second-growth hickory. Iron rings were tightly driven onto each end to extend the useful life of the mallet. In decent condition, these mallets usually sell from $12 to $15.

Carver's mallets are yet another style that formerly were very popular. They were made in various sizes from 2-1/2 to 3-1/2 inches, and often furnished with lignum vitæ or dogwood heads. Ordinarily, they sell in the $10-$25 range.

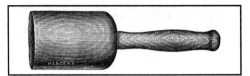

In the early 1900s, the fibre-head mallet appeared. Instead of wood, it was made of vulcanized fibre, reinforced with wrought iron bands. This style is often found in the $5 to $15 range.

Rawhide mallets have long been popular because of their toughness. Rawhide is the untanned, but treated and preserved, hide of cattle. Rawhide mallets are still available, thus they generally have not acquired a substantial value as a collectible.

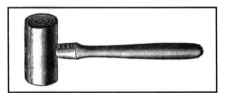

While not properly a mallet, lead hammers are extensively used by machinists and others. Today the lead hammer has been replaced to some extent by 'dead-blow' hammers and other devices. Lead hammer molds have been available in various forms. This one combined the ladle and mold. Usually it was furnished with a metal handle that was placed into the mold prior to pouring the metal. Once the hammer was worn out, it was simply remelted and repoured into a new one. Hammer molds are fairly scarce today.

A catalog of the 1890s illustrates the popular mallet styles of the time. This illustration is included mainly as a guide to identification. In addition to these styles there were numerous others, such as a carriage-maker's mallet.

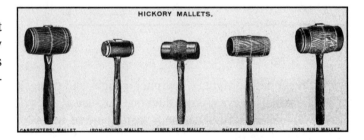

HICKORY MALLETS.

CARPENTERS' MALLET   IRON-BOUND MALLET   FIBRE HEAD MALLET   SHEET IRON MALLET   IRON RING MALLET

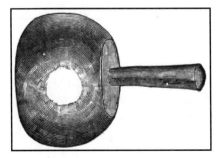

Stonecutters' mallets were usually offered in two sizes, 5-6 inches and 6-7 inches, and they were made of hickory. In 1900, these mallets sold for $1.50 and $2.00 respectively. They sell today in the $15 to $30 range.

Marking Gauges

Occasionally a caliper gauge, as shown here, appears on the market. These gauges were fitted to measure a particular size, and were very accurate. Caliper gauges, while interesting, are not particularly scarce, and gain only passing interest as a collectible.

Many different companies have made many different kinds of gauges over the years. The Brown & Sharpe line began already in 1833. By 1900, it included the Rolling Mill Caliper Gauge shown on the left, as well as a combined Caliper and Wire Gauge on the right. Collectible caliper gauges vary widely in value, depending of course, on their condition. Another fac-

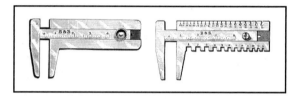

tor is the geographical area. In some areas a particular style of caliper or gauge might have considerable value, while in other areas it might bring but a fraction of the price. Smaller and rather plain calipers seem to be valued at anywhere from $15 to $40, while the better ones, being more ornate, or of a more obviously high quality, might sell anywhere from $40 and upward.

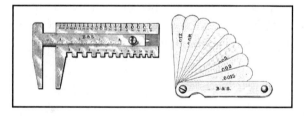

Various kinds of combination gauges were available, including the caliper and wire gauge shown to the left. Thickness gauges have taken on many forms, including the one on the right. The latter is often seen priced anywhere from $5 to $25.

Shown left to right, screw pitch gauges and center gauges are still used every day. Older ones are usually heavier, and were manifestly better built than many of today's styles. Thus, these older devices often sell in the $5 to $25 range.

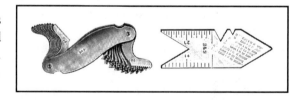

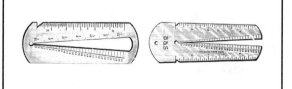

The closed-end wire gauge on the left was sold as a pocket gauge, while the open gauge on the right was designed to gauge the size of all American wire sizes as well as wood screw sizes. Vintage gauges like these often sell from $10 and upward.

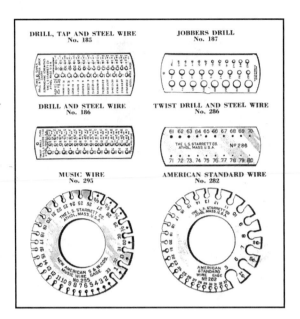

The Starrett gauges of 1920 included numerous kinds of drill gauges and wire gauges. This firm was organized by Laroy S. Starrett in 1880 and incorporated in 1900. Various styles of these gauges are still available, but older and collectible styles often sell in the range of $10 and upward.

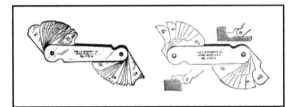

Fillet or radius gauges have been available for a century, and are still made. A nice older set of these might fetch $20 or more today. As noted many times throughout this book, the price at an upscale shop might be much higher than at a remote auction held miles away from the nearest town.

For purposes of illustration, the Starrett and the Brown & Sharpe product lines are mainly shown in this section. It should be noted, however, that there were many other companies who have, and still are, producing most of the tools shown in this section. Among these tools are surface gauges used by machinists and tool makers. Good surface gauges are expensive items today; one can easily spend $100 for a new one.

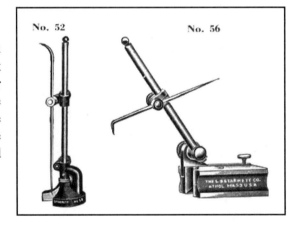

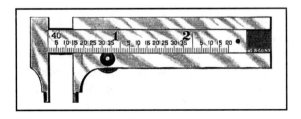

Starrett, among others, offered a combined caliper and button gauge for a time. It was similar to other caliper gauges, but was graduated in 40ths of an inch. Usually the figure "40" was stamped or engraved somewhere on the slide. This style is fairly scarce; it can be found in areas where buttons were produced, as in certain areas along the Mississippi River.

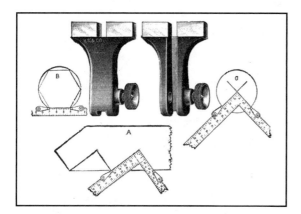

Several companies made stair gauges. A pair of these was clamped to a framing square. It could be used for laying out stair stringers, laying off hexagon angles, or for quartering a circle. Stair gauges are still available, but vintage ones are sometimes rather fancy, even being made of solid brass.

The plane gauge shown here was clamped to the side of a plane and could be set at an appropriate angle for planing an angled edge on a board. These gauges are seldom seen today, since power machinery has all but eliminated the need for this device.

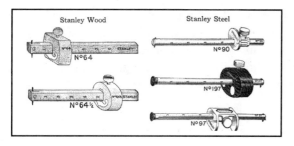

Marking gauges are still in use today, but many of the early ones were very ornate, using expensive hardwoods and brass facings and reinforcements. The single beam styles illustrated here are called marking gauges. Ordinary wood-marking gauges often bring upwards of $20. The better ones have rosewood or boxwood facings, and often bring $40 or more. The metal styles sell in the $20 to $40 range, and perhaps higher in certain instances.

Mortise or double-beam gauges were offered in wood and metal styles. The wooden beam model, complete with a brass-covered boxwood head and brass thumbscrew will likely bring $50 to $100, or perhaps even more today. Steel beam styles often bring $50 or more, especially with roller markers rather than pin markers.

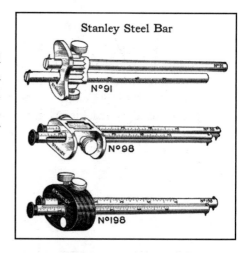

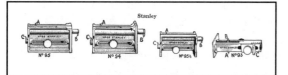

In today's collectible market, the butt gauges shown here might bring anywhere from $15 to $30. Three measurements were needed for hanging doors; the location of the butt on the casing, the location of the butt on the door, and the thickness of the butt on both the casing and the door. The butt gauge was designed to embrace all three of these functions into a single device.

Organian Building

Organ building is an ancient art, and many of the methods used centuries ago are still used today. Only a few companies in the United States still manufacture organ pipes, although there are a number of such companies still operating in Europe.

Much of the organ builder's art is acquired through apprenticeship, as it has been for centuries. Although certain rules apply to the various steps of actually building the pipes, whether of wood or metal, much of the final result depends directly on the craftsmen involved. Thus, certain pipe organs with the finest tonal characteristics still exist, and have never been duplicated, despite many attempts.

Rarely does a tool collector come across even the simplest tools of the organ builder or the organ technician. These tools are usually handed down from one generation to the other, and are rarely found in an antique shop, no matter how extensive. A very few are included in this section on the outside chance that a collector might finally be able to identify them.

Proportional dividers are a necessity for those making organ pipes. Oftentimes, the builder scales pipes so that they halve on the seventeenth pipe of the rank. The intervening pipes are scaled accordingly, and for this purpose the proportional dividers are an essential tool.

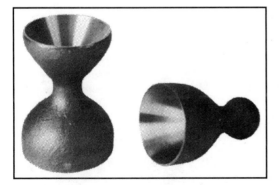

Various kinds of fitting tools are required by the organ builder. Each pipe rests over a rounded hole on the toe board above the windchest. When fitting the toe of the pipe to the toe board it is sometimes necessary to round it slightly so it fits tightly without wind leakage between toe and board. For this purpose, various kinds of toe cones have been made.

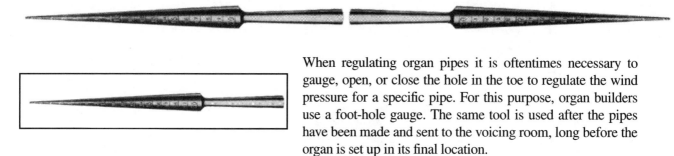

When regulating organ pipes it is oftentimes necessary to gauge, open, or close the hole in the toe to regulate the wind pressure for a specific pipe. For this purpose, organ builders use a foot-hole gauge. The same tool is used after the pipes have been made and sent to the voicing room, long before the organ is set up in its final location.

Tuning cones or "tuning horns" are used to open or close the top opening of certain kinds of organ pipes in the tuning process. These are made in various sizes, since some pipes might be as small as a pencil, and others might weigh several hundred pounds. Other organ builder's accessories might include tuning forks, as well as many different kinds of carpenter's tools needed to build wood pipes.

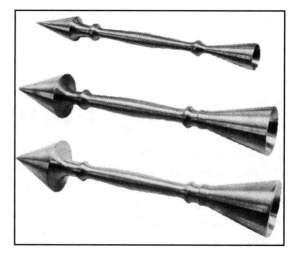

P

Planes

Planes have been used for centuries, going back to ancient times. In fact, the Romans used a plane, calling it *runcina*. *Knight's American Mechanical Dictionary* by Edward H. Knight was released by Hurd & Houghton (New York) in 1876. It lists the following categories of planes then in use:

Angle-plane	A plane whose bit reaches into a re-entering angle
Astragal plane	For cutting astragal moldings
Badger plane	A panel plane set on a skew to work up close to corners
Banding plane	For cutting grooves to lay in string or wire bands
Bead plane	A semi-cylindrical plane for sticking a bead or molding
Bench plane	For working a flat surface
Border plane	A joiner's edging plane
Break-iron	The iron on top of the bit to break the shaving
Capping plane	For the slightly rounded upper surfaces of staircase rails
Carpenter's plane	In this class are jack, smoothing, grooving and molding planes
Compass plane	Uses a curved face for circular work
Concave plane	A compass plane for curved surfaces
Cooper's plane	Long plane upon which staves are jointed
Core-box plane	Used to plow grooves within a corebox (foundry)
Cornice plane	An ogee plane for making moldings
Counter-check	For cutting the groove uniting two window sashes
Covetta	For molding, as with a quarter-round plane
Cutting plane	A carpenter's smoothing plane
Cutting thrust	For grooving the sides of boxes
Dovetail	Used for dressing dovetails
Dovetail box-plane	A form of a rabbet plane used for cutting dovetails
Edge plane	For edging boards
Fillet plane	For dressing a fillet or square bead
Fillister	Used for making a rabbet, such as side or sash fillisters
Fluting plane	Used for cutting flutes or grooves
Fore plane	Intermediate between a jack plane and a fore plane
Forkstaff plane	For working convex cylindrical surfaces
Grooving plane	Usually in pairs known as *hollows* and *rounds*

Planes

Handrail plane . . . . Same as a capping plane

Hollows and rounds . . . . Concave and convex planes, also forkstaff plane

Hollow sash plane . . . . Uses a convex sole, also a round sole plane

Howel . . . . Used for smoothing the insides of barrels

Ice plane . . . . For smoothing ice preparatory to cutting

In-shave . . . . Has a convex bit for dressing inner faces of barrel staves

Jack plane . . . . Coarsest of the bench planes, usually about 18 inches

Joiner's plane . . . . Used for facing and matching boards

Jointer . . . . A plane 5 or 6 feet long, used by coopers

Jointing plane . . . . A 2-1/2 foot plane used by coopers for "shooting the joints"

Lamb's tongue . . . . Has a deep narrow bit for making quirks

Long plane . . . . A joiner's plane with a length of 27 inches

Matching plane . . . . A pair of planes used for tongue-and-groove joinery

Metal plane . . . . A plane made entirely of metal

Miter plane . . . . A plane working with a draw-cut and within a fence

Modeling plane . . . . Short plane (1-5 inches) for smoothing rounded surfaces

Molding plane . . . . Joiner's planes for making moldings; also match-planes

Ogee plane . . . . Joiner's plane for ogee moldings

Overshave . . . . Coopers used it for dressing the back of barrel staves

Ovolo plane . . . . For working ovolo molding on round window sash

Panel plane . . . . A long-stock plane somewhat deeper than a jack plane

Panel plow . . . . For raising panels

Pistol router . . . . A router with a handle like a pistol stock

Plane guide . . . . An attachment for beveling the edge of a board, etc.

Plane iron . . . . The cutting iron inserted in the stock and held by a wedge

Plow . . . . Used for grooving edges of door stiles, etc.

Quarter round . . . . Used for molding framework, or an ovolo

Quirking plane . . . . Molding plane for convex surfaces

Rabbet plane . . . . For plowing grooves on the edge of a board, many styles

Reed plane . . . . Has a concave sole for cutting beads

Reglet plane . . . . Used by printers to fit wooden reglet or printer's furniture

Rounding plane . . . . For making handles for forks, hoes, spades, etc.

Round nose plane . . . . Has a rounded sole and used for rough work

Router . . . . Sash plane like a spokeshave to work on circular sash

Sash fillister . . . . For rabbeting window sash to receive the glass

Sash plane . . . . For molding stiles and bars of window sash

Scaleboard plane . . . . Used to cut a wide chip for picture frame backs, etc.

Scraping plane . . . . Used for scraping steel, iron, ivory and very hardwoods

Shooting plane . . . . Used with a shooting board for squaring edges of stock

Side fillister . . . . For making a rabbet. Used mainly in window sash work

Side plane . . . . Has the bit on the side, used with a shooting board

Side rabbet plane . . . . Joiner's plane for working rabbets from the side

Side round plane . . . . For making half-round moldings

Side snipe . . . . Molding plane made like a snipe's mouth

Single reed planes . . . . Beading plane with one hollow in its sole

Skew plane . . . . For cutting rabbets. Blade is oblique to sole

Skew rabbet plane . . . . Another form of skew plane

Slitting plane	Used for cutting boards into strips
Smoothing plane	Finishing plane, usually 7-1/2-inches long
Snipe-bill plane	Narrow and deep plane for working quirks
Splint plane	For riving splints for small boxes, blind-slats, etc.
Spokeshave	Form of plane with two handles, developed by wheelwrights
Spout plane	For hollowing out spouting and eaves troughs
Square rabbet plane	For cutting a rabbet at 90° to the working face
Stock shave	A shave used by blockmakers
Sun plane	Circular form of jack plane, used by coopers
Table plane	Furniture makers used it for making rule joints on tables
Tonguing plane	Used in pairs for cutting tongues and grooves
Toothing plane	Uses a serrated cutting edge for roughing before veneering
Try plane	Used after the jack plane for smoothing a board
Whisk	A plane used by coopers
Witchet	A rounding plane

Subsequent to this listing of 1876, numerous other styles of planes were developed. All this changed with the widespread use of jointers, shapers and other machines in the early 1900s. Hand planes in all their variety were largely relegated to obsolescence with the coming of electric routers, jointers and planers in the 1940s and 1950s. These hand-held electric machines did the work in a fraction of the time required by hand methods.

The parts of a plane are:

• The *stock,* which is the frame of the plane, wood or metal.

• The *bit* is the cutting edge; it is also called the *iron.*

• The *iron* is held in the stock with a *wedge.*

• The *wedge* is driven tight between the *iron* and the *abutment* or *shoulder.*

• The *bottom* of the stock is the *sole.*

• The *toat* is the handle.

For tool collectors, planes seem to be the most popular device of all. There are probably thousands of different planes that have been built. Some very old ones still exist, and of course, most of them sell at very high prices. Many newer and more common styles still sell in the $15 to $30 range, but it is not at all uncommon for a nice plane to sell for $50 to $100. At the other end of the scale is the Stanley No. 55 combination plane. One of these that is in good condition will likely sell for $200 to $400, with a mint No. 55 perhaps selling as high as $500.

This section makes no pretense of illustrating every style of plane built, much less the great variety within each style. Obtaining values for each style that is shown has likewise been a futile venture, since prices vary widely among the shops we have visited. This market is so vast that compiling a value guide to planes would likely be no more than a compilation of auction results and the perusing of hobby tabloids. As noted throughout this book, auction prices are often driven by a local interest, or a relative who has decided to "bid in" a certain item, regardless of price. Interested buyers are advised to arm themselves with enough information to ensure wise buying before ever beginning to collect planes.

Stanley Works was the largest manufacturer of planes and offered the largest variety. It is said that Stanley built over 250 distinct styles of planes. There were others who built planes, and the 1922 issue of *Hardware Buyer's Directory* lists the following firms:

• Buckeye Mfg. & Foundry Co., Cleveland, Ohio

• Cassady-Fairbank Mfg. Co., Chicago, Illinois

• Central Hardware Co., Philadelphia, Pennsylvania (Goodall)

• Chapin-Stevens Co., Pine Meadow, Connecticut (C-S Co.)

• Clipper Tool Co., Buffalo, New York

• Consolidated Tool Works, New York, New York

Planes

- Kensington Hdwe. & Tool Mfg. Co., Philadephia, Pennsylvania
- Mack & Co., Rochester, New York (D. R. Barton)
- Sandusky Tool Co., Sandusky, Ohio
- Sargent & Co., New Haven, Connecticut
- Otis A. Smith, Rockfall, Connecticut (Fales)
- Stanley Works, New Britain, Connecticut (Bailey, Bed Rock)
- Union Mfg. Co., New Britain, Connecticut
- Vaughan & Bushnell Mfg. Co., Chicago, Illinois
    A few other firms have been found from the early 1900s from magazines and other sources:

- Detrick & Harvey Machine Co., Baltimore, Maryland
- Snell & Atherton, Brockton, Massachusetts
- Iver Johnson Arms & Cycle Works, Fitchburg, Massachusetts
- F. Lettelier & Co., Grand Rapids, Michigan
- Gage Tool Co., Vineland, New Jersey
- L. & I. J. White Co., Buffalo, New York
- C. E. Jennings & Co., New York, New York
- Tower & Lyon Co., New York, New York
- Ohio Tool Co., Columbus, Ohio

The design of planes was well established after 1850. The 1876 edition of *Knight's American Mechanical Dictionary* cited above gives the following general dimensions for the major styles:

Type	Length in inches	Width in inches	Width of Irons
Modeling plane	1 to 5	1/4 to 2	3/16 to 1-1/2
Smoothing plane	6-1/2 to 8	2-3/8 to 3-1/2	1-3/4 to 2 3/8
Rabbet plane	9-1/2	3/8 to 2	3/8 to 2
Jack plane	12 to 17	2-1/2 to 3	2 to 2-1/4
Panel plane	14-1/2	3-1/2	2-1/2
Trying plane	20 to 22	3-1/4 to 3-3/8	2-3/8 to 2-1/2
Long plane	24 to 26	3 5/8	2 5/8
Jointer plane	28 to 30	3-3/4	2-3/4
Cooper's plane	60 to 72	5 to 5-1/4	3-1/2 to 3-3/4

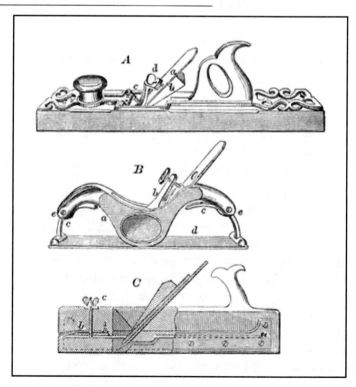

In this engraving of 1875, the Smith & Carpenter plane is shown (A). It used a wooden stock, stiffened by an upper metallic frame. Shown at (B) is the Evans plane. It was designed to be used either as a straight or as a curved plane. Buckel's plane shown at (C) is a two-part design. It was designed to cut more or less wood on each stroke, depending on the downward pressure placed on the plane. Any one of these designs is very rare today.

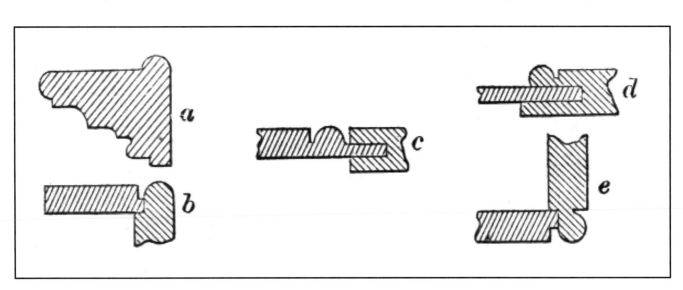

Beading was very popular into the early 1900s. Many different forms of beads were possible, and a few of the most important ones are shown here. At the top, *a* is called a cock-bead; *b* is a quirk bead; *c* is bead-butt joint, and *d* is a bead-flush joint. The double-quirked bead is shown at *e*. All of these forms could be derived with the proper planes.

The bench plane was a joiner's plane used for working a flat surface. In order of their fineness they were named: *jack, long, trying, smooth,* and *jointer* planes. This one is an 1875 model.

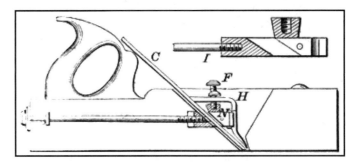

This 1902 catalog illustration shows the No. 122 Stanley smooth on the left, the No. 135 handle smooth in the center, and the No. 127, 129, and 132 planes to the right. The 127 was a 15-inch jack plane, the No. 129 was a 20-inch fore plane, and the No. 132 was a 26-inch jointer.

Smooth planes were furnished with a handle or without, as shown in the two planes on the left. The No. 21 Stanley fore plane on the right was 22 inches in length.

Shown at right, Jack planes were very popular because they were of convenient length and could be adapted to many uses. The 28-inch jointer plane on the right sold for $1.60 in 1902.

The razee or recessed plane was another style popular in the early 1900s. It is shown here in jack plane (left) and fore plane (right) styles.

These Bailey smooth planes of 1902 were adjustable and dispensed with the usual wedge for holding the iron. Shown left to right are two examples.

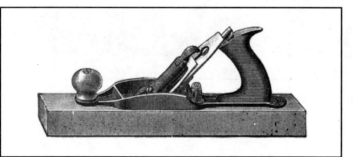

Jack, fore, and jointer planes were available in the Bailey adjustable design by 1900, but we have not researched the production years of various Stanley planes. The 28-inch style jointer plane retailed for $3.25 in those days.

The carriage rabbet plane shown here is easily distinguished. An opening is evident next to the iron and on each side of the stock.

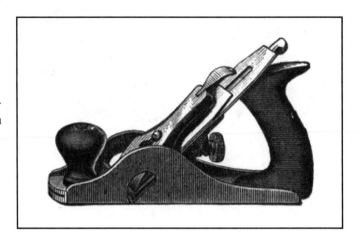

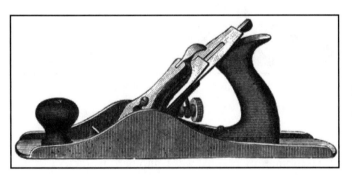

Certain styles of planes were also available with a corrugated bottom. In 1902 a No. 7 Stanley 22-inch jointer plane sold for $5.50.

Perhaps one of the most desirable collectible planes is the Stanley No. 55 Universal. First built in the 1890s, it remained in production for at least sixty years. On the left, it is shown as a moulding plane, and on the right it is set up as a chamfer plane. Complete No. 55 outfits with all the knives often bring $200 to $400, maybe more for one in mint condition.

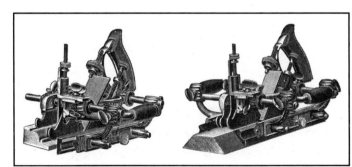

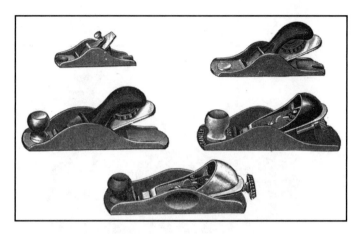

Many different kinds of block planes have been made, with a very few of them being shown here. Usually they are from 3-1/2 to 7 inches in length.

The No. 9-1/2 and No. 18 Bailey block planes are shown here. They were built by Stanley Works. Some planes, including the No. 18 were nickel plated both for appearance, and for durability.

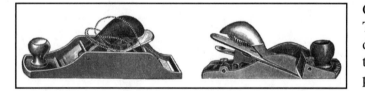

Combination planes were another distinctive style. The No. 130 Stanley block plane was also known as a double-ender. It could be used as a block plane, but the knife could be turned the other way to permit planing into corners.

By adjusting the flexible steel face, these planes could be adapted to concave or convex circles. These specialized planes were fairly expensive for 1900, selling in the $4 to $6 range.

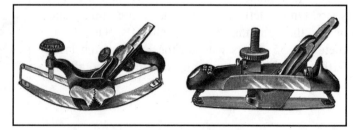

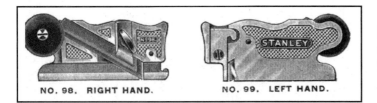

NO. 98. RIGHT HAND.   NO. 99. LEFT HAND.

Side rabbet planes were used for side rabbeting as well as trimming dados, mouldings, and grooves. They were made in right-hand and left-hand styles.

Router planes were used to smooth the bottom of grooves or depressions below the surface of the work. Fillister planes were used either right-hand or left-hand to plane into corners or against partitions. Fillister planes could also be used as a bullnose rabbet plane. Shown at left is a handy router plane and at right is a Fillister plane.

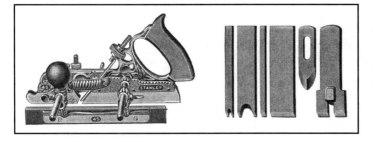

The Stanley No. 45 was a combination beading, rabbet and matching plane. It could also be used as a dado, sash, and slitting plane. In 1902 this model sold for $8.00 and was supplied in a fitted wooden box.

The Stanley No. 46 was also known as Traut's Dado, Plow and Filister Plane. It had a nickel plated stock and fence, and could be adapted to many different jobs with relative ease.

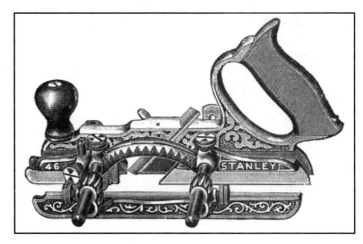

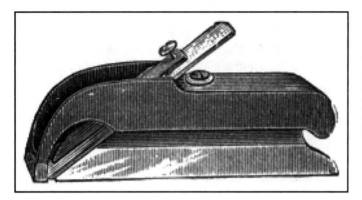

The bullnose rabbet plane was intended for working into corners and other difficult places. Ordinarily a larger plane was used as far into a corner as possible, leaving very little surface to be finished with this small device.

Numerous kinds of beading tools have been made; they were intended for decorative work on furniture and millwork. Priced at only $1 in 1900, this tool was furnished with seven different reversible cutters having a range up to 1/4-inch. Shown is a Stanley Universal Hand Beader. Also shown is a sample of what these beaders would do.

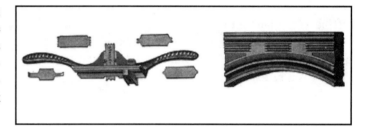

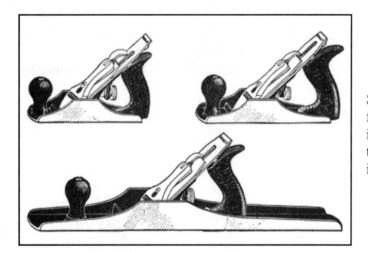

Stanley Bedrock planes were made in smooth, jack, fore, and jointer styles with a total range of 7 to 24 inches. While a smooth sole was standard, any of these planes could be furnished with a corrugated sole if so desired.

The No. 196 Stanley Curve Rabbet was a unique design intended to cut rabbets on circular, curved, or irregular edges. This unusual design is seldom found today.

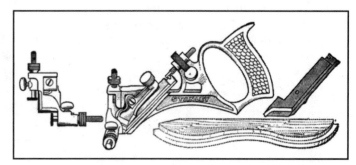

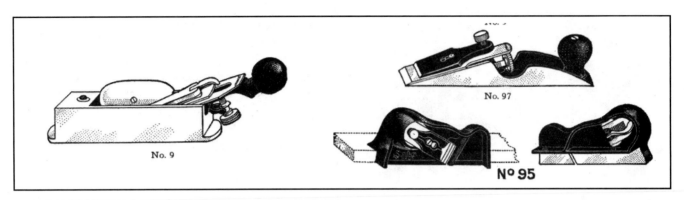

Cabinet planes such as the Stanley No. 9 were made for piano makers and fine cabinet work anywhere that (extreme) accuracy was required. These planes are not often found today.

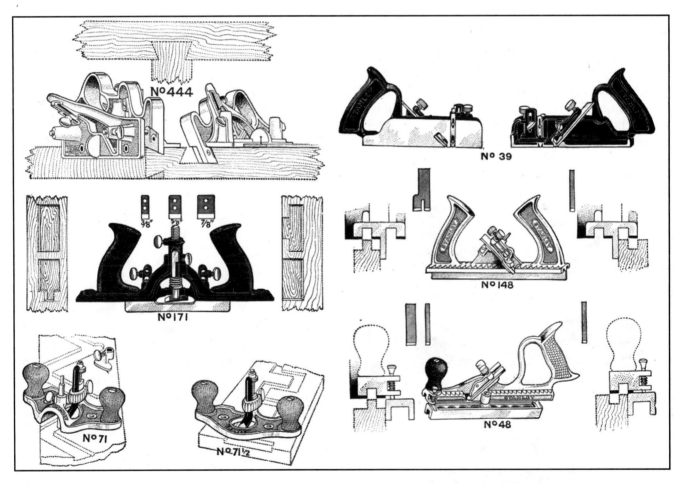

The Stanley No. 444 was a dovetail plane, while the No. 171 was for door trim. Router planes, No. 71 and No. 71-1/2 are also shown, along with the No. 39 dado plane. Matching planes included Stanley No's. 146, 147, and 148. Matching planes like the No. 146, 147, and 148 models were made primarily for tongue-and-groove work, while the No. 48 and No. 49 Stanley models used an unusual swinging fence design.

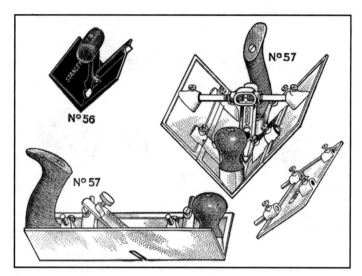

Core box planes were designed for making circular core boxes as used in foundry work. Stanley offered their No. 56 and No. 57 models. While there were other companies that made core box planes and many other styles, Stanley was no doubt the largest maker of planes, and data concerning their styles is the most accessible. Perhaps future editions of this book will include the offerings of other manufacturers.

The No. 40 (right) Stanley scrub plane could be used to quickly "hog" down the edge of a board that otherwise would have to be sawed with a rip saw. This style used an iron with a rounded edge. The No. 340 (left) Stanley Furring plane was used for smoothing rough-cut lumber from a sawmill. It was used to clean up lumber prior to using a bench plane.

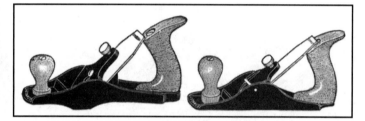

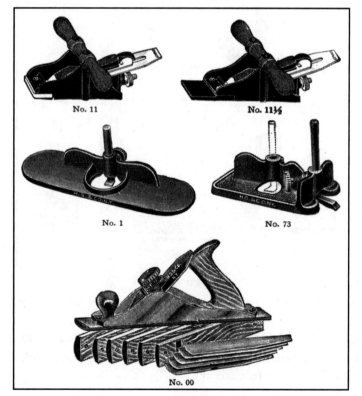

The No. 11 Stanley Belt Makers Plane was used to chamfer the ends of leather belting for making a glued lap joint. No. 11-1/2 Special Floor Planes were used for smoothing wood floors. The No. 1 Pattern Makers Router is but one of numerous styles made for this trade, with the No. 73 Sargent being another. Simplex Pattern Makers Sole Planes are quite unusual because they were furnished with wooden soles of six different radii.

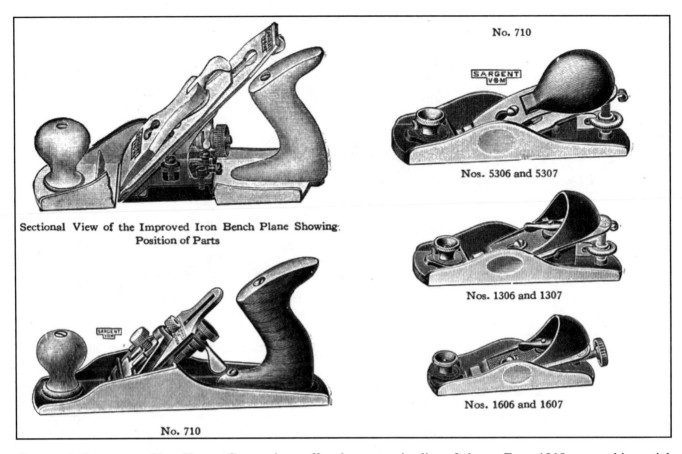

Sectional View of the Improved Iron Bench Plane Showing Position of Parts

No. 710

No. 710

Nos. 5306 and 5307

Nos. 1306 and 1307

Nos. 1606 and 1607

Sargent & Company at New Haven, Connecticut, offered an extensive line of planes. From 1910 comes this partial showing of the Sargent line. Their bench planes were available in smooth, jack, fore, and jointer styles, and all were available with a smooth or corrugated sole.

Gage offered a series of self-setting planes in the early 1900s. Accurately setting the iron for the job at hand was often a time-consuming task. The self-setting design was a great advantage because of the savings in time.

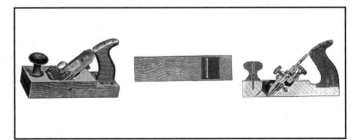

Wooden bench planes remained popular for years after the introduction of the iron stock. The styles shown here were usually made of red beech or white German beech. Shrup planes, at center, were furnished with round nose cutters. To the right is a jack plane. At left is the Horn smooth plane.

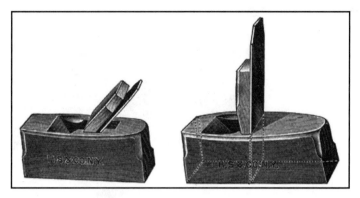

A double smooth plane is shown at left, with a tooth plane to its right. Wooden fore planes were usually 20 to 22 inches in length.

Oval planes (center) and small straight planes (left) were generally used by piano makers, and are quite scarce today. The big jointer plane on the right was usually 24 to 28 inches in length.

Wooden moulding planes have been made in literally hundreds of different styles. Many of them were equipped with irons ground to order for a specific job, and for many of them, the stock was made by the craftsman who was going to use it. Shown here from left, are rabbet, dado, and single bead designs.

Hollow, round, and center bead designs are shown here from left. The hollow and round styles were available with radii from 1/4 to 2 inches.

Tongue and groove moulding planes were furnished in matching pairs. They were used for tongue-and-groove work or anywhere that an accurate match was needed. Nosing planes were generally used for the top of handrails and similar applications. Shown from left are a tongue, a groove, and a nosing plane.

Table moulding planes were used for the matching edges of drop leaves and similar applications. They were furnished only in pairs. Quarter-round planes (right) were designed specifically for making quarter rounds.

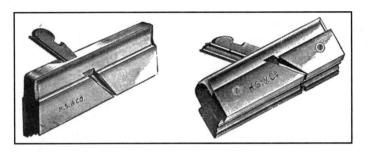

An ogee molding is one having a wave-like form, and has an inner and outer curve. Ogee moulding planes were available in various sizes from 1/2 to 1-inch. Sash moulding planes were made especially for window sash and similar duties. Shown from left are an ogee moulding plane and a sash moulding plane.

Sash and fillister moulding planes were available in numerous sizes and styles, although the sash plane shown to the left was adjustable from 1-1/4 to 1-1/2 inches. For all the moulding planes shown here, there are no doubt hundreds of others in different styles and from different manufacturers. Not to be forgotten are those locally created styles as well.

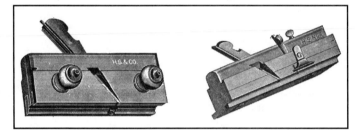

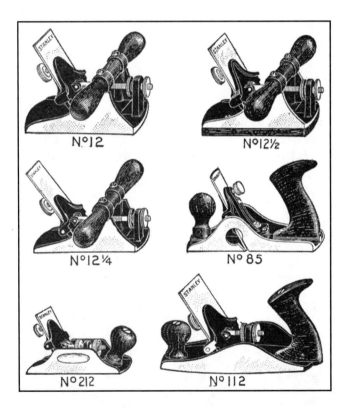

Stanley and numerous other manufacturers also offered a wide variety of scraper planes for fine finishing work. Some were furnished with a rosewood sole since it was less likely to scratch the finish than a metal sole. Toothed veneer scrapers were also available. They provided a tooth on the backside to permit a better glue bond when attaching to the base.

Spoke shaves are illustrated elsewhere in this book. They were developed by wheelwrights, but their use was widespread among other carpentry trades. Spokeshaves have been made in many different styles and sizes, with only a few of them being shown here.

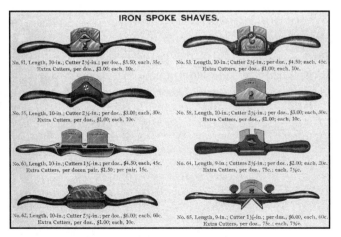

Plastering Tools

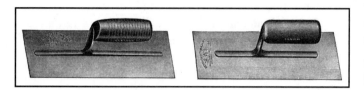

Various kinds of plastering trowels have been used. Two popular styles from Disston were the No. 118 Western Pattern shown on the left and the No. 21 Cincinnati Pattern shown on the right. The latter was made in various sizes ranging in length from 10 to 12 inches.

A gauging trowel is shown on the left of this illustration; it is distinctive because of the rounded tip. This style was made in sizes ranging in length from 7 to 8 inches. The margin trowel on the right was made in 3 x 4 and 3-1/2 x 5-inch sizes.

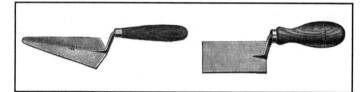

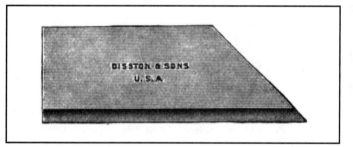

Miter rods as used by plasterers were made in numerous sizes ranging from 4 to 20 inches. Many of these tools have virtually disappeared and are very difficult to find today.

Priced at $1 in 1910, this plasterer's hock was 13 inches, had a wood platform and banded brass sides. Finding one today would likely be quite difficult.

Numerous kinds of mitering tools were used by the plasterer. The leaf and square style at the left was made in half a dozen different sizes, as was the double leaf design shown on the right.

A trowel and quirk is shown to the left of this illustration. This double-ended tool was made in various sizes ranging from 1 to 1-3/8 inches. The trowel and square on the right had a 1-1/2 inch trowel on one end and a 2-inch square on the other.

Pliers and Pincers

One could easily include several pages of pliers within this book. However, the collector value of most pliers is very low. Sometimes one can buy a bucket or box with several pairs of pliers and other assorted "junque" for only a few dollars. Certain brand names have a higher value than others, but for the most part,

pliers are very plentiful and do not generally bring high collector prices.

In this section we have included some of the older and unusual styles that perhaps have a higher collector value than the common varieties.

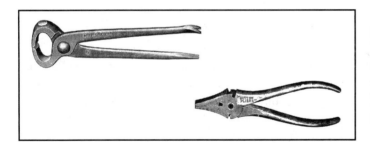

Carpenters' pincers were usually made in 6, 8, and 10-inch sizes. The style shown here included a pincer, tack puller, screw driver, and the side of the jaw was flattened so that it could serve as a tack hammer. Button pliers are also an old design, with both of these pliers dating back to 1900.

Various kinds of cutting nippers have been developed, with the Acme (left) and Bernard's (right) being products of 1900 technology. The Acme had the great advantage of using replaceable cutting jaws.

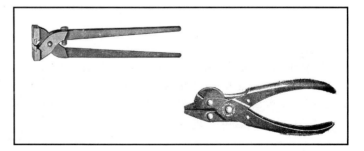

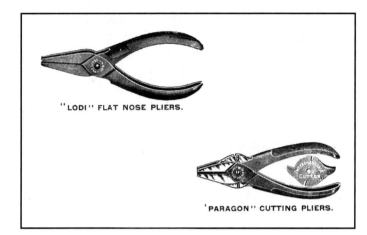

"LODI" FLAT NOSE PLIERS.

'PARAGON" CUTTING PLIERS.

The Lodi flat nose pliers (left) were made from steel stampings and intended solely for household use. Likewise for household use, the Paragon Cutting pliers (right) were a light duty design.

Numerous kinds of fencing pliers have been produced, with Cronk's (left) and the Elm City (right) styles being shown here. Both had flattened jaws so that the same tool could serve as a hammer, albeit a poor one.

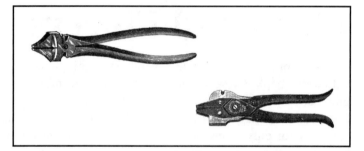

Gas pliers were ostensibly intended for tightening gas fittings, but found their way to other crafts needing to hold or tighten bolts, pipes, and other items. These early designs have long been replaced and are now fairly scarce.

An early slip-joint pliers was Pease's Combination Pliers of 1890. It was advertised as a combination "Pliers, Wire Cutters, Wrench and Screw Driver." Slip joint pliers are very common, so it would be easy to pass this one by while sorting through a box of junk at an auction.

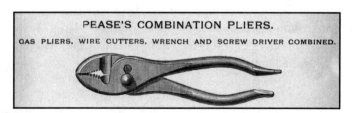

PEASE'S COMBINATION PLIERS.
GAS PLIERS, WIRE CUTTERS, WRENCH AND SCREW DRIVER COMBINED.

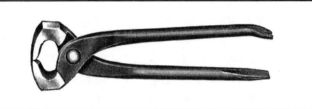

From 1910 comes this high-quality carpenter's pliers. Made of Swedish steel, it combined the essential features of pincers, tack claw and hammer within a single tool. Depending on the size, it sold for $1 to $1.50 at the time.

A furriers pliers is shown here from a 1910 listing. Many unusual plier designs were made to suit a specific need, with this one being an example.

Furriers Pliers

H. S. & Co.
Forged steel, black finish handles

Glaziers required a pliers with smooth jaws. This one was made in 8 and 10-inch sizes. Glaziers still use pliers like this today, so they have not attained a great value as a collectible.

Basket pliers were an essential tool for closing wooden fruit baskets prior to shipment. The pliers shown here from 1910 were made of forged steel and doubled as a nail driver when necessary.

Plumb Bobs

Among tool collectors, plumb bobs are nearly as popular as planes. The plumb bob in some form or other is probably about as old as civilization itself. Although the common forms are not at all expensive, some of the ornate, fancy styles can bring $100 or far more. Those of European origin, especially England and Germany, are among the most valuable. Simple cast iron bobs that were mass produced are worth very little in the collectibles market.

Old machinist's magazines frequently provided the dimensions for making certain styles of plumb bobs, and a fair number of these locally made products still exist. For example, I once made a heavy steel bob weighing about 24 pounds for a millwright. It is still being used when setting elevator legs. Heavy bobs are often suspended with piano wire, especially when the bob will be in position for several days or even weeks. A heavy bob keeps the wire very tight. An old millwright's trick for a bob that is exposed to the wind is to put the lower part of the bob in a bucket with some oil. This dampens the effect of the wind.

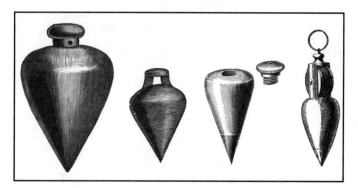

The plumb bobs shown on the left are of cast iron. These bobs of 1910 vintage were made in various sizes. Cast brass and bronze bobs were also very popular, but more expensive. The adjustable or spring check plumb bobs had the advantage of a reel for the line, and could be extended or retracted at will.

Another offering of 1910 included the usual cast iron bobs with an "adjusted" top, meaning that the center hole was accurately drilled in relation to the tip of the bob. An unusual variety is the lead bob used by masons; it is shown on the right.

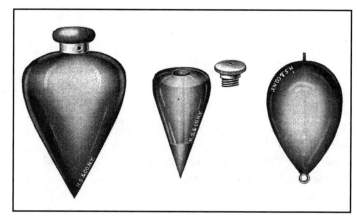

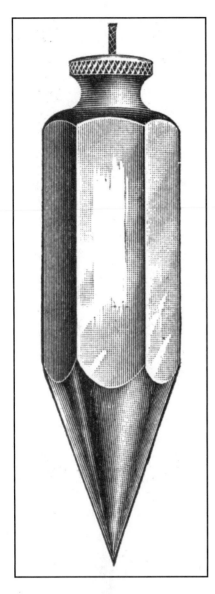

This hexagonal plumb bob was (and still is) very popular. It was called the "Can't Roll" model and was made in several sizes. For great accuracy, special means were used to ensure that the string attachment was perfectly in alignment with the point.

One of the most popular plumb bobs was machined from brass and was fitted with a replaceable tip. The tip was of hardened steel. This style has generally been made in sizes from 4 to 24 ounces.

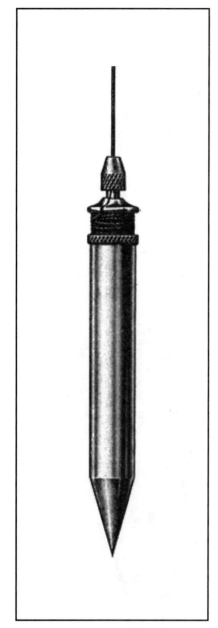

Several companies have made mercury plumb bobs. The inside of the bob was bored out and partially filled with mercury. This made the bob very heavy for its size, and accounted for great accuracy. Machine erectors and others looking for extreme precision have often looked to the mercury plumb bob. However, modern laser instruments have all but eliminated the need for these time-honored devices.

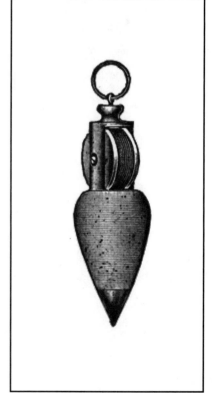

Numerous firms have offered adjustable plumb bobs. Starrett even made one that attached to a special tape measure. It was used to measure the fuel in tanks, both underground and on ships at sea. As with any collectible, buyers should familiarize themselves with the market before placing any reliance on "prices realized" lists from auction houses, electronic auctions, or printed price guides.

Plumbing Tools

From ancient times until the early 1900s, lead piping was used almost exclusively for water supplies. Eventually, galvanized iron pipe was introduced, along with copper tubing. Finally, the industry has come to the extensive use of plastic piping of various kinds.

This section illustrates many of the tools used in lead work. Unfortunately, these tools are now difficult to find. After lead piping disappeared there was no apparent use for the tools, so most of them were discarded. Many of the ordinary tools such as pipe threading dies are not included, especially since they seem to hold little interest with tool collectors.

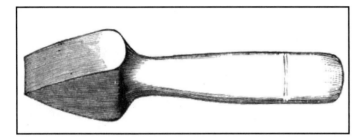

Various tools were used for shaping lead piping during the fitting-up process. Most of these were of boxwood, dogwood, or hickory. Shown here is a Side Edge tool.

The Dresser was used mostly for smoothing lead pipe as it was fitted up. Unfortunately, most of these tools have long since vanished. Lead piping wasn't used much after the early 1900s.

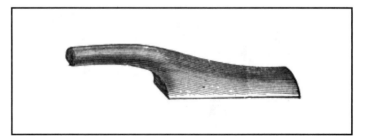

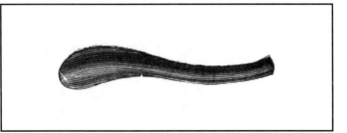

A Bossing Stick was part of the tool kit for working lead pipe. It was used for forming fittings and the like. Fittings were formed on the job. A tee-joint for instance, was created by using a tap borer to open the main. After this, the opening thus made was formed to fit the branch pipe.

The Drift Plug was used to form pipe at an end or at a fitting so that it would fit a mating piece. Fitting lead pipe was an art that is now nearly forgotten, and one that required great skill.

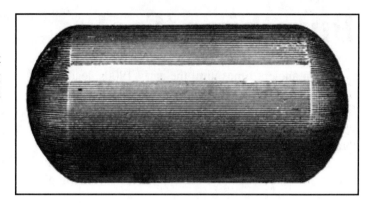

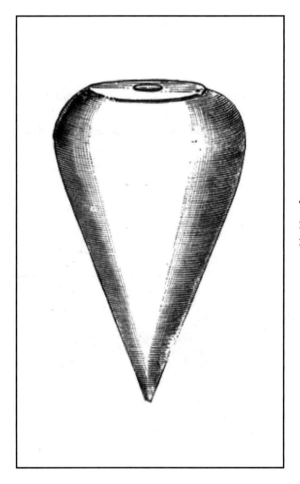

To plug a pipe, a Turn Pin was used. It also could be used for flaring out the end of a pipe or various other tasks. Turn pins were made in several sizes to accommodate varying sizes of pipe.

Occasionally it was necessary to plane the lead while fitting up. A special steel face plane was available for this purpose. We would suppose that this style is difficult to locate today.

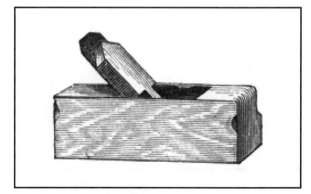

Alcohol torches were made in various styles. The better ones were of brass, and others were of tin. Torches like this are seldom seen today, probably because they lost their usefulness many decades ago.

A pocket level was necessary for laying out pipe, setting fixtures, and other tasks. This one could also be attached to a rule for greater distances. In 1890, this small level with a brass top sold for $2.75.

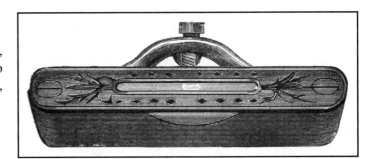

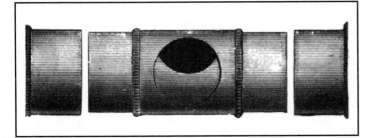

Grease, rosin, and flour were all necessary in the soldering process of assembling the joints of lead pipe. These combination brass boxes were made in at least three different sizes.

Soldering coppers of all shapes and sizes were needed for sealing the joints in lead piping. Since they were also used extensively in the tinner's trade, a great many are still available. In recent years, soldering coppers have come up in collector value. This one is a hatchet form.

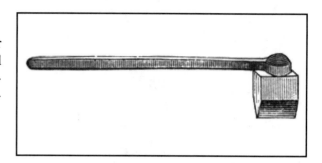

Soldered joints were used almost exclusively in tin work, and thus the need for many different kinds of soldering coppers. Likewise, lead pipe work was joined by means of a soldering iron. They were often heated with an alcohol torch, a charcoal fire or, later on, with a gasoline-fired plumber's furnace.

Double-edge plumbers' saws are now difficult to find. Usually they were made in various sizes from 12 to 18 inches. Most often this saw was connected with lead pipe work.

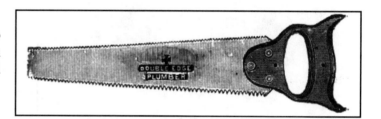

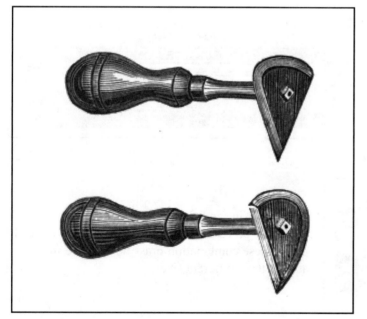

Shave hooks of various sizes were a necessity for lead pipe work. Subsequently, some forms, especially the triangular style were used in specialized wood finishing operations.

The Tap Borer was used to penetrate a main line so that a branch line could be fed. By carefully working the lead outward, a skillful plumber could fit the pipe and solder the joint so as to give the appearance of a single piece of pipe, with no signs of a joint.

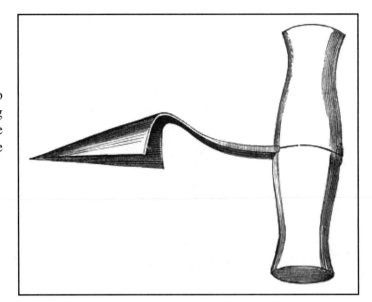

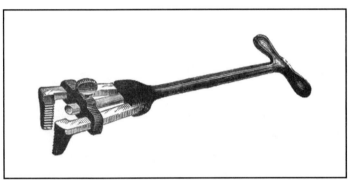

Shown here is Buzzel's Patent Basin Wrench. Finding a way to tighten deeply recessed fittings under a sink or basin required a special tool, and this was the answer for the plumber of 1890.

Priced at $2.50 in 1890, the Drummond Pipe, Cock and Coupling Holder was a universal tool. As the various diagrams show, it could be used to hold pieces in alignment as the plumber wiped the joints.

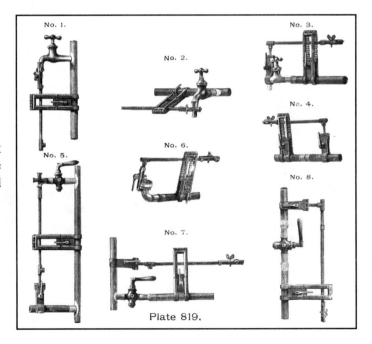

By 1890, a few gasoline-fired plumbers furnaces were available. Included was the Star Soldering Furnace. Priced at $7, it was an expensive, but practically alternative to an alcohol torch.

When used with a plumber's furnace, the Thawing Steamer of 1890 could be used for thawing frozen water pipes. The steamer was made of heavy copper. It sold for $6.75.

Until the early 1900s, threaded pipe was tightened into the threads with pipe tongs. The adjustable styles included Brown's design shown here. Although it had a slight range, it required the plumber to have several different sizes on hand to accommodate the average piping job.

By the 1920s, the gasoline firepot had come into extensive use, and remained there for forty years or more, until finally being replaced with propane-fired models. The C & L (Clayton & Lambert) firepot was one of the most popular and was made in several sizes. In the 1920s, these pots sold from $15 to $35, depending on size and features.

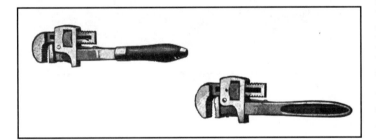

Pipe wrenches of the 1920s were generally of the Stillson pattern shown here or the Trimo pattern. Both were of good quality, so choosing between them depended mainly on personal preference. These Stillson wrenches were available with a wood handle or a steel handle, as desired. Today, the wood handle wrenches have a far greater collector value.

Monkey wrenches were another popular item for the plumber of the 1920s. The knife-handle design shown on the left was made in sizes upward from 6 inches. The Trimo basin wrenches on the right are another peculiar design that is not often found today.

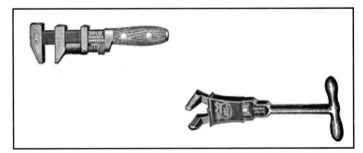

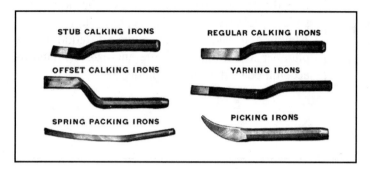

Cast iron drainage lines of days gone by used a plain end of pipe into a bell end. Oakum was packed into the joint with a yarning iron. Once it was in place, heated lead was poured into the joint. After solidifying, it was then driven tight with a calking iron. Several different styles are shown here.

On soil pipe joint with the bell standing vertical, it was a simple matter to pour the lead into the joint. If however, the joint was horizontal, then a joint runner was put around the joint as shown. Made of asbestos rope, it was furnished with a clamping device set at the top of the joint. Molten lead was then poured into the joint through the small opening left at the clamp. Plumbers usually coated the runner with old crankcase oil or perhaps pipe cutting oil to keep the lead from sticking to the rope.

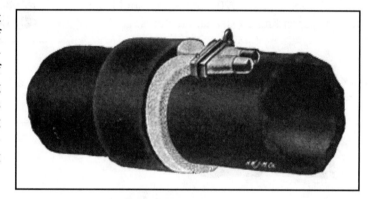

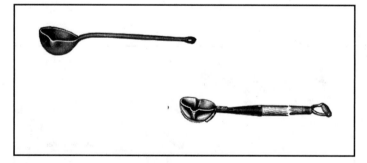

Many different kinds and styles of ladles were used for running lead. A cast iron kettle was placed atop the plumber's furnace, and as lead was used, it was constantly replenished. The ladle was used to dip from the kettle to pour the joint. Cast iron ladles invariably would crack after a certain length of time, and were discarded. Thus, there are few old cast iron ladles to be found...more often, collectors will find ladles formed of steel.

This simple cultivator performed anything but simple tasks.

It took a lot to move a log, ergo the log hook with chain at left, followed by a cant, and another single hook.

Shown from left are a pair of clevises, three different types of planes, and a gouge.

There were many ways of planting everything from potatoes to seed. Shown from top to bottom are a bow seeder, and several planters, including a potato planter at bottom left.

The weight and measurement devices shown from top to bottom are two scales, a triangle, folding zigzag measuring stick, divider, scribe, and square.

Hand-powered fanning mills were used to clean the chaff from the grain.

Condition plays an important role in collecting. Tools in prime condition are often hard to find. You can still have great nostalgic conversations about pieces in lesser conditions. It really comes down to why you collect. Shown from left are a maul, axe, and mattock.

Sometimes it took a big saw to get the job done. This two-person saw is missing one handle, but it is still an impressive display piece. Also notice the antique lunch pail placed on the barrel below. The top functioned as a built-in canteen.

Printing Equipment

This section covers only some of the tools involved with letter press printing. No presses, cutters or other heavy equipment is included. Printer's tools are not often seen in antique shops. Little of this equipment remains in existence, and much of that remaining has been garnered by those perpetuating the old letter press. Composing sticks are found occasionally, but items like mitering machines are rarely found. The most common of these is the Hansen, shown in this section. Most of the others are extremely rare.

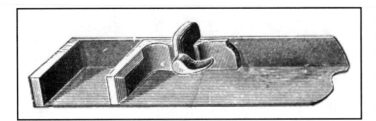

Composing sticks are used for composing the lines of type. When the stick is full, the printer deftly sets the lines onto a stone and continues the work. The Buckeye was an early design going back to the 1800s, but remained available early into the twentieth century.

The Yankee job stick, like most others, was available in several different lengths. Usually a printer selected a stick as short as possible for the job, since it weighed less and was easier to handle. This one was made in lengths ranging from 6 to 20 inches.

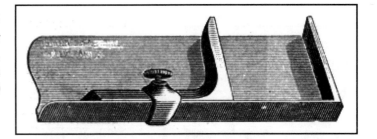

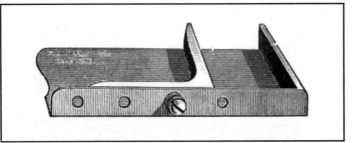

Common Screw composing sticks could be set for specific line lengths. These were preset by the accurately spaced holes in the stick itself. By the early 1900s, the common stick was replaced by improved designs.

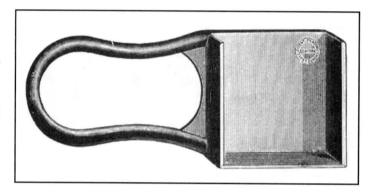

Grover composing sticks go back to 1855. However, the design was so popular that it was closely copied by others, and many so-called Grover sticks really were not the *original* Grover stick at all.

Perfect news sticks were made particularly for the newspaper compositor. They were uniformly 13 or 13-1/2 picas wide and had a depth of 2-1/4 inches. The stick shown here was made of wrought iron, but they could also be furnished in an all-steel design.

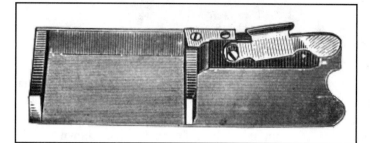

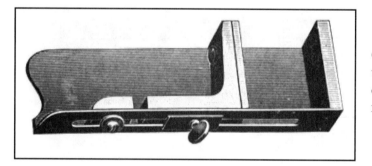

C-Slot composing sticks were made in sizes from 6 to 12 inches. This style had some advantages over others of the day, but still required setting to a pica measure for the column width desired.

Accurately punched holes on the back rail of the Standard Job Stick permitted the compositor to accurately set the knee to any desired width. This style was available in 6, 8, 10, and 12-inch sizes. Frequently, a composing stick was used by a printer during an entire career. Needless to say, no one even dared to suggest borrowing it!

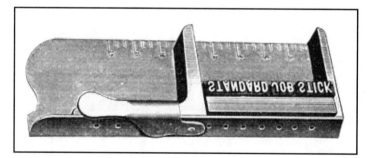

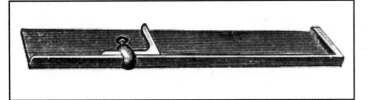

Wooden poster sticks were used for setting large wood type, as when making up a poster or banner. These sticks were available in sizes up to 42 inches, and often had brass-lined ends for greater durability. Time, fire, and termites have all taken their toll; few of these sticks remain.

Composing and makeup rules were a part of every early letterpress shop. Composing rules were accurately made and used for setting a composing stick to say, 14 picas (or whatever width was needed). The makeup rule was a handy device that was at virtually every composing stone. A complete set of composing rules is shown here, along with a leather case. It was priced at $1.50 in 1897. Today, a complete set of composing rules in a leather or wooden case is quite rare.

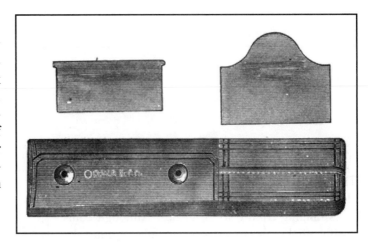

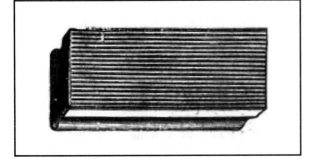

An interesting tool that is rarely found today is the Linotype Planer. It was designed to remove the burr from Linotype slugs. A corrugated rubber face was a salient feature.

After a page was composed and corrected it was placed inside a *chase* or frame and securely locked in place with *quoins*. Especially with newspaper pages, this was done with tapered wooden quoins. They were driven tight with a shooting stick, as shown here, and a mallet. Shooting sticks are fairly scarce today.

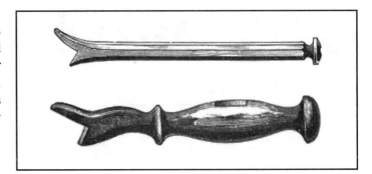

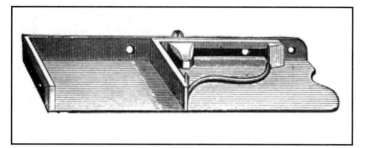

The Albion composing stick was also known as the English Pattern composing stick. It is distinguished with the curved reinforcing brace on the knee. Albion composing sticks were copied to some extent. They are generally found (but rarely) in 6 and 8-inch sizes. They were most often made of plain steel, but were also plated with German silver or nickel.

The Reversible Knee Stick was developed by R. Hoe Company during the late 1800s. It was made in sizes ranging from 6 to 20 inches. Although composing sticks are found occasionally, it must be remembered that production was never very high, since most journeyman printers used the same stick during their entire career.

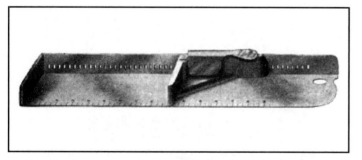

Rouse Job Sticks were introduced about 1920, and served to end the career of many others that had been in use for decades before. The Rouse was easily adjustable, it held the knee securely, and eventually it could even be furnished in a no-rust stainless steel design. Later on, the Rouse was also available in a special micrometer design that permitted small, but precise changes, in the width. This made the micrometer stick quite expensive; it was never sold in large quantity, and is quite scarce today. Numerous other unique composing sticks were also made during the long career of the letterpress.

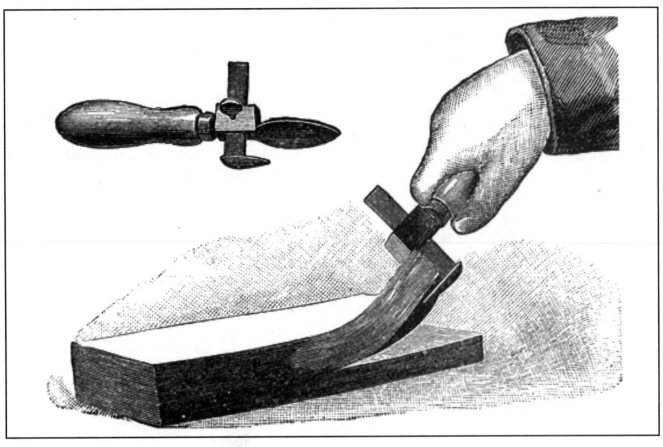

Paper counters have been made for centuries, perhaps this one has been around for well over a hundred years. It was a simple device. A certain number of sheets were counted by hand. The counter was set to this thickness, and the printer could then count off as many of these lifts of paper as necessary for the job at hand.

Particularly in the last quarter of the nineteenth century, printers were overwhelmed by artistic flourishes. Annealed brass rule was bent to every conceivable form in making borders, flourishes and ornaments. The Golding Curving Machine was one such device; it could form curves with a diameter ranging from 1/4 to 8 inches. In 1890, this machine sold for $18!

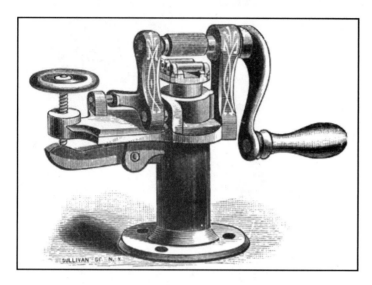

The Printers' Curving Machine could form circles, ovals, or serpentine bends, using annealed brass rule or soft lead rule. In 1890 it was priced at $21.50. These machines were found only in a few shops originally, and today they are extremely rare.

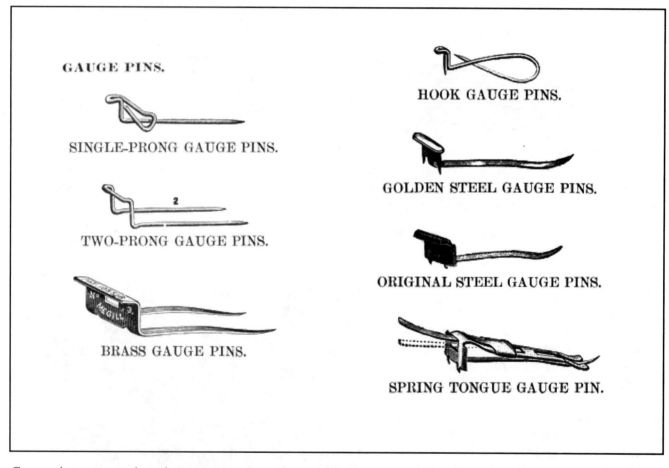

GAUGE PINS.

SINGLE-PRONG GAUGE PINS.

TWO-PRONG GAUGE PINS.

BRASS GAUGE PINS.

HOOK GAUGE PINS.

GOLDEN STEEL GAUGE PINS.

ORIGINAL STEEL GAUGE PINS.

SPRING TONGUE GAUGE PIN.

Gauge pins were used on the press to register the paper in the same position for each impression. Accurate work was required, particularly if a second or even a third color was added. Dozens of different gauge pins were attached to the *tympan* for this purpose. Only a few of them are shown here. Many of these styles have not been made for decades. Still others were made that are not shown here.

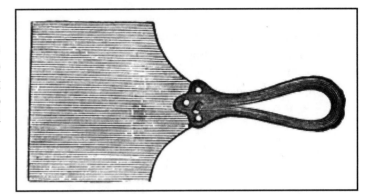

Among the printer's rarities is the Ink Slice. It was used for scooping ink out of drums and getting it to the ink stone. Only newspapers and large printing plants used this device. Ordinary job shops had no need for it, and consequently, it is rarely found today.

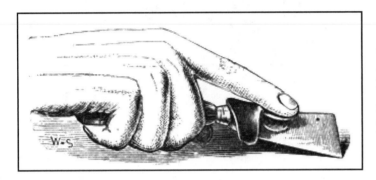

The St. John paper knife is another of those printer's rarities that is hardly ever found. It is distinguished by the finger guard, used to control the movement of the knife. It was illustrated in an 1890 printer's catalog.

Ink knives are found occasionally today, although many print shops used nothing more than an ordinary putty knife. Some ink knives have a broad face and heavier back as marks that distinguished them from a putty knife.

Mitering machines took many different forms. They were designed to miter the ends of brass or lead rule in making designs. The Perfection shown here is from the 1890s; it sold for $10 at the time.

Golding offered this mitering machine in 1890. A knife worked in the vertical column. The lead was held next to the anvil and was shaved to whatever angle was set by the swinging, adjustable vise. This machine sold for $14.

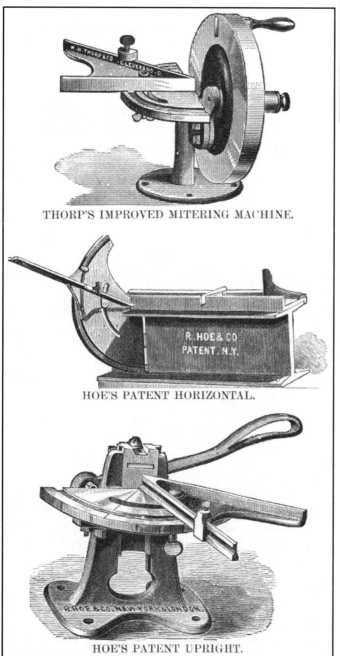

THORP'S IMPROVED MITERING MACHINE.

HOE'S PATENT HORIZONTAL.

HOE'S PATENT UPRIGHT.

Numerous kinds of mitering machines were available by 1890. All of them had the same purpose, that of mitering the ends of rule for fitting up borders and other designs. These various models were priced from $15 to $18.

Sophisticated mitering machines like this Golding Little Giant of 1890 are extremely rare, if in fact, any of them still exist. Priced at $35 it likely found its way only to the larger shops or to those who had some extra money!

The Hansen mitering machine of the early 1900s effectually ended the career of most other mitering devices. Priced at only $18.50 it came with full instructions on how to set the machine for cutting virtually any kind of miter. A Hansen, complete with all its gauges and other parts, might bring $50 or more today. However, vintage letterpress enthusiasts rarely use one, and keep one around mainly as a conversation piece.

Lead and rule cutters were an essential tool for the letter press printer. They had to be accurate, and had to cut the leaden strips without leaving an undesirable burr. Numerous kinds of lead cutters have been made, including this Little Giant style of the 1890s.

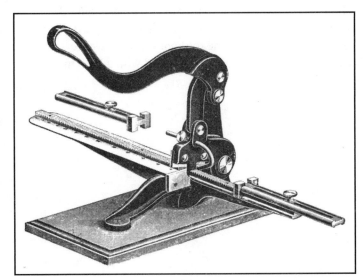

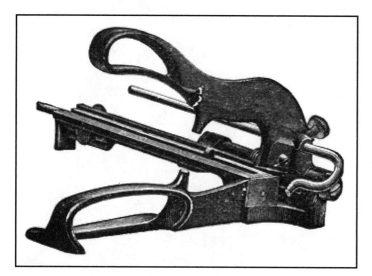

While the Little Giant lead cutter was priced at $14, the Nonpareil shown here was only $4. The $10 difference was an important one for the 1890s, especially to the ordinary country printer. Lead cutters are occasionally found in antique shops, but seldom bring more than $10 to $20.

Bodkins and tweezers were essential to letter press work. The term *bodkin* goes back for centuries, and often refers to a lancet, stilletto, or other pointed instrument. As used by the printer, the bodkin differs somewhat from the ordinary awl. Tweezers were, as shown here, often combined with a bodkin.

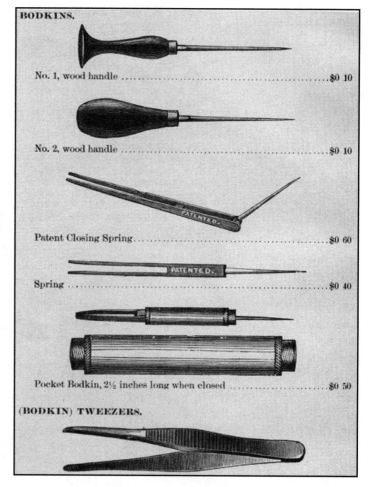

BODKINS.

No. 1, wood handle $0 10

No. 2, wood handle $0 10

Patent Closing Spring $0 60

Spring $0 40

Pocket Bodkin, 2½ inches long when closed $0 50

(BODKIN) TWEEZERS.

Type gauges are found occasionally. They were used for measuring type for wear, or plates for being the required height. (The standard type height in the United States is .918 inch.) Occasionally a type gauge will fetch from $15 to $25 today.

Usually made of maple, the planer was used to level up the type after it was set into the chase. Planers were made in various sizes, and sometimes fetch $10 to $20 today. Some show the signs of abuse with the top being beaten to death by hammer blows over the decades.

The *type gauge* as shown here is also called a line gauge, pica pole, and various other titles. It is always calibrated in picas (about 1/12 of an inch), and some are graduated in points as well. Others combine agate rule, and inch rule. Early styles were of steel or brass; later ones might be made of aluminum or stainless steel. Usually they sell for only a few dollars.

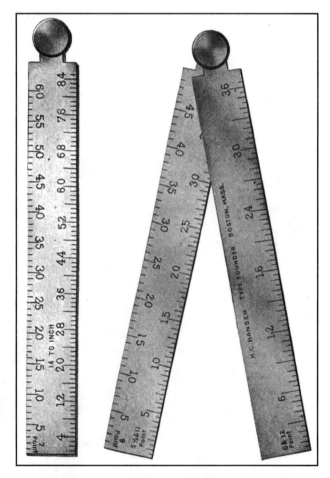

An unusual type gauge is the Hansen Folding Gauge of the early 1900s. It was well designed, and could be folded to fit into the printer's apron. Numerous kinds and styles of type gauges have been made.

Pumps

My book, *Encyclopedia of American Farm Implements* (Krause Publications, 1997) includes several pages of pumps. Thus, it would be redundant to plow the same ground a second time. However, an overview of pumps is shown here, along with some styles not presented in the previous title.

Pumps, especially those whimsical cistern pumps and kitchen pumps, always seem to have a substantial collector value. A well standard that is complete and not badly cracked or otherwise damaged often brings $75 or more. The fancy styles typical of the late 1800s bring substantially more. Broken pieces, welded parts, and other major damage discount the value substantially.

The power pumps have begun to acquire a collector value, probably because most of these larger units have been scrapped, and are now quite scarce.

Pitcher pumps were frequently found in the kitchen, particularly in farm houses and small villages. Oftentimes they were connected to a cistern; the latter was installed to collect rainwater. There are many different makes and styles of pitcher pumps. Some are particularly desirable because they were made with an exposed brass cylinder.

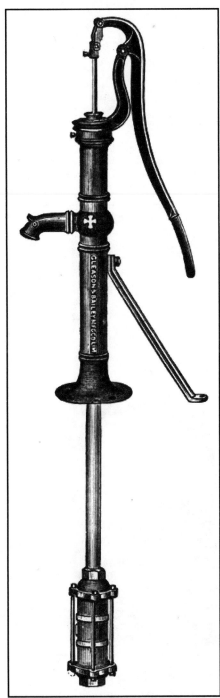

Among the common and highly desirable pumps looked for by collectors is the shallow well variety shown here. Oftentimes these were placed over a dug well. The latter was literally dug by hand, sometimes to a depth of thirty feet or more. As digging proceeded, the dirt was put into a bucket and lifted out by hand. These wells were often lined with brick.

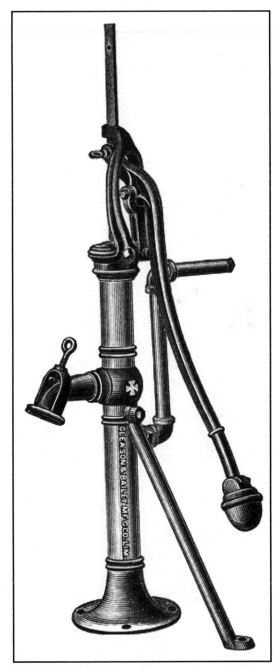

The windmill pump shown here was especially adapted for use with a windmill, and at that time the pump handle was disconnected. However, when the wind didn't blow for several days, the water supply ran out, so it was necessary to connect the handle and pump water by hand.

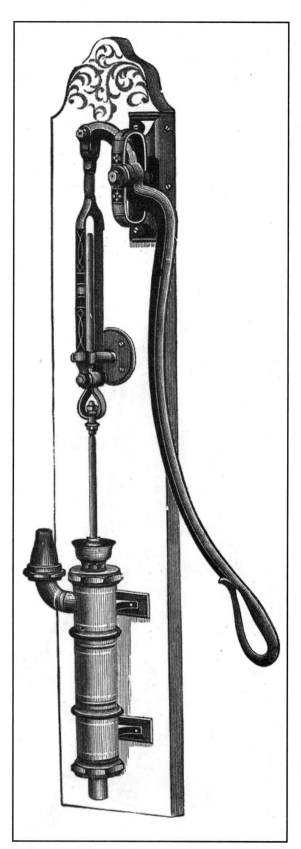

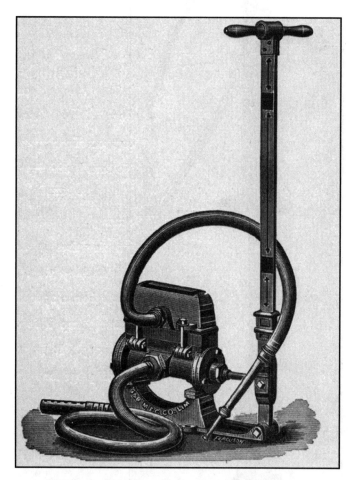

Various kinds of force pumps were available by the 1890s. This was a house force pump. It was used to draw water from a shallow well or a cistern and force it to anywhere in the house. Compared to carrying water into the house with a pail, this was a great improvement.

Listed in an 1891 catalog, this House Pump was "Fitted either for iron, lead or rubber pipe." Pumps like this were used to raise water to other tanks, and occasionally a home would have a supply tank in the attic to which water could be raised with a pump. From the supply tank, water was available by gravity flow throughout the house. This one is from Gleason & Bailey Mfg. Company at Seneca Falls, New York.

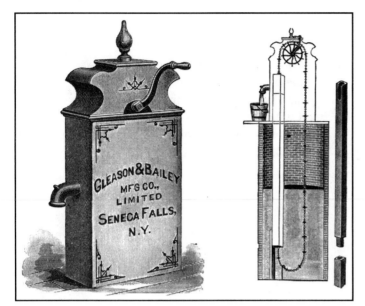

Chain pumps were fairly popular into the 1920s and remained available until about World War II. This was a very simple design that carried water upward from a shallow well and delivered it at a spout. Many different styles of chain pumps were built, but few still exist.

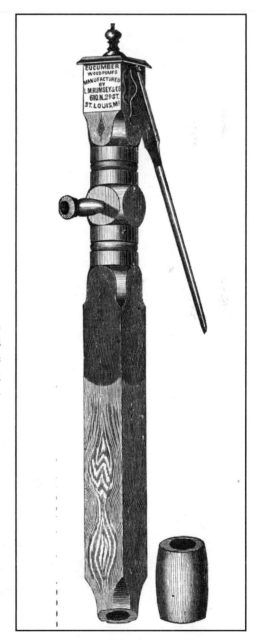

Wood pumps remained on the market until about 1920, and by then the market had all but vanished. Usually a wooden pump was also furnished with wood drop pipe and sometimes even a wood cylinder was at the bottom of the well. It is interesting to note that wooden cylinders were sometimes made with a porcelain liner.

Large wooden handles, not shown here, were fitted to these big pumps. The largest of these 1890 force pumps had a pair of cylinders 6 inches in diameter and with a capacity of 1-3/4 gallons per stroke. The big pump on the right of this engraving sold for $155 in 1890.

By the early 1900s, the power pump had become a reality. A country home of 1910 probably did not have electric power; if it did, electricity was used only for lights. Instead, a small gasoline engine was put into the basement, and some overhead lineshafting was installed. From it, the pump, the washing machine, and perhaps a cream separator could be operated. Mechanizing these jobs was a major step in relieving the hard and heavy work of previous years. Pumps like this Myers Bulldozer were sold by the thousands for just such an application.

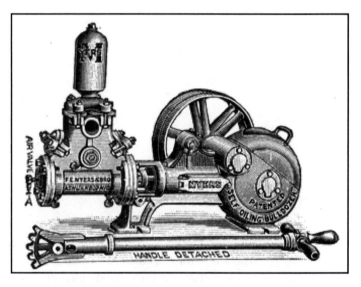

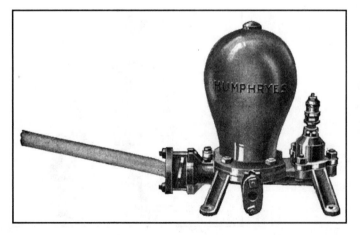

The hydraulic ram is in reality a combination of a water motor and a pump working in a pulsating fashion. The ram works because of the pulsations caused by starting and stopping the flow in the feed pipe. This permits the ram to deliver water to a distant higher point. The water used in this action is drained away. Hydraulic rams are highly desired by collectors, but are not often found. In some countries, such as Australia, hydraulic rams were widely used and are still plentiful.

An 1896 catalog from Goulds Mfg. Co. at Seneca Falls, New York, illustrates their Triplex Pump with an automatic electric motor drive. Certainly this looks nothing like electric pumps would in another twenty years, but it was a beginning to totally mechanized and automatic water systems.

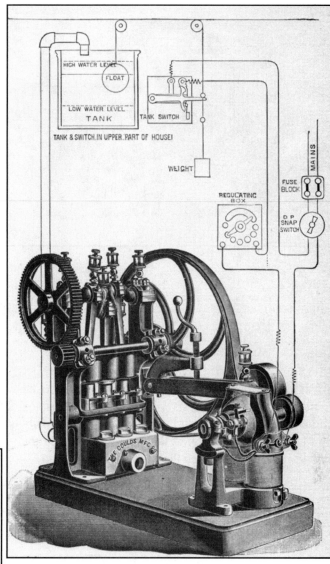

Undoubtedly it was the talk of any small town of the 1890s to get a pump like this for their municipal water system. This Goulds Triplex was built in several sizes. The largest had 12-inch diameter pistons, with a 12-inch stroke. Maximum speed of the crank shaft was 40 rpm. With a capacity of 17-1/2 gallons for every revolution of the crankshaft, this pump could deliver 700 gallons per minute.

During the 1890s companies like Fairbanks-Morse developed their gasoline engine line. Along with the engines, the company designed integral pumping units as shown here. These were available in numerous sizes and configurations. At the small end was a 1-1/2 horsepower model, with the 22 horsepower size topping the 1895 line. The latter was capable of pumping nearly 450 gallons per minute. However this unit weighed 6-1/2 tons!

Small towns often had a "first" water plant that looked something like the one shown here. A huge triplex pump was direct-coupled to the engine through a friction clutch. A close look at the engraving reveals the operator standing between the engine and the pump.

R

Railroad Tools

Railroads developed their own tools for handling and setting track and ties. Conditions varied widely across the country, so specialized tools were often found in certain areas. Rail tools are not commonly found except perhaps among collectors specializing in railroad items. The tools were ordinarily owned by the railroad. When they became worn out or obsolete they were scrapped and seldom got into the ordinary consumer market. Occasionally track bars and spike mauls are found, but these are the exception rather than the rule. Spike mauls often bring $20 and more today. Many of the other items so seldom surface, that accurate values have been difficult or impossible to establish.

Various kinds of bars were needed for building and maintaining track. Their use is self-explanatory. Railroads always used high quality tools, and these bars were usually made of the best steel. Today, a nice bar might bring anywhere upward from $10.

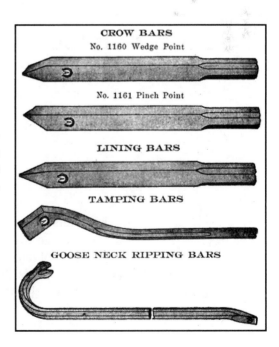

CROW BARS
No. 1160 Wedge Point

No. 1161 Pinch Point

LINING BARS

TAMPING BARS

GOOSE NECK RIPPING BARS

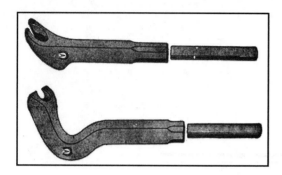

Claw bars were made for pulling rail spikes from the wooden ties. These bars were usually between 5 and 5-1/2 feet in length and often weighed 30 pounds or even more. A gooseneck bar might have sold for $5 or more in 1910. Shown left to right are a claw bar and a gooseneck bar.

Rail tongs were used to pick up rail and move it about. Each track crew had several pairs on hand. They are seldom seen today, especially since most track work has been mechanized for many years.

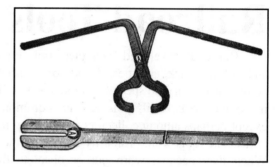

Track wrenches were made in various sizes, depending on the type of joint and the size of the rail. In addition, many rail lines developed their own ideas and thus there were a great many specialized tools used on one railroad line that might not have been used on another.

Spike pullers are another unusual tool seldom found today. Shown here are two-knob and three-knob sizes. An interesting aspect of railroad building is that the work practices, methods, and tools that were used in Pennsylvania might have been entirely different in Indiana or Idaho.

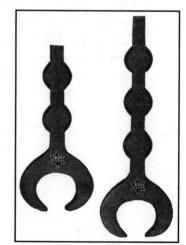

The tie holder was intended to hold the tie against the rail when spiking. A No. 1 size was available for 12 and 16 lb. Rails, and the No. 2 size was for 20 and 25 lb. Rails.

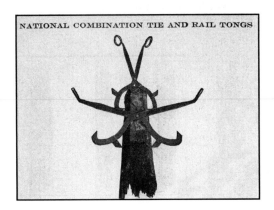

From an early twentieth century catalog comes the National Combination Tie and Rail Tongs. To what extent this tool came into use is unknown, but certain rail lines may have adopted the design for a few years. Since most track tools never got into the public domain, few of them still remain.

Various kinds of picks were used in track work. To the left, is the ordinary clay or railroad pick. The wide chisel and pick combination was another tool. Shown to the right is the combination pick and tamper, also known as a tamping pick, which had some obvious advantages. The latter style was available in sizes up to about 9 pounds.

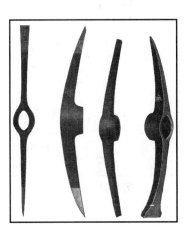

Many different kinds of rail benders were made, although very few can be found today. With the mechanization of track work in recent decades, the need for these hand tools evaporated, and the vast majority were scrapped.

Track was uniformly set to gauge, and numerous styles were available. In addition, some rail companies apparently developed their own designs and used them to the exclusion of all others. Shown is a Huntington Pattern.

Occasionally a track level appears. This specialized instrument was developed only for railroads and had little use outside of this industry. The Buda Company formerly at Harvey, Illinois, built an extensive line of railroad supplies, hand cars, and other equipment for the railroad industry. This firm offered the levels shown for many years.

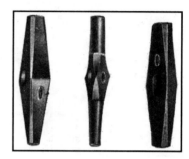

A standard pattern spike maul is shown on the left. It was made in 6, 8, and 10-pound sizes. The Bell or Pittsburgh Pattern is shown in the center; it was generally made in a 10-pound size with a length of 15-1/4 inches. The Pennsylvania Railroad pattern on the right was a 10-pounder with a length of 13 inches. In addition to these styles, there were numerous others used on American railroads.

In the early days of railroading, rail was cut with a chisel, or perhaps a special hacksaw device. Holes were drilled or punched, and overall, the work was hard, heavy, and tedious. Eventually, power tools eliminated much of the hand work of earlier times. Shown left to right are a track punch, a track chisel, and a spike maul.

S

Sawmill Equipment

Various kinds of equipment and tools used around a sawmill are illustrated in this section. Sawmills are illustrated on page 306ff of my book, *Encyclopedia of American Farm Implements,* Krause Publications, 1997.

Sawmills and sawmilling have always carried a special mystique in American culture. Many communities boasted at least one sawmill, and of course, there were some of good size. A special fascination was a big steam engine driving the mill. Today, a sawmill demonstration with a steam engine doing the work always draws a crowd. There is something special about one of those big engines at work, along with the ash, the cinders, and the smell of steam cylinder oil.

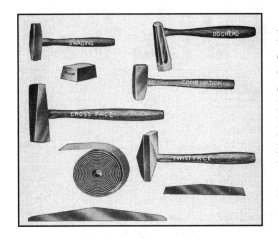

Hanchett Mfg. Co. of Big Rapids, Michigan, published the *Hanchett Saw and Knife Fitting Manual* in 1950. This detailed book gives full details on fitting and managing of saws. The saw mechanics tools consisted primarily of special hammers, anvils, and gauges. At top left is a swaging hammer, and at top right is a doghead hammer. The latter was used for tensioning the blade. Doghead and cross-face hammers were the most commonly used. Combination and twist-face hammers seldom saw any use. Learning to be a saw mechanic was (and is) a job that had to be learned at least in part, from another mechanic. It is not a trade that can readily be picked up from a book.

Solid circular saws were the rule of the day in the 1890s. Replaceable inserted tooth saws did not come into general use until early in the twentieth century. This 1890 showing of circular saws indicates availability in sizes up to 76 inches in diameter. At the time, a huge blade like this sold for $375. The more common size of 52 inches was $90. Many sawyers preferred a beveled blade, that is to say, a blade having a 7-gauge rim and an 8-gauge center. This gave the blade better clearance so it would run easier.

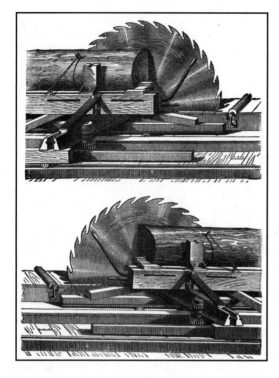

Sawmills were built either as right-hand (top) or as left-hand (bottom). The two different styles are shown here as a matter of curiosity and reference. Usually a first-time buyer would order a right-hand or left-hand mill depending mostly on the location where it would be set, as well as the sawyer's personal preference.

Sawmill teeth are swage-set, that is, the tip of the tooth is spread out with a swaging tool. The tooth cuts a chip or shaving on its way through the log. Cross-cut saws are spring-set, with alternate teeth being bent to the right or left of the saw plate. The saw gauge shown here from 1890 was available in numerous sizes. By gauging the width of each tooth the saw could cut uniformly.

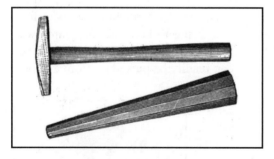

In the 1890s, a sawmill usually had a swage and swage hammer on hand. Occasionally the teeth needed to be revived with a swage, and if a foreign object was encountered, such as a horseshoe that had grown into a tree, there was a lot of work to restore the blade. Sometimes this was impossible, and a great many blades were returned to the factory to repair, or simply scrapped and replaced with a new one.

Morrill's Perfect Saw Set was made in various sizes, and in 1890 it sold for $1.25 to $3.50, depending on the size. Saw sets were used for spring-set blades...the latter arrangement was completely unsatisfactory for mill blades.

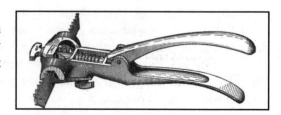

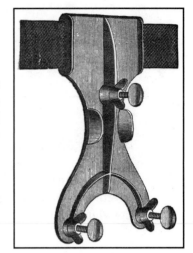

The side file was designed to make all the teeth even on the blade, thus producing a much better grade of lumber. This also had the advantage of making the saw run better and staying sharp for a longer time. Filing was usually done by hand, and required great care.

The saw swage has two halves. One is formed to spread the tip of the tooth. The other levels up the tip of the tooth. Properly done, little filing is then necessary. Using a swage correctly requires considerable skill and experience.

After considerable filing, the tooth gullets in the plate became smaller. This created a problem as there was insufficient space to accumulate the chip. The saw gummer was used to restore the gullet to its original size. This was all hand work and required considerable time.

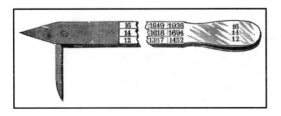

Scribner's Log Rule was used to determine the board feet of lumber in a log through measurements of the log diameter. The Scribner design was intended primarily for logs in water, and was equipped with a lance, steel head, and steel hook. This design was also known as Doyle's Scale.

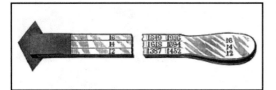

For scaling logs on land, the Flat Log Rule was used. Ordinarily, it was made in a four-foot size, but a six-foot style was also available. Log rules were used to some extent, but experienced country sawyers could usually offer a reasonable guess of the board feet of lumber within a log.

The Flat Board Rule was used to quickly determine the number of board feet in lumber. While these rules were used to some extent, the experienced mill or yard man, given the width, thickness and length of a board or plank, could instantly reel off the answer.

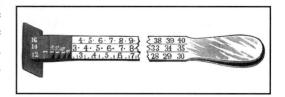

Occasionally a pike pole appears on an auction or at a garage sale. Pikes were used for river driving (of logs). Pike poles were usually made in lengths ranging from 10 to 18-feet.

Shown at the top of this illustration is a peavey (also spelled *pevy*). By definition a peavey has a pointed spike on its end. Below is shown a cant hook, used to roll and turn logs. The latter was made sizes from 4-1/2 to 5-1/2-feet. Cant hooks are still fairly common, and are in fact, still available—and still used.

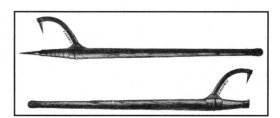

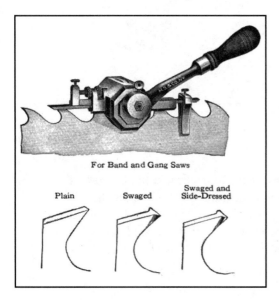

For Band and Gang Saws

Plain   Swaged   Swaged and Side-Dressed

Famous saw makers like Henry Disston & Sons made a great many different saw tools in addition to an endless variety of saws. Their Swage Shaper of 1910 could shape plain, swaged, or swaged and side-dressed blades. A machine like this was much faster than a hand swage, and left each tooth formed exactly the same. Despite its $28 price tag, this and similar machines became popular with mill operators.

Many different kinds of log rules, gauges, and calipers were developed over the years. Included were the log calipers shown here. The calipers on the left were made with a cedar frame, maple jaws, and had the figures burnt into the wood for permanence. It was designed to read diameter and board feet in a log. The calipers on the right would read diameters only. This device would measure logs up to 36 inches in diameter. In 1920, these nickel-plated calipers sold for $22.50.

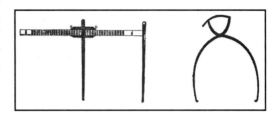

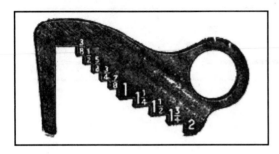

Interesting gauges for measuring lumber have been devised over the years. This Lumber Gauge of 1920 consisted of precisely located notches in a machined aluminum casting. As noted with some of the other gauges shown here, experienced lumbermen seldom resorted to a gauge, being able to judge thickness merely by sight.

Saws and Saw Vises

For every saw and accessory shown in this section there are probably dozens of other examples. Instead we attempted a representative showing of saws and accessories of the late 1800s and early 1900s. Some are found frequently and others rarely. For example, the pedal-powered scroll saws in this section are seldom seen and are likely to sell in the $300 to $600 range, or even higher.

Hacksaws initially were of a fixed frame design, using cast iron. Oftentimes a blacksmith would buy the blade stock in a roll, cut off the required length, and then punch holes in the ends for attaching to the frame. A few companies persisted in making this design into the early 1900s.

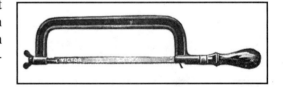

The Star Extension Frame Hack Saw was made by Millers Falls in the early 1900s. This was an adjustable frame design that permitted using blades up to 12 inches long. At that time, hacksaw blades were available in a range from 6 to 12 inches. I came across a couple of new 6-inch hacksaw blades several years ago, but none have been seen since that time.

Millers Falls offered these two pistol-grip designs in the early 1900s. They could handle blades ranging in length from 8 to 12 inches. Numerous companies made hacksaws, and all of them differed slightly in design. Nice older hacksaws usually do not fetch high prices. A nice saw can be bought in the $5 to $10 range.

Henry Disston & Sons was a well-known saw maker with a history going well back into the nineteenth century. By the early 1900s, their line was quite extensive, and included the saws shown here. The saw on the left was nickel plated and had a polished applewood handle; the saw on the right was similar but had a closed handle.

Various kinds of deep saws were developed by the early 1900s. The Universal on the right of this engraving was designed for architectural iron workers and others needing a frame deeper than the ordinary. The handle on the Universal was adjustable on the frame.

For cutting rails, girders, and other heavy pieces, Disston and others provided a special hacksaw in various sizes up to an 18-inch blade. Some styles had the handles in a fixed position, while others had adjustable handles. These styles are quite scarce.

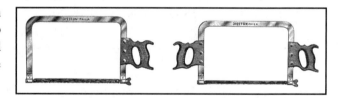

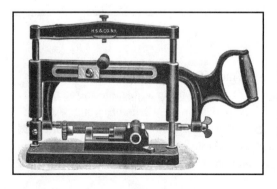

A 9-inch blade was used in this Bench Hack Saw of 1910. Priced at $3.50, it included a swivel vise to permit cutting angles and miters when necessary. Today, one of these saws would be considered rare indeed, and would likely fetch a decent price on auction.

Hand saws were generally made in rip, crosscut, and panel saw styles. Rip saws, as shown in this diagram were usually available with 4 to 7 points per inch. Crosscut saws were ordinarily available in a range of 6 to 12 points per inch. Carpenters often carried two or three different saws of varying point size to accommodate various needs.

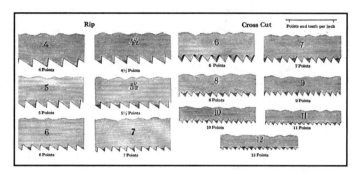

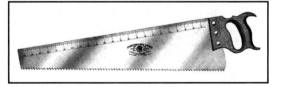

Ordinarily, hand saws were made in lengths ranging from 22 to 26 inches. When buying a saw, one could select either a crosscut or rip pattern. Saw backs were either straight or skew-backed. The Disston No. 120 was made of London spring steel, had a skew back, and was sold with special instructions for filing. In 1910, this saw was nearly $3 a copy.

E. C. Atkins & Company at Indianapolis was established in 1857. However, at that point the Atkins family had already been making saws for about 250 years. Their 1914 catalog illustrates the Atkins No. 400 which they claimed to be one of the finest hand saws ever made. It was made of the finest Atkins Silver Steel, had a polished rosewood handle, attached with three silver-plated screws. The No. 400 was made in sizes ranging from 16 to 30 inches. Shown here are the Rip, Hand, and Panel Saw designs.

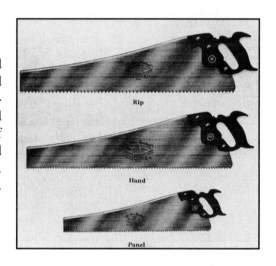

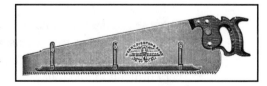

The No. 60 Atkins saw shown here was a combined saw, rule and square. Combination saws were offered by several different companies, and are now quite scarce. Today, they oftentimes fetch $150 or more.

In 1910, Disston offered this special crosscut saw, complete with a gauge for tenoning or shouldering. This unusual style was probably made in relatively small quantities. Finding one in good shape, and complete with the gauge and screws would likely be difficult.

Besides being used in a miter box, the back saw was frequently use for cutting miters, tenons and dovetails. Usually, the back saw was furnished with an elegant handle and epitomized the art of saw making.

Dovetail saws are nothing more than a small version of a back saw. Usually made in sizes from 6 to 12 inches, ordinarily they had teeth at 17 points per inch. Dovetail saws were made with a straight handle (left) as well as an offset handle (right).

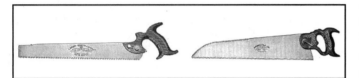

Joiner saws and floor saws are both quite scarce today. The joiners saw (left) was made with a 16-inch blade with teeth at 15 points per inch. Flooring saws (right) have a unique double-sided blade, and another significant feature is the adjustable handle.

Plumbers saws were designed to cut openings in walls, floors and ceilings as they did their work. These saws are among the styles that are now difficult to find. Once power tools came into general use in the 1950s, the need for many of these tools ended and they made their way to the scrap yard.

It would be nearly impossible to list all the saw styles produced over the past century. However, the compass saw was commonly used by the early 1900s, in sizes ranging from 10 to 16 inches. Nice ones are not easy to find today, although there seems to be a host of cheaply made, rusty, and worn-out ones available. Shown at left is an H.S. & Co. Model; at right is a Disston.

The pattern-maker's saw is an unusual design that is not often seen. Compared to the overall labor market, there weren't a great number of pattern makers, and it isn't at all likely that more than a portion of them ever owned one of these saws. Add to that the usual attrition of fire, neglect, and the salvage bin, and it is easy to see why this design is very difficult to find today.

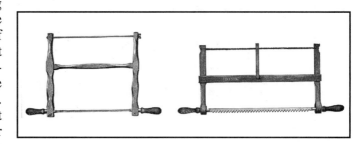

Turning saws and cabinet saws were found in nearly every cabinet shop of the early 1900s. The turning saw on the left was made by Millers Falls. The blade was tightened by means of the back screw on top of the frame. Cabinet Saw Frames as shown on the right were offered by Disston in this example, with a German pattern. In addition, a great many of these were made locally by the cabinetmakers who used them. Instead of a backrod, this design used a piece of stout cord to tighten the blade. A small stick in the center twisted the rope until the blade was tight. It was then captive over the frame, as shown here.

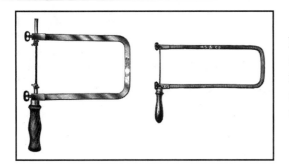

Fret saw frames were entirely different than the ordinary coping saw. The frame was deeper and usually could be purchased for different blade lengths ranging anywhere from 8 to 16 inches. The saw shown here on the right, from H.S. & Co. was intended for amateurs and students. At left is one from M.F. Company.

Jewelers saws used an entirely different approach to adjustable blade length as shown here. The saw back is telescoped into the handle and secured with a thumb screw. Jeweler's saws are not often found today, but nevertheless do not seem to attract the attention of collectors as much as fret saws, certain hacksaw designs, and other styles.

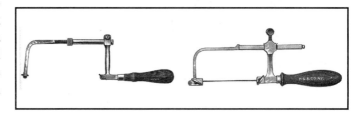

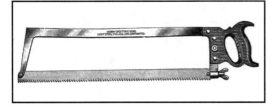

Every butcher had at least one butcher saw. In the early 1900s, there was no other way to split a carcass, except perhaps for an axe. There are numerous styles of butcher saws, made in sizes ranging from 18 to 26 inches. The model shown is a Disston.

Buck saws are frequently found today. As the name implies, they were used to buck or cut firewood. An old saying implied that a fellow got warm twice with one of these saws—first with sawing the wood, and later on, by the heating stove after the wood was cut.

No. 80. DISSTON.   No. 03. MARSHALL.   No. 4. JACKSON.

American Tooth No. 385
Victor No. 386
Victor No. 388

Crosscut saws or felling saws were an important part of life in the early 1900s, and by then, were made in every conceivable size, style, length, and tooth configuration. Many immigrants became cutters and spent their lives in the woods in various parts of the United States. Unfortunately, many of them did not live long…working in the woods was a dangerous occupation. Shown are three Atkins hollow backs.

The one-man saw was fairly popular, since it enabled a person to fell and buck smaller trees without any help. These saws were made in many different styles, and quite a number of them still exist. However, like most saws, their value has increased as a collectible, and will likely continue to do so.

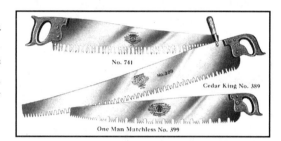

No. 741
Cedar King No. 389
One Man Matchless No. 399

This little machine was intended for setting the teeth on a bandsaw blade. The blade was set in place, the feed was automatically set, and it was simply a matter of cranking the wheel to set the teeth. Doing a fair-sized band only took a few minutes. These machines now fetch $100 or more.

The Cunningham saw-set is another of those unusual designs that has come to be almost extinct. Priced at $12.50 in 1910, it was virtually automatic.

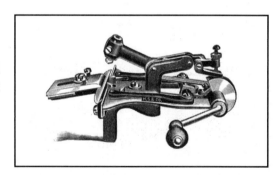

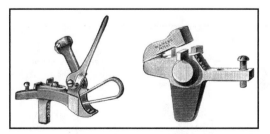

Various kinds of saw-sets were available using either a spring-loaded lever action like the machine on the left, or a light blow with a hammer as with the Aiken saw set on the right. Many of these devices are now very scarce.

Shown here are a couple of plier-type saw-sets of the early 1900s. The Disston to the left was well known, and was available in several sizes. Shown at right, the Taintors saw-set was another design of this period.

While the Monarch saw set on the left was designed only for hand saws, the Morrill on the right was said to be applicable to band saws, circular saws and hand saws. For all the saw-sets shown here, there are dozens more yet to be discovered.

The spring set shown here was intended mainly for band, shingle, and veneer saws. It was made in various sizes, each of which carried several slots to suit the gauge of the blade.

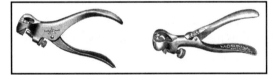

The Morrill saw sets shown here were for hand saws, butcher saws, fret saws, and the like. The No. 10 on the right was intended only for light gauge saws and was unsuitable to hand saws with their heavier gauge.

A decent saw vise was essential for accurate saw filing. Shown in the vertical position, this one of 1910 was factory made. There were undoubtedly thousands more of similar appearance that were made right in the shop where they were used.

Saws and Saw Vises

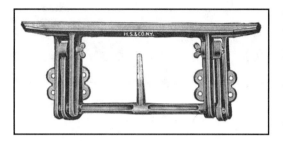

In the early 1900s, this big 23-inch saw vise sold for $9. In looking for saw vises over the past forty years, I have never run across one like this! It was made for mounting directly to a bench, and obviously was heavily built. Saw vises sometimes fetch $25 to $40 and more today, although a decrepit oldtimer covered with rust cannot be expected to bring top dollar.

These three saw vises were all intended for direct mounting to a bench. This style was usually more solid and secure than a clamp-on vise, but strangely, the clamp-on is the most commonly found today.

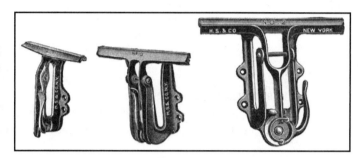

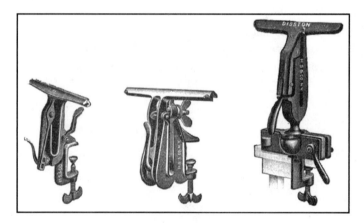

Most saw manufacturers offered saw vises of various kinds, including the Disston shown to the right of this illustration. Shown to the left are two Stearns' models. Numerous other companies also built saw vises. In fact, many foundries welcomed saw vises and other small tools to help fill in their regular work. Most of the vises shown here sold in the $1 to $3 range in 1910.

Early in the twentieth century, foot-powered machines enjoyed great popularity. The Goodell Lathe and Saw was a pedal-powered wood lathe with a scroll saw attachment. This 57-pound machine sold for $15. The scroll saw even had a nickel plated table! By comparison, the Star fret saw shown at right was priced at only $6.50.

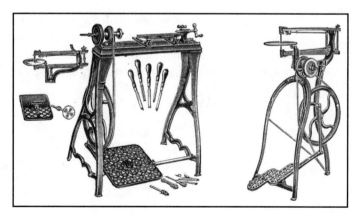

Priced at $21 in 1910, the Fleetwood Scroll Saw was equipped with a small blower to keep the sawdust clear from the work! In addition, the saw table could be tilted, and this was a great advantage. Foot-powered scroll saws in reasonable condition often bring $300, and sometimes much more.

Yet another example of 1910 scroll saws is the Dexter Style C shown here. It was originally priced at $13.50. The Dexter was quite similar to the Fleetwood, but had a wooden arm and was built along lighter lines. Small electric motors began to appear in the early 1900s, and with them came the end of foot-powered machines. Fortunately, a few were sent to the attic and remained there for decades before being once again discovered.

Screw Plates

In 1916, McGraw-Hill Book Co. published *Handbook for Machine Designers, Shop Men and Draftsmen*, compiled by Frederick A. Halsey. On page 210, Halsey discusses Screw Thread Standards. In this regard Halsey writes, "*There is no standard V thread and the continuance of that practice is a simple nuisance.*" Trade magazines of the day encouraged a standardized screw thread system, and apparently the first steps were taken in 1918 toward a unified system. Eventually the NC or coarse series evolved. It was the former United States Standard, supplemented in the

smaller sizes with ASME recommendations established in 1907. The present NF or fine thread series is largely based on recommendations established by the SAE in 1911.

Various changes have taken place since that time.

The 12-pitch thread series remained on the scene. All threads were 12 per inch, regardless of diameter. Boilermakers in particular used this standard. Pump rods for deep wells also retained the 12-pitch thread. Pump rods of 3/8, 7/16, and 1/2-inch were all at 12 tpi. Blacksmiths also favored the 1/2-12 size and this was

sometimes called blacksmiths' thread. Of course, this wouldn't fit with the standard 1/2-13 thread.

Screw plates were usually fitted into a neat wooden case. Today, a nice screw plate set usually brings a decent price. A set ranging from 1/4 to 3/4 of an inch, complete with the taps and tap wrench and in a decent wooden case might bring $50 to $100. An exceptional one might well bring somewhat more. However, it should be remembered that some dies can no longer be purchased for replacement, so this should be a consideration when buying one of these sets.

No. 302, ¼-INCH AND LARGER
NUMBER OF THREADS TO THE INCH

Diam. of Tap Inches	Standard Pitches			Other Pitches Also Furnished U.S. Form	Price	
	U.S. Std.	Whitworth Std.	V Form		Each	Per Set
¼	20	20	20	24, 27, 32	.45	1.35
5⁄16	18	18	18	20, 27, 32	.50	1.50
⅜	16	16	16	20, 27	.55	1.65
7⁄16	14	14	14	24, 27	.60	1.80
½	13	12	12	12, 24, 27	.70	2.10
9⁄16	12	12	12	27	.80	2.40
⅝	11	11	11	12, 27	.90	2.70
11⁄16	11	11	..		1.05	3.15
¾	10	10	10	12, 27	1.20	3.60
13⁄16	10	10	..		1.40	4.20
⅞	9	9	9	12, 27	1.60	4.80
15⁄16	9	9	..		1.80	5.40
1	8	8	8	12, 27	2.00	6.00
1⅛	7	7	..		2.25	6.75
1¼	7	7	..	..	2.60	7.80
1⅜	6	6	..	..	3.00	9.00
1½	6	6	..	..	3.50	10.50
1⅝	5½	5	..	..	4.20	12.60
1¾	5	5	..	..	5.00	15.00
1⅞	5	4½	..	..	5.80	17.40
2	4½	4½	..	..	6.70	20.10
2⅛	4½	4½	..	..	8.00	24.00
2¼	4½	4	..	..	9.20	27.60
2⅜	4	4	..	..	10.50	31.50
2½	4	4	..	..	11.50	34.50

A catalog chart of 1920 illustrates the state of affairs for buying taps and dies at the time. The U.S. Standard uses a slight radius at the root of the thread, compared to the V-thread design also listed in the chart. The latter cut a standard thread except that it used a sharp vee in the root of the thread. The Whitworth was also in use, and it varied from the U.S. Standard. For instance, the U.S. Standard used a pitch of 13 tpi for 1/2-inch, while the Whitworth was 12 tpi. A closer look at the chart shows that a 1/2-inch was also available in 24 and 27 tpi.

Armstrong's Adjustable Stock and Dies was a product of about 1890. Designed primarily for pipe threading, it could also be used for bolt threading when required. When completely equipped with pipe dies from 1/8 to 2 inches, plus seven different bolt sizes, this outfit sold for $40.

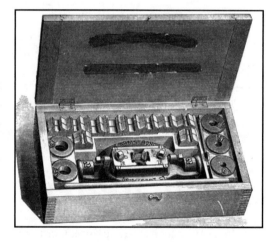

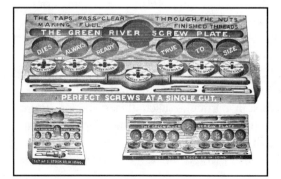

In 1890, this tap and die set from Green River sold for nearly $40. Thus, only machine shops and blacksmith shops were equipped with them. At the time, farmers and ordinary mechanics could not afford this equipment, and when any kind of threading was necessary they made a trip to a local shop equipped for this work.

This attractive screw plate of 1890 from Lightning sold for only $17. However, it was virtually a jeweler's set since the largest die was only 1/4-inch! Occasionally a nice set like this appears at auction, and if reasonably complete will often bring a considerable price.

Jarecki Mfg. Co. at Erie, Pennsylvania, was the builder of this Combination Screw Plate and Pipe Cutter. Five different sizes were made to accommodate pipe ranging up to 6 inches in diameter. Three different sizes covered all pipes up to 2 inches. The big No. 5 plate had a total of five handles, and it is probable that a big crew was needed to cut a thread on 6-inch pipe!

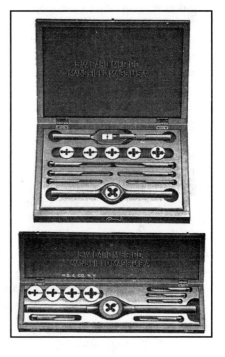

S. W. Dard Mfg. Company at Mansfield, Massachusetts, offered many different sets of Machinists Screw Plates in 1910. By this time, the price for these sets had dropped somewhat from earlier years. A nice set encompassing the range from 1/4 to 1/2-inch sold for under $10.

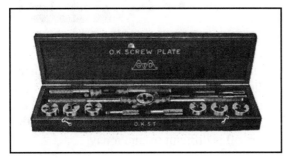

Greenfield Tap & Die Company offered their O. K. Screw Plates in many different sets by 1920. A set of NC coarse-thread taps and dies ranging from 1/4 to 3/4 inch sold for about $28, and a similar set in NF fine threads fetched the same price. The Greenfield line became very popular and was a leader in the field. During the 1930s, the ASME and SAE helped to solidify a National Standard. However, in recent years the Metric System has also appeared, so mechanics now are forced to keep both styles on hand.

Screwdrivers

Screwdrivers of the late 1800s followed the same pattern of decades before. Usually they featured a flat blade, and flattened sides on the handle. This 1890 example was made in sizes from 3 to 10 inches.

The double-grip design was popular in the early 1900s. Stanley and others offered various styles of double-grip screwdrivers. Piano screwdrivers were fairly popular because of their light design. This made them popular for small work.

Clock screwdrivers are a bit out of the ordinary, but were often purchased for small screws and light work. As noted previously, ordinary screwdrivers have only a small collector value, but specialty drivers can easily bring $5 to $10. Handmade screwdrivers and unique designs will bring much more.

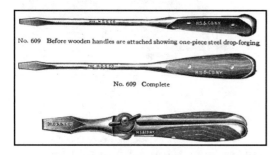

The so-called Perfect Handle screwdrivers had a forged blade to which wooden handles were attached. This style was especially desired by carpenters and machinists for everyday use. An unusual style was the triple lever design. The handles could be set in different positions to provide maximum leverage.

Many different companies made screwdrivers with this 1910 showing representing the average of the time. Ordinary screwdrivers have only a small collector value, partially because they are so plentiful.

Screwdriver sets began to proliferate in the early 1900s. This set typifies what was available at the time. Three different blades were furnished in this set, making it handy for the handyman or in the kitchen.

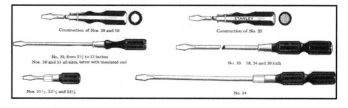

Stanley brought out their Hurwood line in the early 1900s. They were made in several different styles. The No. 20 Regular series was available in sizes ranging from 2-1/2 to 30 inches.

The Disston No. 50 screwdriver of 1910 was furnished with an insulated hard rubber handle. This design was made especially for electricians. Eventually many of the hard rubber handles broke or disintegrated, so the No. 50 is difficult to find today.

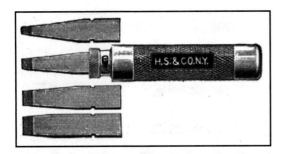

The No. 60 Yankee Magazine screwdriver is seldom found today. In retracted position it was only three inches in length, making it a convenient pocket screwdriver. This style had a nickel plated brass case.

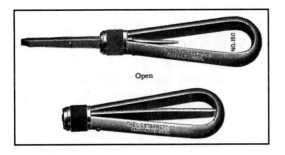

An awl and screwdriver were combined in the Starrett No. 150 screwdriver of 1910. In addition the handle was formed so that it could be used as an emergency wrench.

Jewelers screwdrivers were often furnished in sets, and in 1910 a set of five Starrett jewelers screwdrivers sold for $1.60. Single ones frequently appear, but complete sets are seldom found.

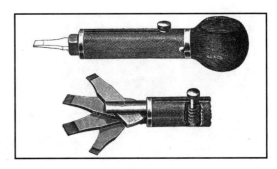

Four different blades were included within the Billings Magazine screwdriver of 1910. A rosewood handle was furnished, and the retracted magazine was under four inches in length.

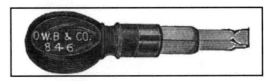

Locksmiths and gunsmiths appreciated this little screwdriver with its short and stout point. Unique designs like this often sell for $10 to $20 today.

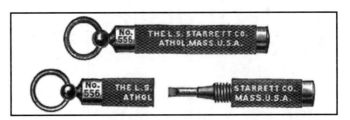

A rather unusual find would be the Starrett No. 556 eyeglass screwdriver. It was a neat compact little driver that could be carried in the pocket, on a keychain, or even on a watch chain.

Various kinds of right angle screwdrivers have been marketed over the years. However, the early ratcheting styles always gain interest, such as these 1910 examples. The Lane ratchet driver on the right of this illustration sold for $3 in 1910.

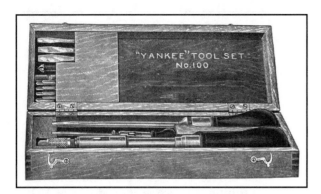

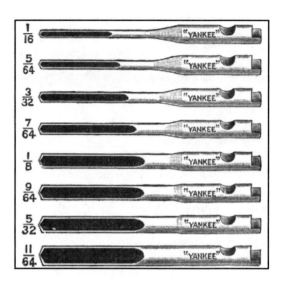

The set shown here includes a Yankee No. 30 spiral ratchet screwdriver plus a set of drill points and screwdriver blades. Originally, this boxed set sold for $6. A complete set in its original case would bring several times its original value today.

Yankee drills became very popular in the early 1900s. The complete set of eight drill points shown here sold for less than a dollar. These drills were very popular with finish carpenters and cabinetmakers for spotting and drilling pilot holes and similar duties.

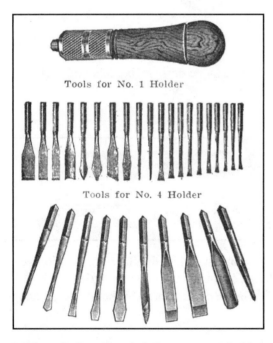

The No. 50 Yankee Reciprocating Drill shown here was a popular early version. Retailing at about $4, it was 16 inches long and had a traverse movement of over 8 inches.

Millers Falls offered their own tool holder set in the early 1900s. It consisted of an awl, reamer, screwdriver, and even a tiny saw. It also included a scraper, a chisel and a gouge for wood. These sets retailed at $1.50 to $2 in about 1920.

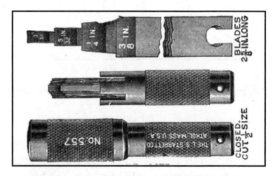

Starrett's No. 557 Patent Magazine Screw Driver of the 1920s retailed for about $1. It included four different blades, all of which could be retracted into the magazine for a small pocket driver.

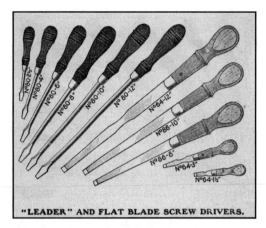

"LEADER" AND FLAT BLADE SCREW DRIVERS.

The No. 75 Yankee Push Brace featured a right and left hand ratchet, and could also be used as a rigid screw driver when required. The chuck would hold auger bits up to 1/2-inch. With a socket bit, it could even drive small lag screws. This one sold for under $5 in the early 1920s.

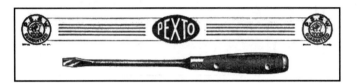

Many different companies have made screwdrivers, this one from Pexto being an example. Pexto has been widely known for its sheet metal machinery, but for many years the company also made an extensive line of hand tools.

Stanley offered a wide variety of screwdrivers including this series in their 1912 catalog. Flat blade screwdrivers remained quite popular, even though the newer round shank had become an attractive alternative. Flat blade screwdrivers are still plentiful, but not so easy to find as formerly.

Scythes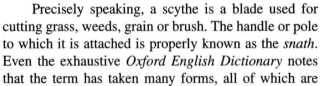

Precisely speaking, a scythe is a blade used for cutting grass, weeds, grain or brush. The handle or pole to which it is attached is properly known as the *snath*. Even the exhaustive *Oxford English Dictionary* notes that the term has taken many forms, all of which are difficult to follow. One would conclude that the term simply evolved for lack of a better word.

A form of scythe created in the 1800s was the grain cradle. The cradle or rack behind the blade served to gather the grain, making it easier to bind into sheaves. (I recall from the family history of how my great-grandfather used a grain cradle while the rest of the family that were able-bodied followed behind and bound the sheaves of grain. No wonder the family was delighted to have their first grain binder in the late 1880s!)

By 1900, the scythe was used mainly for cutting small areas inaccessible to a mowing machine. It was also used for cutting weeds along fencelines and similar locations. On occasion, a farmer would have a brush snath with a heavier shank and a short bush scythe to trim small brush or heavy weeds. Today a nice snath is becoming difficult to find, and oftentimes one that is complete with its handles and the clamping device at the shank might bring $20 to $30 and perhaps more in some areas. Sometimes a snath is simply referred to as a scythe handle.

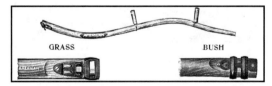

GRASS   BUSH

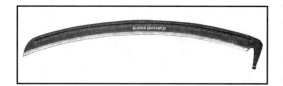

The grass scythe was probably the most popular, although various references indicate that a grain scythe was somewhat different in design. In addition to those scythes produced in quantity from various factories, there were also those of local origin. Local blacksmiths often made scythes one of their specialties, producing them during the cold winter months or other slack times.

Bush scythes were used mainly for clearing weeds and small brush. Those who have used a scythe know that there are few ways known to man that will bring up a sweat. The author recalls that on those days when work was slack around the farm there was always a fresh crop of weeds along a fenceline that had to be cut *that day!* Invariably, it was behind growing crops, the humidity was 100%, the wind was completely calm, and the temperature seemed like it was way past 100°…add to this the wide range of bugs and insects that gathered as we mowed down their protective cover!

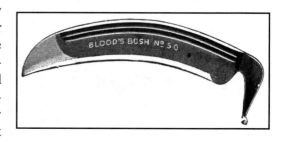

Perhaps as an excuse to take a rest, it was necessary to touch up the scythe with a stone at frequent intervals. In reality, grass and weeds all took their toll on the cutting edge, and it was much easier to touch it up with a stone at regular intervals than to let it become dull. That made cutting difficult. Even with careful honing of the scythe, it was necessary to put it on the grindstone to bring up the edge. Of importance was keeping the edge thin for easy cutting. For this job, there was nothing of those days that beat the old-fashioned grindstone!

Spades and Shovels

Drain spades are easily identified because they taper down about an inch from top to bottom. There are various styles of drain spades, but all seem to have this identifying feature. Drain spades usually were fitted with a D-handle.

Ditching or posthole spades generally are wider at the bottom, narrowing at the step. The reverse taper helped to lift the entire spade out of soil to the side of the ditch, making for less dirt to be shoveled out later.

Post and drain spades were available in numerous sizes. The No. 2 had a blade length of 14 inches, while the No. 6 had a length of 26 inches. High quality spades were shipped with polished blades. Shown top to bottom are a post spade and a drain spade.

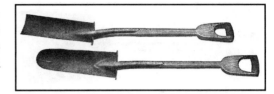

Open tiling spades are becoming difficult to locate today. They were never made in great quantity, and many of them were broken by ineptitude. The Queen Tiling Spades shown here were made in 6 x 18, 6 x 20, and 6 x 22 inch sizes. A four-inch style is found occasionally, the three-inch style is quite rare.

The needs of the nurseryman were different than other occupations and a special nursery spade was developed for this purpose. Usually they were made with a 7-1/2 x 12-inch blade.

Early shovels and spades had the back riveted to the blade. This method was largely dispensed with by the early 1900s. A riveted back generally indicates an early design.

Solid, one-piece cast steel shovels, spades, and scoops made their appearance by 1890. This was a much stronger design than the riveted style. Round point and square point shovels were made in various sizes.

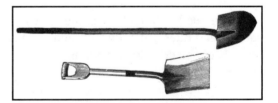

Contractor's shovels, whether in round or square point design, ordinarily have long handles. Numerous other trades used a short or D-handle shovel such as the mining shovel shown here. This one was specifically made for use with iron or copper ore.

The molder's shovel was specifically made for the foundryman to fill his molds. It was of a special flat design, unlike any other shovel on the market. Shown is a model from Fox.

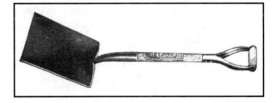

Spades and Shovels

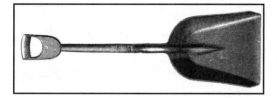

Steel scoops of the 1890s were available with long handle or D-handle at the choice of the buyer. It appears though that the D-handle was far more popular. At the time, scoops were made in four usual sizes, with the No. 2 being the smallest and the No. 6 being the largest.

Coal shovels were a design especially adapted to handling this material. Until recent decades, coal dealers flourished as they hauled coal to homes and businesses. Today, coal shovels are difficult to find.

These cast steel socket strap shovels of the 1890s were made in square point and round point styles. However, for railroad and road work they were furnished with sharpened ends. These styles are seldom found today.

Squares and Rules

This section provides a representative showing of squares and rules. Literally thousands of different rules have been made, along with hundreds of different squares. Many of these are quite old, but are still in use. The carpenter's framing square for example, is commonly made and used today. Except for the older and unusual designs, their value is utilitarian, rather than having a great appeal to the tool collector.

Carpenter's framing squares that are very old or perhaps from a small manufacturer, can sometimes

bring $50 to $100, and even more for an exceptional one. Precision-made machinist's squares are often highly polished and are a very attractive collectible. Boxwood rules are always a desirable collectible and have been made in countless varieties over the years. Common ones often fetch $10 to $25, but those with caliper attachments or other refinements can be in the $30 to $75 range. Rules with ivory inlays might sell upwards from $100 to $500.

By 1900, the carpenter's framing square had been highly developed. The Nicholls for instance, included charts on the body and tongue for calculating common, hip, valley, jack and cripple rafters. Many other functions could be performed using the tables stamped into the square. Books were written on using the steel square as well.

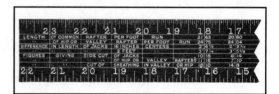

The take-down square is fairly scarce today. It was designed to be taken apart for easy storage within a supplied leather or canvas case. Some of these squares had a copper finish and could even be furnished in a nickel plated version.

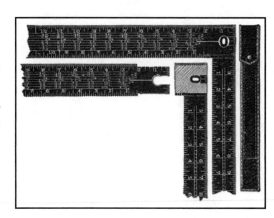

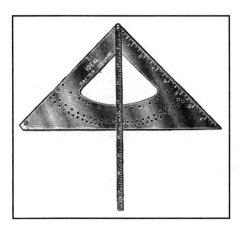

Carpenter's combination squares abounded in the early 1900s, including the Ideal shown here. By properly setting the adjustable tongue, virtually any angle problem could be solved quickly and accurately. Squares like this one are not at all common, especially if in good condition, and even more so if they are still complete with their instruction book.

Starrett offered their No. 439 Patent Builders Combination Tool in the early 1900s. It was intended to replace an entire kit of special tools. It was calibrated for setting pitch angles, as well as serving as a depth gauge, try square, or bevel protractor. In 1910, this instrument with a 24-inch blade sold for $7.

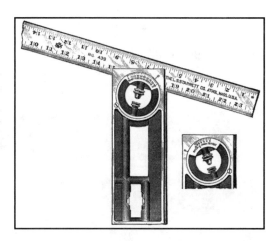

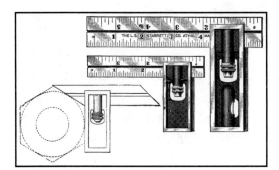

Designed especially for machinists the Starrett No. 13 double square was available with 4, 6, 9 and 12-inch blades. It was also furnished with an extra blade set for hexagon and octagon angles.

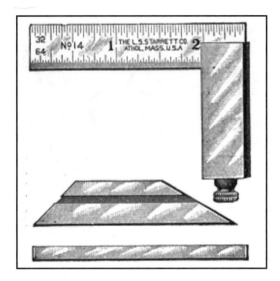

Various kinds of double squares have been produced. Toolmakers often needed a double square, and companies like Starrett could furnish them in English measure or in metric scales.

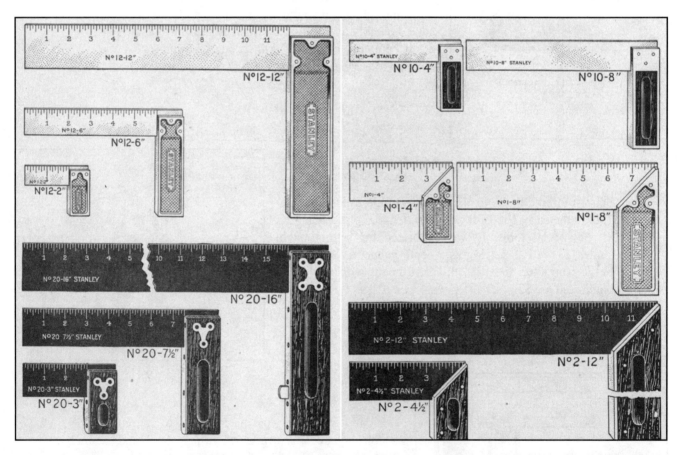

Stanley Rule & Level Company offered an extensive line of try squares, along with try and mitre squares in their 1911 catalog. Included were squares with an iron handle, a rosewood handle, and an iron frame inlaid with rosewood. They were made in sizes ranging from a little 2 x 2-inch size up to one having an 8-inch handle and a 12-inch blade.

Tailors and dressmakers used a square adapted to their specific needs. Those from Lufkin featured a brass corner plate and corner brace, using either maple or boxwood for the blade and tongue. Usually the markings were in 32nds on one side, and in 24ths, 12ths, 6ths, thirds, and two-thirds (of an inch) on the other.

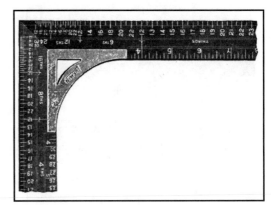

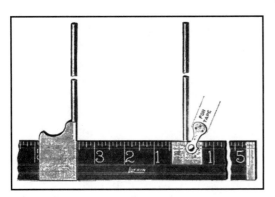

Lufkin, among others, offered various kinds of tailors measuring squares. The most common size was the 9 x 24-inch style, but these squares were also made in 7 x 14 and 14 x 24-inch versions. In addition, Lufkin also made a 6 x 10-inch Arm Square.

There have been countless varieties of wood and steel rules produced. Those from tool companies usually are more accurate and sometimes bring a better price than the plain ones. However, many companies gave out rules as a promotional piece, and one with "International Harvester Company" for instance, might bring far more than a nice machinist's rule. Shown here are a couple of examples from the early 1900s. Many of these were made in sizes ranging up to 6 feet.

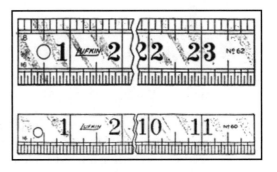

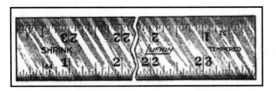

Shrink rules are essential for pattern makers and foundry workers. Owing to the varying shrinkage of various metals, it was necessary to compensate for this during the making of the pattern. Shrink rules ordinarily have their shrink stamped in place, such as 1/10-inch, 1/8-inch (per foot) and so on.

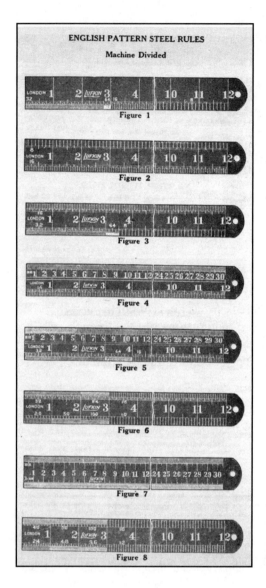

English pattern steel rules have been made in many different styles and graduations. This illustration from a 1911 Lufkin catalog shows eight basic patterns. With the various graduations and lengths available, there would be 64 different combinations available within these eight basic styles.

In machine shops and other industries where an ordinary wooden rule would easily be damaged or broken, companies such as Lufkin offered a folding steel rule. These were available in various styles ranging from 2 to 8-feet in length. Lufkin was also offering an aluminum folding rule at this time.

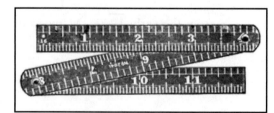

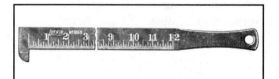

The folding brass rule was used by blacksmiths and other metal workers. It was made in a two-foot size that folded in the center. The blacksmiths' brass hook and handle rule was another Lufkin offering. It was made for measuring hot metal.

Already in the 1890s, Lufkin was offering the Tinners Steel Circumference Rule. It could read in inches on the top scale, with the bottom one giving the circumference for any inch or fraction shown at the top. The back side of the rule also gave the dimensions for fabricating various kinds of vessels, tanks, and the like.

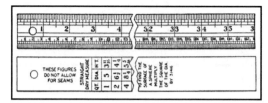

Boxwood rules were very popular into the early 1900s, but were largely displaced by the folding or zig-zag rule. They were eventually replaced by the tape measure. From 1900, comes this showing of rather plain rules with square (right) or round joints (left). They sold in the range of 30 to 60 cents.

The arch joint rule was of substantial design, but cost twice as much as the ordinary bound joint styles. In addition, this style was often available with a built-in caliper. This style, full, brass bound, sold for $2 in 1900!

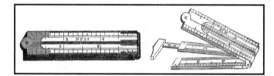

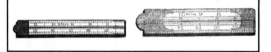

A double arch joint boxwood rule, fully brass bound, and two feet long, sold for the princely sum of $2.40 in 1900. Yet another style was the carriage-maker's boxwood rule. It was 4 feet long and sold for $4.

Numerous kinds of folding steel rules were available by 1900. Usually the steel rule was preferred by those working with metal, especially blacksmiths in their work around hot metals.

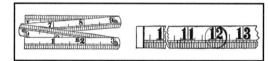

The blacksmith's rule was usually two feet long. Some were made of wrought iron, and others were of steel. The marks were deeply cut for permanence, given the extreme conditions under which they were used.

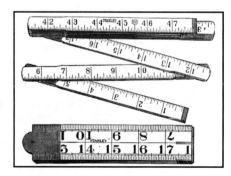

Stanley offered an extensive line of zig-zag or folding rules by the early 1900s. These were made of hardwood, and were available in several different styles. Also available was the Blindman's Rule. It was made especially for work in areas of poor lighting or visibility, as well as for those who had poor eyesight.

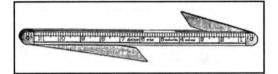

The four-foot carriage-makers boxwood rule was an expensive rule in its time, and is not often found today. Most boxwood rules folded out to two feet, and a few were made of three-foot length. In ordinary use, the numbers and graduations eventually wore away, and the joints became loose, so the rule was discarded.

Disston and others offered a wide variety of Sliding T Bevels. One of the most interesting was the Disston model on the right. It was clamped in place with a thumb nut on the bottom of the handle. This was advantageous since it was easier to position without having the thumbnut at the pivot point. Several other companies offered a similar design.

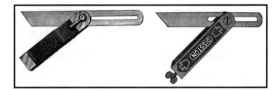

The ship carpenter's bevel was a tool developed especially for the needs of this industry. Today, an early example of a ship bevel is not easy to find.

Lufkin offered this Spoke Caliper Rule early in the twentieth century. As the name implies, it was designed especially to caliper the size of spokes in wagon and automobile wheels.

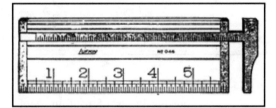

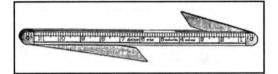

Coopers likely welcomed this Hook Stave Rule from Lufkin. It was designed especially for the cooper or barrel-maker and featured a brass hook and a brass endcap.

One of the most interesting boxwood rules we have found is the Lufkin 873 Combination Rule, Level and Protractor. Combining all these features into a folded six-inch pocket tool was quite a feat. This one had a retail price of about $4. I have tried to find one of these for several years, but with no success.

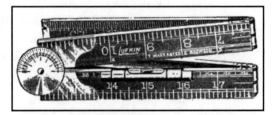

Surveying

This section illustrates some of the common surveying devices, mainly from the early twentieth century. Those of earlier date are not often found, and usually are fairly expensive…prices of $500 and more not being uncommon. Many of the early instruments are virtual museum pieces, and were elaborate in every detail. Those used for land surveys are probably among the highest quality.

Edmund Gunter in England invented what is still known as Gunter's Chain in the early 1600s. Gunter was a mathematician with numerous inventions to his credit. Gunter's chain was originally 100 links, each being 7.92 inches long. In American practice, this works out to 25 links, 1 rod or 16-1/2 feet. Then, 4 rods equals 100 links or 66 feet, or one chain. There are 80 chains in a mile. Of note, many rural roads are still laid out as 66 feet right-of-way. That was one chain, and that made it easier for the surveyors.

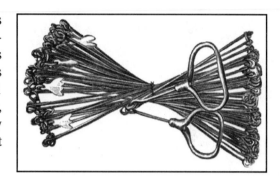

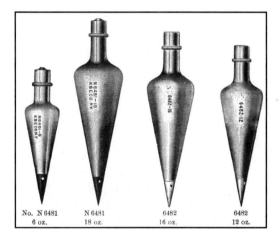

A plumb bob is essential to establish a reference point. Keuffel & Esser for instance, offered numerous kinds, and all of them were very precise. The brass bob with a replaceable steel tip is still the most common style used in surveying work.

The Abney hand level is an instrument that reads level as well as determining angles and grades. In experienced hands this level is fairly accurate. These are found only occasionally today.

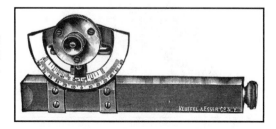

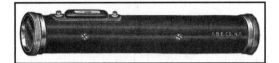

Simple hand levels are found occasionally today. They were used mainly for rough calculations of grade, and for this they were entirely satisfactory.

A fancy compass like this surveyor's style is found only occasionally today. In fact, those of any value are still in use, otherwise they have likely been discarded.

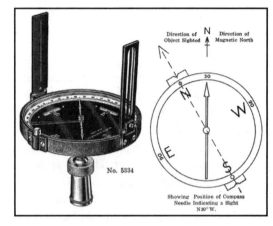

Numerous companies have built transits over the years. These instruments have always been expensive to build, and a decent one still can bring $200. Very nice transits, especially very old ones can easily bring $1,000 or more.

The dumpy level was able to read level only, and unlike the transit could not read angles or slopes. These levels were, of course, much cheaper than a transit, and were widely used by contractors and builders. Today, these instruments have largely been replaced with laser levels.

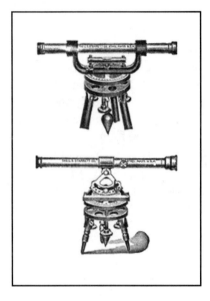

Starrett built levels for a number of years. They were designed mainly for contractors and carpenters for laying out buildings and similar jobs. In the 1920s, these instruments were priced at $15 to $30, depending on the accessories furnished with the level.

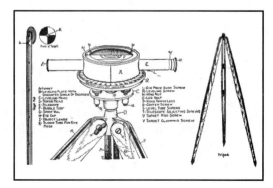

By the early 1900s this level was on the market. It was low-priced and came complete with a tripod and a wooden case for only $15. Farmers and carpenters alike used the Bostrom, and it appears that this one was widely sold.

T

Tinsmithing

Not only did the tinsmith need to be a person possessing extraordinary craft skills; a thorough knowledge of mathematics, especially geometry, was also required. Although a few books on the trade were available prior to 1900, they were few indeed. Thus, most tinsmiths learned their trade as apprentices in the shop of another. There they toiled for several years until finally becoming skillful at this craft.

The tools required by the tinsmith were indeed very few. The shop owned all the larger machines, leaving the tinsmith to own his snips, rules, awls, and other hand tools.

Most of the usual hand tools are shown here, along with larger tools such as seamers. In addition, there is a showing of heavy equipment found in only the larger shops. It is displayed here simply because any images of these machines are seldom to be found.

Common tools such as dividers, awls, and the like are found in various sections of this book. Many of the tools used in the sheet metal trades are little different than they were a century ago, and are not included in this section.

Peck, Stow & Wilcox Company began business in 1819. A century later, industry catalogs still illustrated the original Pexto Tinner's Hand Shears. They were made in several sizes, cutting from 1-3/4 to 4-1/2 inches.

Like the original 1819 pattern, the Pexto Samson Snips were available in a straight or a circular pattern. Except for a slightly different design, both the Samson and the Original were of the same quality.

Although there were numerous companies offering tinner's snips by the early 1900s, the firm of J. Wiss & Sons Co. at Newark, New Jersey, stands prominently in the list. The Wiss Tinner Snips shown here were made in right hand or left hand. They were available in seven different sizes.

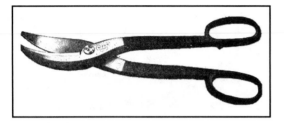

Wiss Circular Blade Tinner Snips were made especially for cutting curved work. Seven different sizes were available. The handles could also be furnished for left-handed workers.

Combination snips were available from Wiss by the early 1920s. This style was made in four different sizes, and was intended to handle straight or curved work equally well.

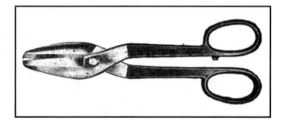

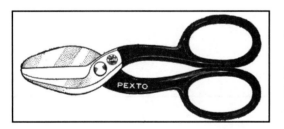

The No. 82 Pexto Pocket Snips was available in the 1920s…this small pair was only 7 inches long, and as the title implies, could be carried in the pocket. Tinner's snips usually bring only a few dollars in today's collectibles market.

Bench shears are seldom found today. They were for heavy cuts, and were made in nearly a dozen different sizes. The largest size weighed 48 pounds, it was 46 inches in length, and had a cut length of 7-1/2 inches.

Slitting shears were developed by the early 1900s. They were made especially for cutting corrugated metal sheets lengthwise. Both handles remained above the work.

Double cutting snips were designed especially for cutting stove pipe and similar applications. This style cut out a narrow ribbon of tin at the center of the cut. Another feature was a small crimper mounted on the side of the snips.

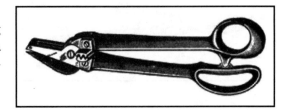

Compound snips were used for cutting heavy sheets that could not be handled with an ordinary snips. These were available from various companies and in numerous styles. The aviation snips so common today actually evolved from the aviation industry and did not become popular until after World War II.

Tinners' stakes were used for hand forming of tin and other light metals. Mounted to the holder is a Beakhorn stake. Beneath it in order are: Double Seaming, Candle Mould, Needle Case, Creasing and Horn, Conductor, Conductor, second half of Beakhorn stake, Blowhorn stake. Numerous other stakes were available, with these being the most commonly used. Tinners' stakes are difficult to find today.

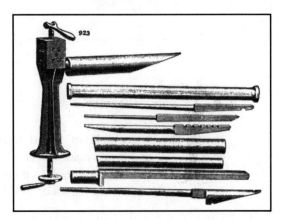

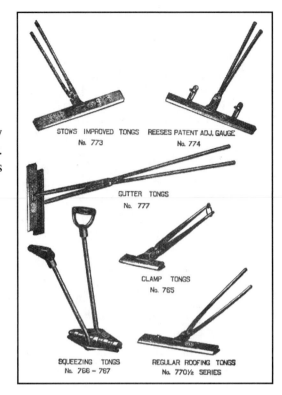

In the days of standing seam roofs, especially in the early 1900s, numerous tools were developed for the tinner. Shown here are some of the major tools, including various kinds of tongs for flat work and gutters.

STOWS IMPROVED TONGS No. 773

REESES PATENT ADJ. GAUGE No. 774

GUTTER TONGS No. 777

CLAMP TONGS No. 765

SQUEEZING TONGS No. 766 – 767

REGULAR ROOFING TONGS No. 770½ SERIES

Tinners' Fire Pots of the 1890s were fired with charcoal, and as shown here, had a small opening for the soldering coppers. Coppers generally were used in pairs, with one being reheated while the other was being used to solder a joint.

Soldering coppers came in all shapes and sizes, with the Roofers' Copper being shown here. These were generally sold in pairs, with the largest usually being about 14 pounds a pair, or 7 pounds each. Larger coppers held their heat longer, but were not necessarily as useful as an intermediate size.

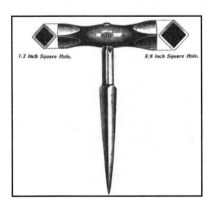

1/2 inch Square Hole.   5/8 inch Square Hole.

About 1900, Pexto offered a combination wrench and and sheet metal reamer. This unusual tool was designed to open holes in ordinary tin roofing when necessary, and the wrench could be used on 1/2 or 5/8-inch square nuts.

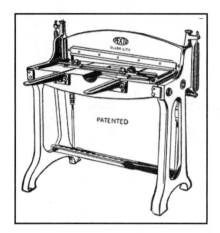

Squaring shears, or treadle shears of the early 1900s, were offered from Pexto in four sizes from 22 to 42 inches. They could cut steel up to 18 gauge. Many a shear was ruined by cutting heavier metal...I have seen treadle shears with broken beds, broken treadles, and other damage caused by ineptitude. With decent care, a treadle shear is able to cut a sheet of paper, even though it might be approaching the century mark in age.

Slip rolls are used to form circular parts; pipes, cones, and other objects. Pexto, among others offered a variety of hand and power-operated slip rolls with the smallest model being only 30 inches wide.

Setting down machines were used to start seams inward. However, this machine was not often seen in vintage sheet metal shops, and is seldom found today.

Turning machines are used for jobs such as preparing stove pipe elbows or preparing the tin for a wired edge. Many different sizes and styles have been offered over the decades. Using a turning machine requires considerable skill and practice.

Wiring machines are used to form the metal over a wire, as in a wired edge. As with many bench machines, the success of the job lies primarily in operator's skill.

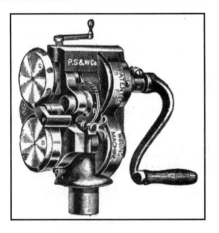

Pexto offered many of its bench machines in an "encased" design as compared to the regular open design. The encased design was virtually identical except that the gearing was enclosed behind a cast-iron shield.

Burring machines are used to turn up an edge or a flange on vessels. After the edge has been turned up, the mating piece is put in place and the flange is turned over with a setting down machine. In reality, many tinners simply turned the edge down with a hammer.

For making up stove pipe, the combination beading and crimping machine is used. These machines are relatively easy to use and are probably the most commonly found of all bench machines.

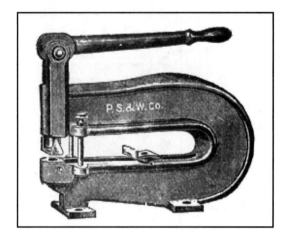

Numerous kinds of hand and bench punches are available to the tinner today as they have been for a century. Most of these have little collectible value, but instead, are purchased for continuing use by trade craftsmen.

Oftentimes, tin shops were required to fabricate steel frames for boxes and other items which were then covered with tin. Besides blacksmiths, the tinsmith was the most likely to use the heavy machines shown here. Tinsmiths, much like the blacksmith, had to have an excellent knowledge of mathematics, especially geometry. In the early days it was up to the individual craftsman to calculate the measurements for laying out a pattern.

From the 1890s comes this slip roll forming machine. It was built by J. M. Robinson & Co. at Cincinnati, Ohio. Equipped with 31-inch rolls, this machine sold for $63 at the time!

For simple work, the Folder was an obvious choice. It was easily portable and could turn an edge from 3/16 to 3/8 of an inch up to its maximum length. For this style from Robinson, the largest folder could handle 60 inches.

The big Robinson Squaring Shear shown here was made in sizes from 4 to 10 feet. It could shear metal up to 14 gauge, and could be operated either with a foot treadle or with the hand-operated reduction gear shown here. The 4-foot size weighed a ton and sold for $300 in 1894. By comparison, the 10-foot size weighed 2-1/2 tons and sold for $650.

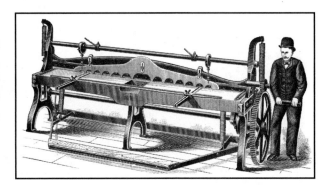

By the 1890s, corrugated metal had become very popular for roofing, siding, and other uses. Creative ways were found to incorporate this material into architecture by way of curves and bends. It was also used to make tubes and culverts. J. M. Robinson & Company illustrated their Improved Curving Rolls for corrugated metal in their 1894 catalog. It sold for $150.

V

Vises

No attempt has been made in this section to illustrate vises made after the 1920s. Many of the designs built after that time are still in use today. However, some very interesting vises, such as the carriage-makers designs are included. There are probably a great many unusual designs not included here, but hopefully we will be able to include them in future editions of this book. Many of the vises shown here still sell very cheaply, despite their age. A notable exception is the box vise shown below. A box or post vise in reasonably good condition almost always brings $50 or more at auction. A very nice one might bring over $100.

From the 1870s, come these machinist vises, available with a flat bottom (stationary) or a swivel base design. They were made in various sizes from 3-1/2 to 7-inch jaws. Shown left to right are flat bottom and swivel base models.

The special needs of the coach-maker were addressed in the Prentiss designs shown here. They were made in 3-1/2 and 4-1/2-inch sizes. Prentiss Vise Company in New York City was an early manufacturer specializing in vises of all kinds. The Bingham, Monarch, and Shepard vises all came from Prentiss.

The Patent Sudden Grip Vise of 1880 was made in regular, jewelers, and coach-makers designs. It featured a swivel base, and a quick-closing design. Except for a catalog illustration, no other information has been located on this vise.

Combination vises were on the market by 1880. They were intended to combine the ordinary machinists vise with pipe vise jaws. Also shown here is an extra heavy machinist vise with 5-inch jaws.

The Solid Box Vise, shown here at right, is from 1880. This design was also known as a blacksmiths' vise or a post vise. Many different companies made post vises, and almost always at an auction they will bring $50 or more if they are in decent shape.   Shown at left is a Nason's improved pipe vise.

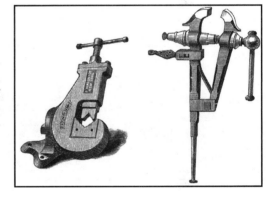

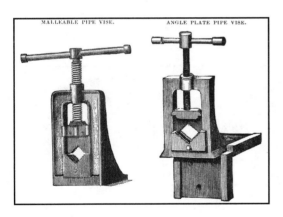

Numerous kinds of pipe vises were available by 1880. At this point in time, pipe vises were made with a solid frame. Pipe had to be pushed through the opening in the vise, and if a fitting was to be mounted on each end, it was impossible to remove. This eventually led to development of the split pipe vise, made so that the top half could hinge open to release the pipe.

Parker vises were made by Chas. Parker Company at Meriden, Connecticut. From the 1880s, comes this showing of Parker's woodworking vises. The best of this series had 4-1/2-inch saws that would open 9 inches. The base and jaws could be swiveled for holding irregular shaped pieces...this vise weighed 65 pounds and sold for $18.

Parker filers and finishers vises of the 1880s included a swivel back jaw that would adjust to articles of irregular shape. At the time, many articles were finished by hand filing, so vises like this were an important part of the machine shop.

Combination machinist and pipe vises were a part of the 1890 Parker vise line. The largest of these was furnished with 5-1/2-inch jaws and could hold up to 6-inch pipe. This huge vise weighed 155 pounds and sold for $35.

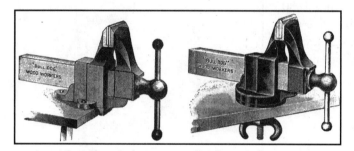

In 1890, coach-making was a thriving business. The needs of the coach-maker required a special vise, and numerous companies offered this design. Shown here is the Bulldog in plain and swivel base designs. The latter weighed 58 pounds and sold for $11.50.

Coach maker's vises are typified by their very high jaws, and many of them, such as the Prentiss designs shown here had a swivel back jaw to accommodate pieces of irregular shape.

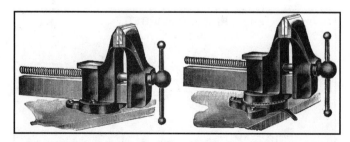

Shepard's coach makers' vises differed somewhat from most in having the screw open-mounted instead of shrouded beneath the ram as will be noted for most other vises. This style is from 1890.

Woodworkers vises were offered in many designs, ranging from the plain vise on the left, to the quick-acting design on the right. Eventually most of these designs for woodworker's vises would be abandoned.

This interesting little vise of 1910 was called the Auto and Motor Boat Vise. It was intended to be secured to the running board of an automobile or the deck of a boat for on-site repair work. It had 2-inch jaws, and in a nickel plated version it sold for $10.

Emmert's Patternmakers Vise of 1910 was an unusual design that included seven different pairs of jaws. This design was intended for clamping almost any object in virtually any position. At the time, this vise sold for $15.

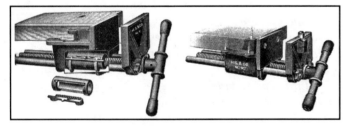

The Richards-Wilcox vise and others of this general design virtually replaced the earlier woodworker's vises. An extendable tab on the top of the movable jaw permitted clamping work against a bench stop.

Emmert Mfg. Company at Waynesboro, Pennsylvania, offered this unusual vise in the 1920s. Dubbed as Emmert's Universal Vise, it was adaptable to almost any clamping need for toolmakers and machinists. The Emmert Universal was supplied with five different pairs of jaws. It sold for $25 in 1920.

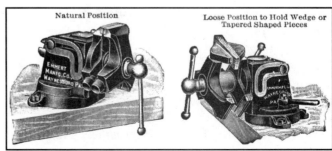

W

Wrenches

The first significant development in adjustable wrenches came with Loring Coes first patent in 1843. From here came a variety of Coes wrenches. In 1903, Coes Wrench Company at Worcester, Massachusetts, noted the sixtieth anniversary of the wrench, noting that "The best wrench of today is a Coes, not a 'Coes Pattern.'"

Although this section attempts to illustrate the major styles of wrenches into the 1920s, there is no attempt whatever to show the myriad of farm machinery and other special wrenches that have been made. Special identification and price guides on wrenches have been compiled, and trying to replicate this work seemed to me like a futile effort. Some of the wrenches from John Deere, International Harvester, and other companies command very high prices today, as do some of those from Ford and other automobile manufacturers.

For the benefit of wrench collectors, the following names have been gleaned from the 1922 edition of Hardware Buyers Directory:

Adjustable Wrenches

Allan-Diffenbaugh Wrench & Tool Co., Baraboo, Wisconsin (Kant Slip)

Anderson Wrench Co., Portland, Connecticut (Turnmore)

Arrow Tool Co., Buffalo, New York

Art Metal Works, Newark, New Jersey

Barcalo Mfg. Co., Buffalo, New York

Barnes Tool Co., New Haven, Connecticut

Bayer Steam Soot Blower Co., St. Louis, Missouri

Bemis & Call Hdwe. & Tool Co., Springfield, Massachusetts

Bergman Tool Mfg. Co., Buffalo, New York (Queen City)

Billings & Spencer Co., Hartford, Connecticut (Triangle B)

Boston Auto Wrench Co., Boston, Massachusetts

Bullock Mfg. Associates, Springfield, Massachusetts

Clipper Tool Co., Buffalo, New York

Coes Wrench Co., Worcester, Massachusetts

Coleman Railway Supply Co., New York, New York (Craft)

Corry Wrench Co., Corry, Pennsylvania

Craftsman Tool Co., Conneaut, Ohio

Crescent Tool Co., Jamestown, New York

Cronk & Carrier Mfg. Co., Elmira, New York

Cushman Co., Champaign, Illinois

Cygnet Mfg. Co., Buffalo, New York

Diamond Calk Horseshoe Co., Duluth, Minnesota

Erie Tool Works, Erie, Pennsylvania

Fairmount Tool & Forging Co., Cleveland, Ohio

Goodell-Pratt Company, Greenfield, Massachusetts

Greene, Tweed & Co., New York, New York (Baxter)

Greenfield Tap & Die Corp., Greenfield, Massachusetts (Little Giant and GTD)

Herbrand Co., Fremont, Ohio

Wm. Hjorth & Co., Jamestown, New York

Hy-Speed Wrench Co., Chicago, Illinois

Imperial Tool Co., Bloomington, Illinois

Keystone Mfg. Co., Buffalo, New York (Westcott S)

Lakeside Forge Co., Erie, Pennsylvania

Monte Wrench Co., Shelbyville, Indiana

Moore Drop Forging Co., Springfield, Massachusetts (Morco)

Frank Mossberg Co., Attleboro, Massachusetts (A, Alderman, Diamond, F, Junior, K, National, Sterling, X)

Oliver Mfg. Co., DesPlaines, Illinois
Oswego Tool Co., Oswego, New York
Peck, Stow & Wilcox Co., Southington, Connecticut
(Pexto)
Rex Wrench Co., Boston, Massachusetts
Richards-Wilcox Mfg. Co., Aurora, Illinois (Elgin, Shark)
Robert Wrench Co., New York, New York
M. W. Robinson Co., New York, New York (Carl)
Scholler Mfg. Co., Buffalo, New York
H. D. Smith & Co., Plantsville, Connecticut (S)
Star Mfg. Co., Carpentersville, Illinois (Elgin)
Superior Tool Co., Cambridge, Ohio (Du Charme)
Vlchek Tool Co., Cleveland, Ohio
Clarence E. Wakefield, Worcester, Massachusetts
(Wizard)
Walworth Mfg. Co., Boston, Massachusetts (Walco)
T. F. Welch Co., Boston, Massachusetts
J. H. Williams & Co., Brooklyn, New York

Alligator Wrenches

Armstrong Bros. Tool Co., Chicago, Illinois
Atwater Mfg. Co., Southington, Connecticut
Bonney Forge & Tool Works, Allentown, Pennsylvania
Forsyth Metal Goods Co., East Aurora, New York
Harris & Reed, Chicago, Illinois (Sawvian)
Hawkeye Wrench Co., Marshalltown, Iowa
Kilborn & Bishop Co., New Haven, Connecticut
Kraeuter & Co., Newark, New Jersey
John A. Roeblings Sons Co., Trenton, New Jersey
Smith & Hemenway Mfg. Co., New York, New York
(Red Devil)
Vaughan & Bushnell Mfg. Co., Chicago, Illinois (V & B)
J. H. Williams & Co., Brooklyn, New York (Bull Dog)

For all those companies shown in this 1922 listing there are many more firms that made wrenches of various kinds, both before and after this date.

The Coes adjustable wrench had its beginnings in 1843, and sixty years later it still had the same general form. The Coes Knife-Handle wrench shown here from a 1903 advertisement used a hardened steel bar and jaw, steel castings in the handle, and a hardwood handle.

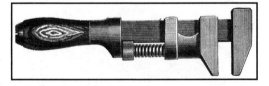

Coes Standard Wrenches of 1880 were made in 6, 8, 10, 12, 15, and 18-inch sizes. The Coe epitomized wrench design for decades, and several different firms copied the wrench insofar as they could avoid patent infringment.

The Girard Patent Wrench differed but slightly from the Coes design. In 1880, it was offered in seven different sizes ranging in length from 6 to 21 inches.

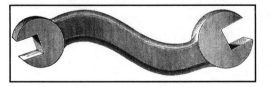

Drop forged wrenches of the 1880s were usually in an S-form. They were made in many different sizes and designs. Despite the fact they were often made of drop forged steel, they were extraordinarily heavy and still could not begin to stand the strains imposed on them.

Wrenches

Baxter wrenches were made by Greene, Tweed & Company noted in the index above. Shown here are two different designs of the Baxter "S" wrenches. Of an adjustable design, they were made in 4, 6, 8, 10, 12 and 15-inch sizes. Shown are an early model at right and an improved version at left.

A popular design that emerged in the 1880s was the Combination Pipe Wrench (and Monkey Wrench). This one was patented in 1868 by Bemis & Call (B&C). It was made in 10, 12, and 15-inch sizes.

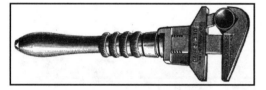

Bemis & Call made this combination wrench, probably under the same 1868 patent issued for another B&C wrench shown in an adjacent engraving. The major difference was that this style used a long nut for adjusting the jaw, and this was a great improvement over the regular model.

The Always Ready was but one of a multitude of alligator wrenches made over the years. This one of 1890 was made in four different sizes ranging from 5 to 11 inches in length.

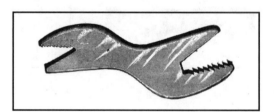

Stillson pipe wrenches were well known by the 1890s. By the 1920s, at least six different companies were manufacturing Stillson Pattern wrenches, although not under the Stillson trademark.

Pipe tongs were an early form of pipe wrench. The single jaw engaged the pipe, but numerous sizes were required to handle the various sizes of pipe. The jaw was subject to wear, and once it was rounded over, the wrench could either be rejuventated by a blacksmith and then retempered, or simply discarded for a new one.

Holdfast wrenches were an interesting and popular alligator design of the early 1900s. The combination wrench on the left is still quite common today. It embodied three different wrench sizes as well as the alligator jaws.

Priced at $1 in 1898, the Elgin Adjustable Wrench (left) was nickel plated, and weighed only 10 ounces, making it a convenient pocket tool. Agricultural wrenches (right) were usually of average quality and lacked the refinements of more expensive styles such as the Coes. The wrenches shown here are furnished with a wooden handle, sometimes known as a perfect handle.

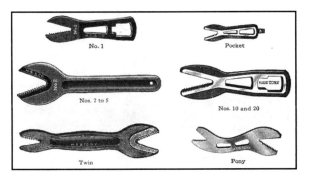

Shown here are a half dozen of the most popular alligator wrenches for 1910. The No. 1 at the top left was only 5 inches long, and the tiny pocket style at the upper right was but 4 inches in length. It sold for under fifty cents in 1910.

Wrenches

The Genuine Stillson Automobile Wrench was offered in a 1910 catalog. It was made in sizes from 8 to 18 inches. Advertising of the day noted that it was "a handsome and strong tool, with Perfect Handle, and comfortable in all weather conditions."

Billings & Spencer, among others, promoted their adjustable wrenches by the early 1900s. The series shown here was available in 6, 8, 10, and 12-inch sizes. Depending on the manufacturer, the range of sizes and the salient features varied considerably.

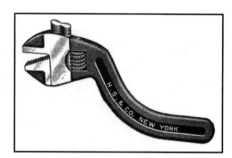

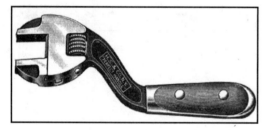

Adjustable "S" wrenches of the early 1900s were also available from Billings & Spencer (and probably others) with a Perfect Handle, as shown here. In many years of looking for old tools, I have yet to find one of these wrenches with a Perfect Handle. I am not saying they don't exist, but I do suggest that they are fairly scarce.

The Duplex Adjustable Wrench from B.M. Co., is another unusual design that is seldom found today. It was designed for access to difficult locations. This style was offered in 6, 8, and 10-inch sizes.

Pocket wrenches became very popular in the early 1900s, including this representative showing from Billings & Spencer. These styles ranged from 4-1/4 to 7 inches long, and were ruled on the inside of the sliding bar. One style even included a pipe wrench attachment.

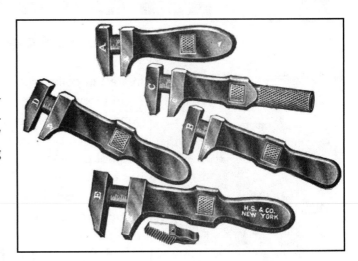

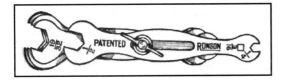

Ronson offered this small wrench set about 1910. At the time it sold for $1.50. It was designed for the automobilist and easily fit into the tool box. As an added feature, it also included a Prest-O-Lite key for those autos fitted with gas lighting.

Mossberg and other companies began offering wrench sets, especially for autombiles by 1910. This one consisted of pressed steel socket wrenches, an Alligator Wrench, spark plug wrenches, and an assortment of double-end wrenches. At the time, this set sold for $12, including a substantial fitted wooden box.

In the 1920s, Crescent offered their Double End Adjustable Wrench. The Crescent name had become nearly synonymous with adjustable wrenches by this time, and to this day, adjustable wrenches of any make are often referred to as "Crescent Wrenches." The adjustable style shown here was available in a combination 6 and 8-inch range, as well as an 8 and 10-inch style. For 1924 the larger one retailed at about $2. This style is relatively scarce today.

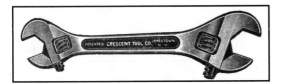

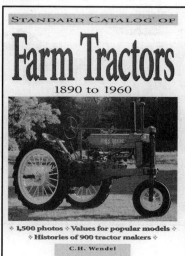
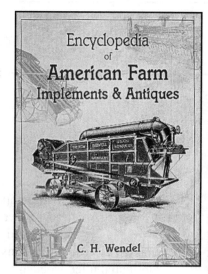
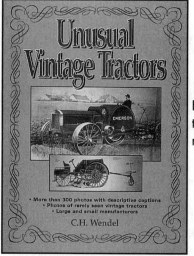